PEAKLAND DAYS

BY THE SAME AUTHOR

Rambles in the Hebrides
Rambles in Peakland
Rambles in North Wales
Portrait of the Pennines

Peakland Days

ROGER A. REDFERN

Photographs by
E. Hector Kyme

ROBERT HALE & COMPANY
LONDON

First published in Great Britain 1970

ISBN 0 7091 1859 7

Robert Hale & Company
63 Old Brompton Road
London S.W.7

PRINTED IN GREAT BRITAIN
BY EBENEZER BAYLIS AND SON LTD.
THE TRINITY PRESS, WORCESTER, AND LONDON

CONTENTS

CONTENTS

ILLUSTRATIONS

ACKNOWLEDGEMENTS

To my good friend E. Hector Kyme go sincere thanks for producing, as usual, a high-class set of photographs to illustrate this book. He has taken infinite pains to comply with my difficult requests, and no trouble has been too great in preparing good reproductions from the old prints I have used to supplement his own photographs where necessary. These old photographs are opposite pages 8, and 12. The photograph facing page 160 is my own, while that of Miss Hannah Smith opposite page 81 is by courtesy of *The Morning Telegraph*, Sheffield.

My thanks go to Mrs. W. Craig of Worcester once more, for her efficient co-operation in typing the manuscript and for helping me to produce an index.

For supplying me with many interesting facts and verifying others I wish to thank heartily the following friends, relatives and acquaintances: Mrs. J. Bailey of Chesterfield, Mr. E. Cooper of Dronfield, Mrs. G. Crawshaw of Bakewell, Lady Hollely of Barlow and Mrs. R. Redfern of Old Brampton for facts contained in Chapter 2; Mr. Wesley Stone of Old Whittington for many historical facts and reminiscences contained in Chapter 3. Mr. R. J. Campbell of Ravenshead, Notts. for corroborating incidents described in Chapter 4; Mr. P. M. Barnes for the unfailing supply of historical data at his command, some of which I have been able to include in Chapter 5; Mr. C. J. Blore of Uttoxeter, Mr. J. R. Bond, O.B.E., of Darley Abbey, the late Harry Fox of Matlock, Mr. E. Lawton of Bradley and Mr. L. M. Waud of Derby for material in Chapter 9; Mrs. D. Black of Old Brampton for reminiscences and Mr. E. Morgan of Ashgate for reminiscences and much technical data contained in Chapter 10, and to the latter also for permission to use the photograph opposite page 96; Mrs. C. Biggin of Cordwell and the late Mr. Isaac Biggin of Unthank for facts contained in Chapter 11; Mr.

F. Heardman, B.E.M., of Edale and Mr. R. B. Bramwell of Calver for much of the fascinating historical information and personal memories contained in Chapter 15; Mr. E. Hasman of Sutton Scarsdale and Mr. R. H. Riggott of Barlow Lees for facts contained in Chapter 20.

ONE

An Expression of Feeling

A pair of heavy horses—one a grey, the other black—ascend the slope towards two great oak trees. They are drawing a mowing machine and behind them an old man controls the reins. The last swaths are being cut, for the headlands, out of sight beyond the two oaks, are being worked and the rest of the field lies striped with yellow-brown lines of freshly fallen mowing grass. Behind the man and his team there is a backcloth of dark-green tree-tops (for we are here at the crown of a slope), while away and beyond a green and wooded valley curves to a high, purple horizon of upland which is set at a distance difficult to judge. Abbey Lane winds away along the valley-bottom, edged by a few red-brick houses. But I must explain that we are looking at an oil painting done by Miss Winifred Wilson in 1928. To see how much the landscape had changed in forty years I went to Beauchief one autumn afternoon and after some exploration found the place from which the view had been painted.

One of the pair of great oaks had been blown down in the great gale of February 1962, and the roots had been dug out, leaving a great hollow of bare soil, weeds and stones. Across the meadow where the horses had ascended with the mowing machine a wire netting fence was stretched incongruously, and a large grass field which had slanted up in the middle distance to the steep wood rising to the 625-foot summit of the knoll called Meadow Head was now filled with the brick, concrete and tarmac of a new housing development. But, surprisingly, the most dramatic evolution in that vista had been wrought by Nature herself. Running across the bottom of the mow meadow, just beyond the horses and the man and unseen in the painting, is an old footpath on the route from Lower Bradway to Abbeydale. Along the edge of this path have grown in the intervening forty years a veritable avenue of tall and slender saplings which effectively interfere with the landscape view. Standing beside the sole surviving oak none of the detail (albeit much altered) depicted by Miss Winifred Wilson can be made out; particularly in summer when those saplings are full with leaves.

The basic lines of the composition remain unaltered—oak filling a third of the canvas, field slope, wooded sweep to Meadow Head and purple vagueness of the ridge above Woodseats—but the effective incision made by the saplings has taken much from that particular viewpoint. And I am certain that Miss Wilson would not have chosen that place to set up her easel in 1928 had it looked as it does over four decades later. Which shows just how much even such a permanent-sounding thing as 'landscape' is really transient; subject to nuances of change or—occasionally—dramatic alteration. The former is Nature's way, an acceptable deceit which leaves the long-duration viewer happy with such change for it is so gradual. The latter is often typical of man's way, greedy and callous and intolerable to even the short-duration viewer who possesses a feeling for landscape.

Had I been able to go to that rise above Beauchief Abbey regularly in those forty years the dramatic change in the view would have been barely discernible between visits. As it was I had something of a disappointment.

Not so with regard to another viewpoint 3½ miles due to the south of the first one. About 1940 Miss Winifred Wilson painted a landscape in her Great Brind Wood, above Highlightley. Again, two trees dominate the composition, a slender silver birch in late spring raiment and a young and still delicate oak. The silver birch is the tree of the painting. Bushes dot the woodland floor about the remains of last year's bracken, and the other trees beyond the clearing fall away on the slope in secondary importance. On the far side of the valley Johnnygate Lane winds up between the fields which rise up in their turn towards Moorhall—one newly drilled cornfield above Peter Wood is just beginning to glisten green as the corn leaves open on the surface. Above the Moorhall horizon another large downpour is imminent for purple-blue clouds are rearing from the west, topped by three steep, white domes of towering cumulus which draw the eye from the delicate branches of the silver birch towards infinity. It is clearly a day of spring showers and sparkling sunlight.

A quarter of a century had passed since the painting had been completed when I went in search of the viewpoint. I found it easily. The silver birch was little changed, the slender oak a little taller and the bushes had doubled their height so that less of the clearing was now visible. Johnnygate Lane still wound up between those fields towards Moorhall. The sky was dotted with rain clouds and the blue between was not so radiant.

The protean nature of landscape can be quite remarkable, as in that view above Beauchief Abbey; it can be (and usually is) much more subtle and acceptable when Nature is left to her own devices, as in the case of Great Brind Wood.

The inter-relation of landscape and views and viewpoints is subtle and almost defies adequate description. None less a master of the subject than John Constable put his finger on the problem. His statement that "landscape is an expression of feeling" comes to the truth of the matter. It is impossible to fully describe the beauty and the meaningfulness of a spectacular view of Nature's making. Only landscape painting and music are capable of expressing the feelings of those views, and then every intelligent human creature has a different interpretation of such expression. Words, on the other hand, must come a very poor third; though poetry can come much closer to expressing our landscape emotions. A. E. Housman knew the secret of verse *vis-à-vis* landscape, in particular concerning his blue hills of Salop. So did John Donne three and a half centuries ago, and John Clare expressed the secret of the countryside in simpler and more direct terms early in the last century.

Then there is Robert Browning who caught so well a breezy April view:

> The year's at the spring,
> And day's at the morn;
> Morning's at seven;
> The hill-side's dew-pearled;
> The lark's on the wing;
> The snail's on the thorn;
> God's in his Heaven—
> All's right with the world!

And three centuries earlier Piae Contiones expressed the same feeling of rejoicing as Winter passed from his particular landscape. He felt able to sing:

All the world with beauty fills,
Gold the green enhancing;
Flowers make merry on the hills,
Set the meadows dancing.

Those are simple landscape joys expressed without fear of being classed naive or sentimental. But to every view each man has his interpretation and expression of feeling. With Peakland in mind, that infinitely varied countryside between the West Riding moors and the Trent and from Cheshire Plain to coalfield fringe of easternmost Derbyshire, there are two broad classes of views.

The first is the sudden, breathtaking, widespread vista over great distances. The place to visit on a day of crystal clarity punctuated by sudden showers. In those conditions the vista is at its best for startling distance, and great area is its characteristic. Such landscapes are not often pretty or necessarily beautiful; their wonder lies in their scale. There are several of these outstanding viewpoints in the area which come to mind. The summit of Shutlingsloe (1,659 feet) gives fine westward panoramas over the Cheshire Plain and, in extremely clear conditions, the Wirral Peninsula can be made out with the glint of the Mersey. A little over 6 miles to the north as the crow flies is the wider summit of Sponds Hill (1,346 feet) overlooking Lyme Park. This is another good place from which to look out over Cheshire; this time there are particularly interesting views over the suburban-type country about Bramhall, Hazel Grove and Romiley, backed by the hazy congestion of Stockport. That long, gracefully curved ridge of north-eastern Staffordshire called Morridge—a corruption of 'moor ridge'—which rises steeply to the west of Onecote in the valley of the upper River Hamps gives different views. These take the eye, in clear weather, far down into the west Midlands and culminate in the fair cone of the Wrekin. It is a comfortable thought to know that from this edge of the Peak District one is able to see those very different heights of Salop across a largely unspoilt countryside of rich farmland and woods.

The high plateaux of the Black Peak don't offer a wealth of distant views because of their very nature. A sudden fall of land is essential to reap the full benefit of a stretch of lower country. However, the western edge of the Kinder Scout plateau has some surprisingly good viewpoints over south Lancashire and north-eastern Cheshire, as have the headlands of Cock Hill and Peaknaze Moor on westernmost Bleaklow.

In the south are two outstanding belvederes, and both easily accessible. Alport Hill rises to 1,032 feet above sea level as an extension of Wirksworth Moor above Wirksworth and Alderwasley. The top has been quarried and the notable Alport Stone tilts its weathered millstone grit towards the lowland view; and

Alport Stone or Rock on Alport Hill from the west

what a view it is in clear conditions. It is a jewel of a panorama towards the south, between south-east and south-west, for the higher land to the west (rising from Madge Hill and Hognaston Winn backwards to the limestone plateau about Brassington and Longcliffe) and the great bulk far to the north prevent extensive sightings that way. The ridges come down on both hands from the Pennine country—brown, blue and gold against the southern sun—to form an intimate, hilly atmosphere. Away to the south sweeps the heart of Midland country; far off lie the gentle Wolds of Leicestershire, little woods, meandering streams of sluggish water and fox coverts. I have been told that the carillon tower at Loughborough may be seen in all that green sweep of England but I have not been so fortunate with atmospheric conditions. The darker profile of Charnwood Forest and Cannock Chase can be readily identified, while far off in the purple-blue of Salop the Clee Hills rise as a bold island of old rock above the rolling seas of the fair West Midlands, more than 60 miles distant. Again, the profile of the Wrekin is easier to separate from other far off heights. And in that same south-western quarter the truly lucky observer may infrequently make out the hazy heights where Salop merges with Wales. Man has come to the aid of our hilltop gazer for in the busy country of the Trent may be distinguished several power stations—like the one at Drakelow 19 miles distant—the telecommunications tower on Cannock Chase and several water towers close to the Trent. What is particularly interesting about Alport Hilltop is that is stands very close to the central point of Derbyshire. Its claim to fame is its fine, tilting gritstone tor and its arresting southerly views out of Derbyshire.

The other belvedere to which I have referred stands only 3½ miles to the north-east, another ridge-end which may quite legitimately claim to be the very ending of the Pennines. It is the limestone height crowned by the Stand above Crich. Crich Stand is a remarkable monument to the Sherwood Foresters who died in two wars and from its topmost point a lantern beams every night. Here is revealed another open view but different for the eye is drawn particularly towards the east, away over countless coalfield ridges. Rolling swells of field and spinney and little towns punctuated by shafts of sunlight across a dozen smoke-screens casting haze over a landscape at once romantic and sad. Towards the north-east are the wooded lands about Hardwick Hall and roving the eye southwards are the little ridges cluttered above the Erewash—in the vicinity of Riddings, Codnor, Westwood and Eastwood. Beyond are the vague suggestions of the remains of Sherwood Forest and the broad slopes of Lincolnshire beyond the imagined curve of the Trent. Southwards the view is over land shared with that wide vista from Alport Hill—blue, green and mauve cast over by sunlight hidden here and there by an intervening island of cloud. Crich Hill is a magnificent place from which to view Derbyshire and Nottinghamshire and a most appropriate site for the Stand.

The second type of view is the landscape of enchantment revealed intimately, a traditionally beautiful or pretty or, at least, memorable assembly of lines and colours and associations. To every man his particular favourite, his landscape combining reality and dreams; for my part there is space here to mention but a handful of vistas attractive on the score of beauty and association with people and events. Maybe this handful will coincide with the choice of others; at least it will focus the reader's eye upon this incomparable land and set him thinking about the elements contributing to his favourites.

From beside Lockerbrook Farm high above the western bank of Derwent Dale the eye ranges over reservoir water to the high pastures rising to Green Sitches, Lost Lad and Howden Moor. It is a downward view to the impounded water, the trees of Nab Wood rising to our viewpoint and here, beside us, the gritstone buildings of the farm. The bold and undulating watershed backs the picture, rising from Derwent Edge by Featherbed Moss to Margery Hill and beyond to the vague cloud-swept mosses of the north. It is a relatively narrow view, confined by the farm buildings on the one hand and the trees on the other—water, field, wood and moor combine with that most important element, the sky. So often a dramatic, brilliant or picturesque sky contributes the major element in a view. Many panoramas are rendered mediocre by an indifferent or uniform sky—

> Skyscape is master,
> Landscape the subject indeed.

Now for a less dramatic but more beautiful viewpoint. Where the Meek Fields slope down from the sky-facing fields about Moorhall there is a place close beside Rose Wood, near its uppermost reach. From this steep, woodside corner the land falls away to the windings of Barlow Vale. The sycamores which dominate this upper side of the wood are an ideal curtain in summer, when their foliage and—in June—their sweet-scented flowers hang thickly. Down curves the edge of the wood leading the eye through a dozen fields to the houses and farm clustered at Cordwell. Beyond rises the ridge topped by Holmesfield and running away by Cowley and hidden nooks to Dronfield Hilltop. This is a particularly good example of a view which retains some of its secrets and is consequently more enchanting because of hidden treasures, wealth imagined but never visible—the mind is richer than the eyes. The culminating point of this wood-side-cum-wood-top vista is the ridge crested by Cobnar Wood, the magic acres of Monk Wood and the far, blue-green line of eastern heights. Distance prevents the identification of detail on the Hundall ridge and far towards Bolsover and Palterton. One interesting thing worth mentioning here is that this view is almost as lovely from 250 feet lower down, in the fields as they level out

The prospect of Seven Woods from Unthank Lane Farm

near Unthank Lane Farm. But here it is a flatter composition and the sky must of necessity play a greater part. Whereas the Lockerbrook view is one for all-seasons, the Meek Fields view is at its best in late spring and early summer, when a hint of wild hyacinth and cool ferns shimmers through the woodland fringe to our open, grassy platform.

For an intimate moorland view I know of none better than the glimpse up Oyster Clough from the sudden turn of the path above where the line of the Roman Road runs north-westwards towards Glossop. The green windings of the little clough lead the eye straight to the cabin, perched gazebo-like close to the sky. A very different panorama lies the other way, the high and undulating profile of Seal Edge cuts across from east to west and its skyline punctuated by the several gritstone tors characteristic of Kinder Scout's northern scarp slopes. The coniferous plantation directly below our viewpoint hides partially the torrent of the River Ashop—altogether a good composition with the several essential elements grouped to best effect.

Occasionally man actually improves a view by creating a contrived landscape. The result is usually surprising and often breathtaking because it is beautiful and unexpected. By far the finest contrived landscaping in Peakland is to be found at Chatsworth, sheltering above the Derwent beneath Eastmoor's western breast. To Sir Joseph Paxton and his patron, the 6th Duke of Devonshire, must go much of the credit for the gardens which flourish today. The architectural garden of flowers beneath the west front of the house was probably proposed by Wyatville before Paxton came to Chatsworth; likewise, it was the Duchess Evelyn who planted the narrow gorge or ravine below the grotto pond after World War I. But between them Paxton and the 6th Duke were responsible for some of the finest features—the great Emperor Fountain fed by water from the lakes up on Eastmoor's edge is notable amongst these features.

The way to Chatsworth formerly was a steep descent off Eastmoor close to the Hunting Stand, and literate travellers regularly remarked on their relief on that descent. In 1697 Celia Fiennes rode from Old Brampton and Chesterfield and hated every mile of the wilderness way until, quite suddenly, she saw "the Duke's house" and noted its position as being "just at the foote of this steepe hill which is like a precipice just at the last". For a long time the rugged profile reared in sight behind the house and gardens, but during the last two centuries the planting of thousands of trees has "driven out of sight" the wild moorland. Up there, by the Emperor Lake, one is at the edge of the moor, and quite suddenly it is possible to look down over the waterfall to that loveliest of contrived landscapes: the water descends as a curtain between the massed rhododendrons and so along the top of the aqueduct, to cascade suddenly to the rocks below and so lead beneath the garden wall to emerge in the Cascade House. From there the wild torrent is a curtailed and cultured watercourse, gently processing towards the south front. But from our elevated viewpoint above the waterfall the formality is barely noticeable, and the watery top of the aqueduct leads our gaze over the top of the house to the tree-edged Derwent and away beyond the spire of Edensor and the woods rising to Calton Pastures and Ballcross to the west. Three well-positioned and mature Scots pines complete the composition by adding a random framework to it. After the breezy moor at one's back this revelation is almost Italianate, and how Paxton and his worthy employer would wonder at its present maturity.

There was once a boy who climbed to the top of the tallest tree in the wood behind his home. In clear weather he had a distant view of the Royal Liver Building across the shining Mersey from his Wirral perch. The other way were revealed the blue distances of Welsh mountains. Wood pigeons were always calling in his wood and their song has ever since reminded him of those sun-filled Cheshire days of the long ago.

To run into the warm fields of early summer and to lie on his back amid the dandelions and the clover, that was his great passion. And so to gaze upwards to the infinities of sky and understand, as few worried adults can, Ruskin's "sensuous rapture" of clouds. Ever changing chariot shapes and steeples and turrets of purity in the sky. That was, and is, a world he can ever return to at almost any time and so refresh a lively, fruitful spirit—the very landscape of the clouds and sky.

I climbed a gorse bank, buttery with bloom, and lay in a cowslip meadow which tilted towards the east. Far away down the valley the deciduous trees had burst forth in brilliant green, russet and yellow leaf. The far-away water reflected accurately the blue above, a lark called distantly, away behind me. And as I lay in the meadow and shared that "sensuous rapture" of occasional cloud-isles awash in their vapoured sea a far-away hilltop came into my view. It was a summery hilltop and I recognized it immediately. An ash tree stood boldly in the hedgerow between two grass fields and from the dusty, level lane where I seemed to be an ascending skylark was clearly visible. Beyond the fields the land fell away towards an unseen valley of woods and red rows of houses, then, beyond, it rose to a broad and plateau-like ridge beneath the eastern sky. The lane where I seemed to stand turned and descended dustily to another green valley, unseen beyond the nearest hedgerows. Far away a dozen horizons rose from the haze for it was certainly a bright day of great promise.

The dusty lane, the nearby fields, the lark and the solitary ash; the distant, green horizons; the unseen land in the voids beneath—all this came into view as I dreamed. A lifetime's thoughts and experiences compressed into but a moment of time. Away in those green and brown spaces, in the town and out of it, on the highest land and in a score of deep woods I had run, climbed, talked and worked. The paints applied separately united on the small canvas of the mind to create a composition of infinite colour and depth. Moments of melancholy and moments of great happiness.

The woods and shaded valley-ways for melancholy and the hilltop fields and open moor for happiness—but not always so in my complex dream. The colours are interwoven and spread about so that there are joyous shadows in the woodland and, often enough, the heights are *bruyère triste.*

The lark descended to the green fields and I turned northwards, looking ahead through a cloudy veil towards the gable ends and chimney pots beside Highgate Lane. The sun was very bright, it was a day of great promise.

TWO

Highgate and Hallowes Lane

You would never have thought that the rough lane winding up from the town had once been the main route southwards from Sheffield and the north. I never realized it, even though our house stood close by it; no, it was simply Highgate Lane, crossing the open, level land at 650 feet above sea level before it descended as a track through the great wood to the mouth of Barlow Vale and so to Chesterfield. Time has fitted the lane into its proper historical pigeon-hole, and it is obvious to me now that the road from Sheffield and Norton which came by Aston End and down to the Drone Valley as Green Lane continued up the other side of the valley as Hallowes Lane and Highgate Lane.

In the Survey of 1561 Green Lane was known as "the Grene lane" and was the lane leading to the original village 'grassy spot' or 'green'. Where this stood is not certain, though it could well have been where Green Lane and Calleywhite Lane meet, a short distance above where the Drone flows in its much altered, semi-subterranean course. There are still the remains of a grassy bank here, called by older generations of Dronfeldians, Dog Turd Hill, for obvious reasons. The green may have been quite large, evidence of which I will mention later.

It is a very ancient route, ten times older than the modern road route which winds up by Unstone and over to Woodseats and Heeley Bottom. Crossing the ancient way on the floor of the Drone Valley is another of equal antiquity. It strikes eastwards as Calleywhite Lane and up the slopes to the ancient settlement of Summerley and beyond to Eckington. The other way the route climbed the steep ridge by way of the present site of Dronfield's railway station, up Church Street and High Street to the open valley leading westwards to Holmesfield and Peakland proper. By coincidence much of my life has been lived along two arms of these crossing routes—one to the south, one to the west.

A dense thicket of rhododendrons, young conifers and hawthorn separates one side of Highgate Lane from the edge of the golf course. We used to spend much time in exploration of this jungle, and, coming out into the bright light of the fairway beyond, it was possible to look away to the west, to far blue hills which were the edge of the Pennines above Totley and Dore. In the fields near the house I remember following Colin Parkin up and down the furrows as he ploughed with a pair of heavy horses. Little did I realize it then, but that was the end of an era; not long afterwards the tractor had ousted the heavy horse for most farm work in the district. Two other characters come to mind when I think of Highgate. One was an ugly, dark-haired young woman who passed by with her brother on regular firewood collecting missions into the wood. She was known as 'Monkey Face' and she was rather frightening. The other character was equally frightening, a dirty little man with a sharp nose and a long overcoat and cloth cap. He was a ne'er-do-well who lived near 'Monkey Face' and spent most of his time on or near the golf course, stealing golf balls and doing a little caddying. He was well known as 'The Rat'. It was my constant worry that I would come face to face with this terrifying character one day, in a lonely spot far from home. That, however, never happened while I was still small.

The highest point of this elevated ridge-end which rolls easily westwards towards the Pennines proper exceeds 700 feet above sea level. The whole area is known as Hill Top. In unpublished documents in the Portland Collection in the Nottinghamshire County Record Office dated 1563 and 1578 it is termed "le Hille Toppe". For at least four centuries the people of this busy, wood-surrounded and field-dotted district have known the district by the same name, and that goes for the majority of the proper names—the fields, farms and woods particularly.

Two paths descending towards the south are memorable from the days of earliest memory. The entire southern and south-eastern flanks of the high ground were (and are still largely) clothed with the trees of Monk Wood. To everyone in the district the wood—one of the largest in Derbyshire—is known by this name, though it really consists of several areas of woodland which merge to form a delightful and quiet world. Brierley Wood hangs above Unstone Green and the meandering Drone and much of it has gone, felled for opencast coal mining and turned subsequently to farmland. Cobnar Wood clothes a conspicuous knoll across the Barlow Brook, a remnant of ancient wood occupying the medieval "Cobba's bank or slope". (In the 1324 Calendar of Inquisitions the wood was called "Cobbenouere".) Black Piece, Grasscroft, Loundes and Lees Woods are other parts of what is commonly termed Monk Wood. The true Monk Wood occupies the greater part of the western woods, extending from Bull Close to Lees Common. For the sake of simplicity though, the entire woodland is referred to here by its common name. The first known reference to the area by the name we know today seems to be in the Calendar of Patent Rolls for 1327, when "le Monkeswoode" was presumably derived from the Old English 'munuc' and 'wudu'. The reason for this ecclesiastical connection is simple. Southward from Beauchief Abbey ran a trackway to the penitentiary at Harewood Grange, above Holymoorside, some miles to the south. The Premonstratentian monks and others travelling between the two places would pass through Dronfield up Hallowes Lane (the Old English for a 'nook or corner of land'—but isn't it possible that this is the 'hallowed' lane?) and so through the woods associated with the passage of monks, by Abbey Farm between Barlow and Cutthorpe, to ancient Linacre House where a rest would be taken before the last, long walk over the hills by Wadshelf and Upper Loads or by Chander Hill (maybe from the Middle English 'chauntour'—a chanter or a chorister) and Holymoorside and Cat Hole.

The first path associated with my earliest memories of the world of woodland is a continuation of Highgate Lane, the original route-way continuing southwards towards Chesterfield. Just beyond the edge of the golf course are the vague ruins of Highgate House. It is a long time since this place was inhabited but there are still people living who remember it. The last occupants were a local family called Booker, and Mr. 'Teddy' Cooper recalls that there was a drift mine in the upper part of Loundes Wood and coal was brought up the slope by a narrow-gauge tramway. Ponies drew three full tubs at a time to the vicinity of Highgate House and there the coal was loaded into carts and taken down to Dronfield and district. He used to climb between the laden tubs and enjoy the ride to the top of the slope, and slowly down again with the tub wheels sledging on runners. It is a long, long time since that drift mine produced coal. Beyond the inconspicuous ruins of Highgate House the lane turns down through a deep cutting, hedged on either side above steep banks near to which the tramway ran. The isolated smallholding by the lane is called Ouzelbank Cottage and looks out to the south above a broad meadow which was until twenty or so years ago surrounded by the upper reaches of Loundes Wood. Down across the far side is a spring of clear water emptying into a trough, and Dronfield people have for a very long time visited it to fill bottles which were carried home to be used as a tonic for the delicate and aged. I used to go regularly with my mother to collect the spring water in lemonade bottles for my grandmother. The spring still flows but most of Loundes Wood has gone.

The path wound down ever deeper into the eastern woods and contained many wonderful features to impress a child's mind. Most of these features have gone with the felling and opencast mining of the wood—the Green Pond and the Avenue—but the Blue Mountain remains. It must have been this trackway that King Ecgbert of Mercia followed in A.D. 829 on his way northward from Tamworth, his capital, to meet King Eanred of Northumbria at Dore, 3½ miles to the north-west of Dronfield and just within the Northumbrian border. This extension of Highgate Lane into the wood has the indescribable aura of a living past, it has a charged atmosphere which is apparent even to the stranger.

From Ouzelbank Cottage a path leads steeply down to the east to cross the railway at Unstone Station. I remember that when I was 4 and 5 years old we used to go down that way quite often to meet my father on the main road below the station. He would stop the car and we would have a ride home. Alternatively one could continue down through Brierley Wood, keeping to the ancient route, and so reach the mouth of broad Barlow Vale near Sheepbridge Works. Even though it is a dirty place this old established engineering works has the advantage of being close to the wood and the open fields and it was the proximity of small coalpits in Monk Wood and by the Sud Brook which caused the construction of two railway tracks. They wound enigmatically up their respective valleys between the trees and brought fuel to the Sheepbridge blast furnaces. Sometimes we arrived just in time at the works to catch my father after that longer descent through Brierley Wood.

Another route ran off the last one, and roughly parallel to it, straight by the gone-forever Green Pond where a man's body once was discovered, beneath the heady arch of green and gold which was the famed avenue of great deciduous trees, and so out to the sudden vista over lower Barlow Vale from the top of the Blue Mountain. It was an old colliery tip and shone mauve in the summer sun. Here and there it was colonized by young silver birches; today it is largely hidden by them. From the crest one looked southwards to Cobnar Wood and Dunston. The helter-skelter of the rough run down the face of the Blue Mountain was a special thrill to me and it may have been the site of the birth of my love of steep and mountainous country. Who can ever know exactly the complex construction of a personal enthusiasm which becomes a way of life?

The second path slipped down from the end of Hilltop Road, almost opposite the entrance gates to Highfield House hidden by high hedges and tall trees. The path went down between woodland and fields on one side and the golf links on the other. Not that the golf links are easily visible from this path—now as then—because of a very high hedge. Suddenly, though, there is a gap and here stands a great oak tree. Through the gap by the oak there is a wide and distant panorama away over the golf links to the hidden corners and dotted woods of Barlow Vale, all backed by the open fields stretching upon the horizon to the breezy moors. This part of the golf links has always struck me as having the feel of a seaside course, high on a headland with nothing but the sky beyond; it is a quality gained from its elevation on top of this broad ridge.

A short distance down the path brings one to the top of Monk Wood, at least to where one formerly entered the wood. Away to the east the trees have gone and the area is rough pasture, though some young trees have been planted and are still hidden by the herbs and grasses. When I was very small my mother pushed me in the wheel-chair down this steep and winding path, a staircase of delight between the shaded groves of oak, birch and beech. The path is eroded by running water and sand and stones cover the deep ruts just as they did a century and more ago. The trees were felled at the end of World War II but from the sad, neglected slopes of what I always considered *my* wood have grown sapling silver birch and some young oaks. Now this part of the wood has an appearance very similar, it seems in retrospect, to that of pre-war days. That similarity will increase as this new generation of trees grow up.

At the bottom of the path was a cross-roads at the heart of the wood, where the 'Middle Riding' crossed from east to west on its way between Sheepbridge and Lees Common. Not far forward, along the track towards Barlow, stands Monkwood Farm. Teas were served in the orchard and in those days the place was virtually surrounded by the wood. It is a typical Barlow Vale farm-house and buildings with walls of local coal-measure sandstone and roof of large, stone slabs in the traditional manner. A swing hung for our delight from an old pear tree in that orchard, and if it was wet we sheltered in the open cartshed facing the south-west. The place was probably rebuilt in the seventeenth century, but it is of older foundation as it was known as "Monkwoddfeyld house" in 1581 and at an earlier date, "the Mounks house". Perhaps the monks stayed here and farmed the open fields towards Barlow while their herds of swine were fattened on nuts and roots gleaned in the encircling woods. The other possibility is that it was a resting place for monks making their way between Beauchief Abbey and Harewood Grange at the edge of Holy Moor mentioned earlier in this chapter.

A short distance along the 'Middle Riding' towards the west it is not a difficult thing to find Robin Hood's Well. The water issues from a hollow a little way above the track, surrounded by several trees, notably a venerable pair of hollies. Whether the celebrated outlaw ever drank from this watering hole must remain a subject for conjecture, but it is almost certain that he travelled in this region, *en route* between his Sherwood country and the higher parts of Peakland with which he is so closely linked by tradition. Upon these shading holly trees are some very old initials, with rather indistinct dates, and in 1925 my father carved his initials clearly. Two years later my mother carved hers and both sets are still in perfect condition. In 1948 Alan Watson and I did the same on these trees and so the trunks could be said to comprise a complete family tree.

Along the 'Middle Riding' there are no open views but going towards the west, actually almost north-west, a little valley develops to the left hand and across it is the 530-foot-high eminence of Broombank. The early Ordnance Survey maps in the first quarter of the last century referred to the hillock or knoll by this name; it is derived from the Old English 'brom' (broom or spine-less gorse) and the Old Danish 'banke' (slope of a hill or ridge, or a bank-side). Upon it grows a variety of older trees which were never felled when much of the wood was cleared last. From its top the views it obscured from the 'Middle Riding' are suddenly revealed, views over Barlow Lees and mid-Barlow Vale and backed by the blue haze of the hill slopes rising towards Grange and the moors. On the southern flank of Broombank are the ruins of the colliery of the same name, one of many which were developed in the lower reaches of the valley during the last century and which gave employment to many of the inhabitants of Barlow, Commonside, Unstone and Dronfield. The gaunt red chimney used to rise mysteriously above the trees at the edge of the wood when seen from the lane near Barlow Lees and along the Galloping Close. It used to frighten me and not until several years after it had been demolished did I ever make an expedition into that area, through the butterbur leaves in Broombank Plantation above the lower Lee Bridge.

On the northern flank of Broombank the bluebells are particularly dense, they have colonized a great part of the hollow falling from the 'Middle Riding' and often bloom at the same time as the wild crab-apple blossoms nearby to make a lovely contrast of deepest blue with palest pink. The 'Middle Riding' soon reaches a gate and leaves the western edge of the wood, traversing a steep slope between a coniferous plantation above and pasture field below. This field provides an ideal sledging run, down for several hundred feet to the brook. Beyond the plantation is Lees Common, a farm of considerable antiquity which was modernized in 1960. Here was born in 1872 Arthur Hollely, later to become Sir Arthur Hollely. This son of Derbyshire rose to a situation of note, being a draper in Plymouth. Though he made his home in the West Country the roots were inevitably in native soil, and in later years he and Lady Hollely came to their old cottage at Wilkin Hill, Barlow, two or three times each year. In old age his tall, angular figure could be seen walking the lanes of youth from time to time. In 1961, at the age of 89, he died and his ashes lie in the churchyard at Barlow, close to the remains of other members of the family. Lady Hollely still lives in the finely situated cottage at the top of the hill overlooking the valley of the Sud Brook.

By coincidence Lees Common is today the home of Sir Eric Mensforth, a former Master Cutler. There are comparatively few humble farmsteads in Peakland which can claim to have been in the possession of two knights in such a short period of time in recent centuries. I can remember seeing the new perimeter wall being built for the orchard many years ago. An old craftsman from Barlow erected it with the help of a Standard Fordson tractor. The wall is unique in this district for it consists of alternate layers of stone and turf. The roots in the turf have continued to anchor the soil and this in turn supports the stones. It is a derivation of the traditional bocage walls of Cornwall, Brittany and West Wales.

When the farm-house was modernized in 1960 we had the key to look round and I shall never forget the dramatic appearance of the sky over Barlow Common and Bole Hill as a great thunderstorm approached on that August afternoon. The noise of the thunder rolled nearer and an occasional flicker of lightning sent us from the bedroom windows and away down the lane towards home, but the storm caught us before we had reached Dronfield by way of Hill Top.

From Lees Common a path runs back towards the east, up steeply at first and so onto the crest of the little ridge which leads towards the golf links above Monk Wood. Crossing the eighteenth, the path enters the top of the wood by way of a bridle gate. This is the Pig Gate, a name given by my family because an adjacent dead tree trunk was devoid of bark and had the look of a pig's head. It is a place of magic charm on a quiet, sunny day, for if you are walking westwards out of the wood there is a sudden revelation of the far-off valley and hills beyond the nearer tree-tops. And if one is crossing in the other direction—from golf links into the wood—the contrast of open country with the confines and intimacy of the trees has a memorable charm that does not fade with renewed acquaintance. There is a family photograph which is a particular favourite of mine; it shows my maternal grandparents by the Pig Gate almost half a century ago, looking out to a view I know so well and treasure. For me this picture does more than any fine panorama, my mind illustrates the view which my grandparents were absorbing and the trees and gate close by them suggest the secret arbours of the wood.

Bluebells and bracken, cuckoo calls and the soft and drowsy coo-ing of wood pigeons, a glimpse down some enigmatic ride between silver birches at the end of a warm evening, the many scents of fungi on a September walk; these and a whole miscellany of other sounds and smells and sights are, for me, Monk Wood past and present.

Where Hallowes Lane gives way to Highgate Lane stands Hallowes Farm; or what was formerly Hallowes Farm, now the Hallowes Golf Club. As explained earlier this name has been derived from the Old English word 'halh' meaning 'a nook or corner of land'. By 1342 the name had become 'Le Halughys' and according to unpublished documents at Belvoir Castle, Leicestershire, it had become 'Hallowes' by the year 1594. A deed drawn up in 1342 transferring land "in Selioke and Le Halughys" to a Robert de Sellyok probably refers to the present Hallowes Farm.

Now, the present building was erected by the Morewoods in 1657. This family have a known pedigree which goes back into the fifteenth century. In 1629 Anthony Morewood of Hemsworth, near Sheffield, purchased Alfreton from a Robert Sutton. Some historians believe that the same family built Norton House in 1623, a fine old house demolished in 1868 by its new owner, an industrialist called Charles Cammell, well known in the district. The new Norton House in the suburb of Sheffield occupies the same site. Hallowes Farm has the initials of a member of the Morewood family and the date 1657 over its main door. It seems that there was a family called Hallowes living hereabouts (if not on the site of the farm of the same name) before 1657 because a Samuel Hallowes living at 'Hallowes' in Dronfield had a grandson (also Samuel) who was owner of the old Norton House about 1674. This family came into great wealth through the Woolhouses of Glapwell. In any event Hallowes Farm is a very fine seventeenth-century yeoman farm, the house being particularly complete. It is H-shaped and has gables on its wings, low mullioned windows tied to a long and uninterrupted string course, the purpose of which was partly ornamental and partly to function as an 'eave' from which rain would drip clear of the lower wall and windows.

When the Morewoods built the house they surrounded the level garden at the front by a high, stone wall to keep it sheltered and private. A narrow gateway and steps led from Hallowes Lane, past the lovely stone dovecot to the front door. To reach the back of the house one had to pass in front of this high wall and turn down towards the north just beyond it. The extensive outbuildings lie back behind the house, upon the northern side.

The last people to farm there were the Johnsons. It so happened that a group of keen golfers took to playing their game on the open fields to the south and west of Hallowes Farm in 1892. Their first base was a cottage on Hill Top Road, and later they moved to the top of Salisbury Road and the house which became their club house. A tent was set up in an adjoining field as a locker room. One of these pioneering golfers was Charles Chapman Baggaley, headmaster of Dronfield Grammar School from 1888 until 1926. To this day the house in Salisbury Road is known as the Old Club House. Finally, in 1925, the Johnsons moved out of Hallowes Farm, went into the Old Club House and the club took over the farm-house. From the point of view of preservation of the fabric of the old house this proved a very good thing because the Hallowes Golf Club have been able to maintain the place in an excellent state of repair down the years. One major change was the removal of the high garden wall and the use of the stone to build an airy extension on the western end of the house. This has opened up the frontage so that all passers-by can see to advantage the south front and the dovecot while the views from the house are now extensive, out over the links to a far-away glimpse of Peakland moors in the west. On the links not far from the Hallowes is a pond, a place of fascination and tragedy. On a frosty winter morning a long time ago, when the Hallowes was still a farm-house, a youth went over to the pond to break the ice for the sheep to drink, and as he did so the head of a woman broke the surface. She was a local woman living at Hill Top in reduced circumstances.

Hallowes Lane winds down to the north-west to Dronfield, overhung by tall trees. Before World War I it must have had a very different character; a rural lane climbing between fields on to the windy brow of the hill just beyond Hallowes Farm. Later it became a quiet suburban lane, flanked on the eastern side by interesting houses and bungalows. It is much the same now but the peace is rather spoiled by the noise and fumes of cars ascending and descending the lane.

I can well remember the regular journey up and down the lane, between my Highgate home and my grandparents' house in lower Hallowes Lane. Each house and bungalow interested me because of the unusual and contrasting architecture, and because of the inhabitants—likewise unusual and in great contrast one to the other. In later years a walk up the lane and by those same houses has refreshed early impressions, and the dark shelter of trees and shrubs has remained.

My great-grandfather was William Ward Barker. He was born on 1st July 1830, and lived all his life at Quoit Green House, adjoining Hallowes Lane. The house was built in 1613 and one of its finest features is the ingle nook. The name Quoit Green seems to be a corruption of the Old English terms 'cot' and 'grene' which indicate a cottage or hut upon the village green. The house was formerly a coaching inn on the old road which climbed the hill towards Chesterfield, going by way of the present Cross Lane and Upper School Lane (or 'Back Lane' to give it the usual local

William Ward Barker in the garden at Quoit Green House, Dronfield. About 1915

Hallowes Golf Club House, Dronfield

Old Whittington Manor Farm

(*left*) Doctor George Clifton at work at the Hall, Dronfield in 1949. (*below*) The Monument, High Street, Dronfield in 1949

designation). How long Quoit Green House had been in my great-grandfather's family prior to 1768 is not certain, but in that year William Ward Barker's great-great-grandfather (one, William Ward of Oxclose, Dronfield Woodhouse) sold Quoit Green House and 16 acres of land to his son, also William Ward.

In a letter published in the *Sheffield Telegraph* and dated 15th July 1908 my great-grandfather wrote about this William Ward, his great-grandfather, as follows:

> He farmed this [Quoit Green] and other land, and at his death my grandfather inherited and farmed it, who left it to my mother. My father, Hugh Barker, was killed when I was two years old. I have farmed the land over 50 years up to a few years ago, and am now in my 75th year. . . .
>
> Faithfully yours,
> William Ward Barker.

Actually this letter was prompted by one previously published in the *Sheffield Telegraph* on 15th July 1908. This first letter was from a family called Thornton who lived at Norton Cuckney, and claimed a record for living in the same property over the longest period of time. My great-grandfather's claim to the longest continuous occupation of one property was accepted by the editor as the Thornton's claimed a period less than 140 years.

Over a long period William Ward Barker of Quoit Green was well known—notorious might be a better description—for his regular powerful attacks against injustice and humbug which were published in the local press. He was a fighter for what he considered right and proper, for the weak against the powerful, for the enforcement of justice. Indeed, he adopted the pseudonyms 'Justitia', 'Fair Play' and 'Veritas' in many of the forthright letters written to the press over a long period of time.

In a letter which appeared clear and bold in the *Derbyshire Times* some time during 1882 the following was stated—an example of his strong feelings on matters of local government:

> Ratepayers! Profit by the experience of the past. If the May-Lucas clique retain the reins of office you may expect heavy rates. May has slipped into the Local Board through the back door. Lucas wants to join him, quite natural, after his profitable operations of last year, when his and his son's bills combined amounted to £100.7.9d for Law and Cast Metal! Did not Lucas raise the salary of

their Man Friday last year £10 per annum in defiance to a memorial largely signed by the ratepayers, protesting against such advance by reason of his having received 10 years' salary for doing nothing? If May and the Lucas's bore their own share of the burden they have laid on us they would not be so liberal with the ratepayers' money. If their land and works is taken as the basis of the ratal, every ratepayer in the parish ought to have a large abatement. Note the assessment—

May, 42 acres, 25s 4d per acre.
Lucas, 110 acres, 26s 6d per acre.
Works combined £225

Contrast this with the works of Messrs. Wilson and Cammell, £2,500 and yet the Lucas's say "we did very well before the Steel Works came, and we can do when they have gone". Won't they be the big Bosses once more. Will you again advocate Toadyism and Jobbery?

Is not 16s per cwt rather a high price for cast metal?

PLAYFAIR.

In another communication on the subject of the ultimate removal of the Dronfield Steel Works of Messrs. Wilson, Cammell and Company from Calleywhite Lane, Dronfield, William Ward Barker foresaw troubled times for the people of the town. In a long and scathing attack on local humbug the following was included:

For six months ending February (1882) last 63,000 tons of steel rails left Dronfield Station, and over 60,000 tons of pig iron were delivered at Dronfield Station for the works. . . .

The sum originally asked for the Dronfield works was £165,000, but as the cost of removal was taken into consideration the purchase money was eventually fixed at £132,000, the expense of removing and re-erecting the plant at Workington being set down at £34,000. . . .

The main point of criticism here by my great-grandfather was that valuable and irreplaceable industry was being driven from the environs of Dronfield by the high rates fixed by local 'tin gods' to further their own ends. The same letter continues:

It is hoped that the plant may be transferred to Workington by the end of the summer; and then, with the exodus of the company and its workmen, O, Dronfield, farewell, a long farewell to all thy greatness.

No, not quite. There will still be something great left—the Dronfield rates. Now they are 7s 3½d in the pound; then they will rise to 10s or 12s.

The exodus of the Israelites from Egypt could not distress the subjects of Pharoah half as much as the exodus of Messrs. Wilson, Cammell and Co. has discomforted the good folks of Dronfield.

He went on to suggest that Messrs. Lucas ("who are so patriotic and love Dronfield well") should fill the gap left by the vanished iron and steel company on Calleywhite Lane. This never happened and the long, brick rows of workers' houses erected by Messrs. Wilson, Cammell & Co. years before were left empty for long periods of time.

But as time progressed the temperature of the correspondence rose. My great-grandfather penned the following in the same year (1882):

Don't heed the clap-trap, the lying effusions of the apologists of the May-Lucas clique, these paid scribes, these advocates of communism, these men of straw, are not the parties to advise. . . . Was not £1,900 collected for School Board last year in addition to £440 Government Grant? How much did E. Lucas's brother-in-law take away as Architect's commission for Schools and Cemetery? How much have Lucas's received from the town for their cast metal wares in excess of the time's prices?

These fellows lie when they say Lucas and Baggalley have given "perfect and universal satisfaction". We should be just as well represented by two old washer-women. . . . These paid scribes also lie when they tell you I am thirsting for "official honours". I have no desire to frab with such snobs as are to be found on our Boards, although I don't fear facing them.

I consider the public business of this town has been carried on disgracefully for a great number of years, hence my reasons for making a stand in my own way, and saying it is time we swopped May and the Lucas's, we may get better, but it is impossible to get worse custodians of the public purse.

Then there were several forthright letters telling the general public of "Illegal proceedings of Dronfield School Board", of the promotion of interests of "certain shareholders in the Dronfield Gas Board", of "Alleged Irregularities of the Dronfield Local Board", and so on.

As to the Burial Board and its "crooked affairs", William Ward Barker sent a letter to the *Derbyshire Times* on 23rd February 1882, of which the following is an extract:

The Great Daniel resigned his seat on the Burial Board because of a certain member being distasteful to him, and because he remembered the old proverb his schoolmaster taught him, namely, "Evil communications corrupt good manners". How self-sacrificing of him to resign, and how reckless again to fall into the Lions' Den.

This letter goes on at some length and explains how, one month after resigning from the above-mentioned Burial Board, the "Great Daniel" was re-elected by a mass vote on the part of "the Radicals". The letter goes on to explain that the proceedings were "cut and dried" and that the individual concerned "would do himself a gracious kindness in resigning from *all* the Boards, as I cannot imagine, for a moment, that he represents the intelligence of Dronfield Ratepayers". The above situation had originally arisen because William Ward Barker had recently been elected to the Dronfield Burial Board, the originator of the following attack on "the Great Daniel" some good time before.

> You will know Daniel as the great Spouting Boss of all the Boards, as the pious Baptist. If he is a fair sample of our representatives is there any wonder at the rates being piled on to 6s 11d in the pound?
>
> Dronfield, January 5th 1882

W.W.B's regular questionings of local government proceedings had caused the following letter to the Dronfield Burial Board when he had been elected to this Board: "Gentlemen, Please accept my resignation on the Board as I have too much self-respect to sit with one now elected. D.S."

It seems that more fuel was added to the fire and my great grandfather would enjoy in typically forthright manner the composition of this reply:

> Mr. Daniel S– – –
>
> Sir,
>
> At the Burial Board Meeting today I proposed your resignation be accepted, which was carried. I think we shall very well survive the loss of you. I trust you may profit by the expression of public opinion which awaits you, and that you may not have too much self-respect to retain a seat on the School Board for which your exposition of defective education of today so clearly unfits you.
>
> I am, Sir,
>
> Respectfully yours,
>
> W.W.B.

We cannot know at this distance in time how much this (and great quantities of similar correspondence between W.W.B. and his contemporaries) was the result of deep hatred and feeling for what each thought correct and true, and how much impish, tongue-in-cheek enjoyment the correspondents obtained from the lengthy broadsides fired in the form of regular letters which appeared in print for everyone in the district to read.

Anyhow, things now began to go seriously wrong for the 'Great Daniel' in this particular offensive. In reply to the above letter he sent the following written on a postcard, never thinking that anyone but the recipient would see it: "W. W. Barker, Dronfield. Very dear Cakey, Yours at present lies before me, it will shortly be behind me. I am going up the yard. D.S."

We can imagine the shock felt by D.S. (the 'Great Daniel') when he saw this correspondence in the *Derbyshire Times* the following week, with my great-grandfather's reply below it, as follows:

Mr. D. S.——— Dronfield, January 7th 1882

Sir,

I duly received your postcard, which indicates the fact that you originated from the gutter. Poor Daniel! I sincerely pity you. Do be advised, Daniel, and enlist a boy from the 2nd Standard of the Board School to give you a few lessons in composition and spelling.

I will make an exhibition of your trump card to the ratepayers, as evidence of your fitness to represent them on the School Board. As I should consider it "infra dig" to notice you further, I may say in honour to you that I consider you a very good specimen of the non-conformist Radicals of Dronfield.

I am, yours truly,

W.W.B.

P.S. Remember not to forget your brothers, Jack and Israel, this cold weather.

This letter was returned to its sender with the following written upon the envelope: "My School Master taught Evil Communications corrupt good manners so I return your sweet note without opening for fear of being contaminated with the enclosed Bosh."

W.W.B. had not finished with the incident of the short post-card yet for he included those lines from the envelope in his next published letter, following them with this explanation which must have been too much for the opposition because it seems to have been the end of the incident.

> After being re-sealed, the above was written on the back of my letter and no doubt posted as he went to dispense hot gospel at his Tabernacle. Who would not like to be a Town Counsellor? Who would not like to have the "entre" to Elm Cottage, so as to be able to fraternize with the Proprietor of Beech Works?

Mr. D. S. ——— was, of course, the Proprietor referred to and the demise of this verbose battle must have been something of a disappointment to local readers. But my great-grandfather continued through the years to make his voice heard when he believed it to be necessary. Here there is only space to refer to two more incidents in which he became deeply involved. Both were court cases which received much publicity.

The first began in the 'Yellow Lion' public house in the Haymarket, Sheffield, one August day. W.W.B. became involved in an argument in the bar-parlour with a farmer from Dronfield Hill Top called Richard White. This concerned earlier rumours spread by the latter about the poor quality of a horse my great-grandfather was trying to sell locally. W.W.B. told White that he had been guilty of a dirty trick and that the horse in question was worth all the horses he (White) had about his place. At this White jumped to his feet and threatened to knock the other's head off. Other men present in the room stopped White from doing this and W.W.B. withdrew to another room. Some time later he returned to the bar-parlour where White still sat. The argument re-commenced and White finally struck W.W.B. "over the face and head with both fists about a dozen times". White was dragged away and my great-grandfather was taken to a nearby doctor's surgery for attention to his cuts and bruises. In evidence at the Sheffield County Court the injured party explained that "during the harvest, with the slightest exertion, my nose would start to bleed and keep on bleeding for half an hour or an hour. My nose was knocked on one side and remains so, and I can only blow it through one nostril."

Counsel for the defendant now produced a letter which W.W.B. admitted having written to White some time before. It was unsigned and the handwriting disguised. It read as follows:

> Dear Dick, Tha as been up to thy rowin agean I wore at Scots

dore an herd it ole. He get thy rag out Barker did he teld thee a good deal as I dident kno I knowd tha wor tworst devvel i england tha has had thy foot into my ribs but I shall be strete wi thee dick I kno wo it wor as nobbled the oer t head wi that stone thy hacts an deeds coles for Judgement and tha will die afore long wi thy shoes on an that ivvery boddys hoppinion an ivveryl be glad for Barker spoke t truth when he telled thee as ivvery boddy hated seet on thee tha fowl devvel. . . .

The letter continues at some length. W.W.B. also admitted having written a second letter to the defendant, part of which reads as follows:

Dronfield, April 15th.

Mr. White, Sir, I rite these few lines to inform you that your dauters are deceving you and being foold thereselves Mr. Frances young man is running about with them all day on a tuesday he was trotting the youngest out all afternoon last tuesday week and last tuesday they were all wateing 2 hours on piper wood brig and then they rote on the wole as they wor tired of stopping he ses he will marry the youngest if you will give him a thousand pounds they are spoiling their chances of marrying. . . .

The admission of sending these disguised letters did not help the plaintiff in his action for damages against White for the physical attack in the 'Yellow Lion' at Sheffield. However, the Judge had no option but to decide in favour of the plaintiff as the assault could not be justified. At the same time he did not think it had been wise to bring the case into court because on his own evidence W.W.B. had done quite sufficient "to provoke any man to strike him". As to damages the judge thought that a shilling would have been enough had White struck the plaintiff once or twice; as he had gone to excess and caused permanent damage to his nose he gave the verdict to W.W.B. for £5.

The second court case was heard at Dronfield Petty Sessions in 1883 as a result of threatening letters received by the assistant-overseer for the parish, a new man called George Jenkinson. In all he received six threatening letters; the first was received by post on 21st December 1882 and read as follows:

George Jenkinson, Are yew reedy tow meet yewor God, if no, do so, an lose no time thou has poluted this beautiful earth long enough with thee taxes and thee rates. Thee shalt die so mak ready for thal die.

The second was found fastened to the latch of the door on New Year's Day, 1883: "Death is near so mak ready."

During the night of 5th February a quantity of dirt was thrown at Jenkinson's windows and on the following night the frame of one of his windows was cut. Four nights later several holes were bored in his house door. Then on 13th February the third letter was put under the house door. It read as follows:

> Death is very near, be ready; death is always near. Death has not done its work yet, but it soon will have done so. Bobbies will not save thee; thee sees I know tha as get bobbies. George Jenkinson, be ready for death; it will come very soon. Killing no murder. Nout will save thee.

On the following morning the next letter arrived by post, commencing as follows:

> Killing, no murder, assassination no crime. These are the weapons for the poor man. George Jenkinson thy time has come. The night is not far distant. Dynamite. Thou genteel parish pauper, thou robber of the poor man. . . .

This particular letter was ornamented with "a death's head", cross bones, cross swords and pistols. Two weeks later, on 28th February 1883, the fifth letter was received by post. It went on at some length and contained certain admonitions:

> Our motto, killing no murder; assassination no crime. George Jenkinson, with all thy precautions thou has omitted one, that is to get a dog. A dog would be more use to thee than all the bobbies that were made. A bobby cannot smell and hear like a dog. Thou fool, if thou had got a dog thou sees thou could have caught us, for thou cannot get a dog under a week, and we shall been before a week is past. . . .

On 3rd March 1883 the sixth and last letter was received by Jenkinson. It began:

> George Jenkinson, I heard that you would like to know who sent you the letters and bored the door, and put the papers under etc. It is I, William Ward Barker. It is I who am the avenger of Dronfield. . . . I have seen all your doings. They can take me tomorrow if they like. I mean the bobbys. . . . I defy the law and the bobbys. You will think this bold, I suppose, but you can take me if you like. There is nothing

I would like better, for then I could prove that I was an avenger of Dronfield. Yours truly,

William Ward Barker.

Quoit Green Villas. I would not live with Bobbys. No, infra dig.

The defendant denied any knowledge of these letters and said that two weeks before he had had a letter published in the *Derbyshire Times* and on the same night a threatening letter had been pushed beneath his front door. It read: "We will murder you, sure enuff, then Dronfield will be right."

One of the magistrates ventured the opinion that he did not think it likely that a person in W.W.B.'s position would have written such letters, but that he was well known as a writer in the papers, and it was not surprising that he should be suspected of these compositions, particularly as he was fond of making use of Latin words which few in the parish were able to do. The case was dismissed.

W.W.B. was quick to put the editor of the *Sheffield Daily Telegraph* in his place following the report of the hearing in his paper:

I was not remanded on bail. The justices evidently took in the merits of the case and remanded me at large. . . . A very unwarrantable and unjustifiable outrage has been committed on my person in keeping with Dronfield, but more anon—I am, sir, yours respectfully,

W. W. Barker.

Dronfield, March 6th 1883.

It is something of a relief to find when perusing the voluminous scrap-book containing newspaper cuttings of W.W.B.'s letters to the press that some of them take up the fight on behalf of individuals who he believed were being given a raw deal in a context other than that of local government. There is space here for but one such communication to the *Derbyshire Times*. Even this, though, is directly connected with a facet of local government in so far as it concerns the unfair taxation of traction engines in the district at a time when these mechanical contraptions were becoming a fairly familiar sight in the area.

Dronfield, December 5th 1882

Sir, Scarcely ever a week passes without some record in your journal of the shortcomings of traction engines in general, and of Dronfield engines in particular. The press and the powers that be have risen "en masse" against these machines, which are regarded as an intolerable nuisance, so much so that they have gained for the owner an unenviable notoriety, but as I know you would not willingly kick a man when he is down permit me to offer a few remarks on the other side of the question. . . . I believe the justices have been very severe with Mr. Sheard, and he is of the same opinion for he told the Magistrates at the Dronfield Sessions the other day to shoot him at once. The amount of torture he has been subjected to, physical and mental, consequent on being the owner of these engines, is something awful, and anyone with feeling must be sorry for him; his eldest son was killed by an engine, and he has very narrowly escaped death from the same cause.

Then again he had been called upon to pay in fines and legal expenses more than has been spent on the roads from Dronfield to the Wooden Pole during the last twelve months. . . . In some instances, traction engines are credited with more damage to bridges and roads than is their due, Piper Wood Bridge and road to wit; the slight fracture in that bridge was caused by the subsidence of the foundation more than 25 years ago, and the road has been cut up by timber drags, traction engines having passed over it six times.

The letter is interesting as a document of local history in that by the remarks above it is possible to learn that Piper Wood Bridge (otherwise known as Lee Bridge on the lane between Dronfield and Barlow Lees) suffered foundation settlement only fifteen or sixteen years after its erection in 1841. It continues by pointing out that Mr. Sheard offered to keep "the Holmesfield roads" in good repair for 30 per cent less than such repairs cost before the advent of the traction engine hereabouts. His price was £40 per mile per year. The letter concludes thus:

Mr. Sheard has expended some £1,500 in engines and waggons, he has also paid £17 recently for the licence to run them and I submit he has as much right to run them as any innkeeper to sell wines and spirits, and would suggest that, instead of the authorities seeking to make the restrictions so severe that it is impossible for the engines to be utilized they should, as the more honourable course, petition the Government to repeal the Act of Parliament altogether and make the owners compensation for vested interests.

I am, sir, yours truly,
Fairplay

As we now know the traction engine did get a better deal in following years but this was one of the first suggestions that such a lessening of taxation was desirable. In the years up to and well into the twenties the steam-driven traction engine did a tremendous amount of hard work throughout the town and country; it continued as motive power with threshing contractors up to the end of the forties, losing favour when the diesel engine became relatively commonplace in the agricultural tractor.

Throughout a long and active life W.W.B. kept a diary, as was usually the habit with the literate Victorian man. It is fortunate that the diary for 1916, for the last few months of his life, still exists. There is space for but extracts here:

Saturday, January 1st 1916

Very wet, stormy, uncomfortable day. Stayed close to the fire. F.M. came to tea. H. Allen and Tom Barker called for Bell Ringers' Christmas box (2 shillings) in the evening. Treated them to a glass of rum.

The following Tuesday W.W.B. records, among other things, that Income Tax is 3s. in the pound. On the next day:

Fair, cold, clearer atmosphere. Tried to keep warm by staying by the fireside. Barber came as usual to shave me p.m. Mrs. Thompson returned from London where she went to interview her fiance's family which she alleges is satisfactory.

On Saturday 8th January, we read:

Nice, fine, mild day. Had a walk on Cemetery Road as far as the gates. Mary [daughter] went to Chesterfield to buy me a turkey with which to honour Glady's 23rd birthday [youngest daughter] which falls on 10th instant. She went to Sheffield to dine with Mrs. Thompson. Mary paid nine shillings for turkey, 1 shilling for sausage and 1 shilling bus fare. F. Allen was working in the garden a couple of hours.

At the end of the month, on Friday 28th, the weather was still set fair:

Fine and mild, like early spring. Took a walk to the fowls and on Cemetery Road in a.m.

Thrushes singing, crocuses in bloom in the garden, Gladys took me in the bath chair to the butcher's. Bought beef—6 lbs, 6/-, Suet 2d.

On February 1st the weather was foggy and cold:

Zeppelins have been raiding again, seen at Chesterfield.

Very forward condition of vegetation. Crocuses and snowdrops out, yellow jasmine in full bloom. Roses are in leaf, am afraid they will receive a check before very long.

His fears were realized and on Wednesday 9th February, the diary reads:

Another white world with frost. Very slippery. Mrs. Harrison called, also Mary. Gladys took my teeth back, could not stand them in my mouth. I wrote the Atlas Company, London for quotation for insurance on damage from aerial raids.

Spring weather came in early April. On the 26th—a lovely day—

Gladys went to Sheffield to get some fish for Annie. Dobby took me in the chair to the butcher's. Paid him 7/- for meat. After dinner Gladys and Dobbie took me round Hill Top. Had a man digging in the Croft. Padley came and took tea with me. Mr. Holford came after tea and stayed while his daughters and Gladys had a drive in the trap to Norton. They returned at 7.0 p.m.

The next day was fine and warm, a man was setting potatoes in the Croft for three hours. The vicar, Rev. Groocock, called during the morning. Refreshing sunlight slanted through the mullioned windows of Quoit Green House all day. On the following day, Friday 28th April, the weather was again lovely and fine:

Mr. Johnson brought 4 lbs of King Edward potatoes – paid 3/10d for them. Old man came again and finished setting in the Croft. Slacked some lime, paid him 5/5d.

I have felt very languid all day. Gladys went to Sheffield, paid 2/7d for some bacon.

The weather was again fine and warm on the next day but the diary is written in another hand: "Pa died. Left in purse £4.19.6d."

To most local people my great-grandfather was known as 'Cakey' Barker, a name which lingers on the tongues of the oldest inhabitants. Not long ago an old farmer in Cordwell Valley was recounting some story of over half a century ago, referring to 'Cakey' Barker. "But you wouldn't know him, he's been dead these fifty-odd years," he recalled. I was pleased to be able to tell him that he was a relation of mine! The nickname seems to have been earned by his far-sightedness in being a pioneer of scientific livestock feeding in the district. He was probably the first farmer in the parish to give cakes to his cattle and horses.

Upon much of the 16 acres adjoining Quoit Green he built stone and brick houses, including most of the property on Scarsdale Road. This was once a rough track leading to the west off Hallowes Lane, but he erected rows of brick houses and upon the walls of some he had a layer of concrete applied. Ever afterwards these came to be known as the 'Mud Row'. Only recently have these been demolished.

There is space here to recount only one more memory of William Ward Barker. It was his habit to ride wherever possible on horseback and he sometimes went over the Finney Fields to Holmesfield. Some time after April 1887 (it is impossible to say exactly in what month or year) he was returning over the fields from visiting the Reverend Charles Bradshaw at Holmesfield long after dark. He reached the Big Chestnut two fields from Farwater Lane and proceeded across them. His route took him close by the old, unconsecrated burial ground where victims of the local cholera morbus epidemic of 1832 were buried, but before he reached it he made out the figure of a small child dressed, it seemed, in white. The child approached him and took hold of one of the stirrup irons, walking alongside the horse. Thinking it to be a frightened local child caught in the fields after dusk he said nothing. Only when the child left the horse's side and disappeared over the wall into the burial ground did my great-grandfather realize that what he had seen was an apparition.

His daughter Mary was my maternal grandmother. She married into the Dearden family who lived at Jordanthorpe Hall, Norton. In his historic account of the village of Norton and its environs entitled *Chantrey Land* (published 1910), Harold Armitage describes Jordanthorpe Hall as being ". . . covered with ivy, but a portico stands clear of this green profusion, and the house is one of the most attractive in Norton". The famous cartoonist Linley Sambourne who made his name working for *Punch* was brought up by his aunt Linley in this big house. A member of this Linley family was Elizabeth, the "Maid of Bath" painted by Gainsborough and destined to become Sheridan's wife. The name Jordanthorpe (within Derbyshire until the parish of Norton was transferred to the city of Sheffield in 1934) is very old. There is a reference to it as "Jurdanthorpe" in 1290—meaning 'Jordan's outlying farm'.

My grandparents, the Deardens, lived at Rhyl Cottage in Hallowes Lane and later at adjoining 'Beechcroft'. Both properties were part of the Ward-Barker estate. When I think of 'Beechcroft' it is summer, and the leaves are upon the tall trees, beech and elm, overhanging the lane. The garden is full of the odd and the curious; a young laburnum tree tied in a knot while still a sapling by grandad; a strange glazed drainpipe with several mouths and branches from which grow ferns and geraniums at crazy angles, the work of my grandad when he worked at a brick refractory; the secret arbour beneath a shading mayblob tree, strewn with great, white snowballs in early summer—what a surprise grandma got if I crept down the path by the great, red Californian poppies and jumped out into the arbour where she often sat; then there is the garden shed in the kitchen garden which is really forbidden territory, the preserve of my grandad, where rows of tools await long hours of toil. The rainwater tank beside the garden shed often contains a large bag of soot or farmyard manure suspended in it for some obscure reason and what delight there is in secretly stirring it round to see the black or brown juice whirling, care being taken that no one ever came upon the scene unexpectedly. The delights of the wash-house were many; the highly geared grindstone is turned as fast as possible with one hand while my grandad's files are held against the screaming stone with the other to produce a fine display of golden, blue and red sparks which shower this way and that in the gloom with the door carefully shut. Only once do I remember being caught red-handed as it were, by the mechanic-in-charge! Another instrument of delight in the wash-house which exists now, I imagine, only in the memory was the mechanical washtub. It had a long vertical handle and by pushing and pulling a series of gear wheels spun wooden 'peg legs' inside the wooden butter-churn-like tub and so swirled the contents. What fun there was in driving the gear wheels around at high speed by means of powerful pulls on that handle and in hearing the thunderous reciprocation of these 'peg legs'. With a final effort I let the handle go as Lizzie entered, throwing up her wet, red hands as the contraption rocked across the concrete floor towards her, seeming quite out of control.

Mention of Lizzie reminds me of my grandma's subsequent maid. Ellen was a simple-minded soul of about 60 at the time of which I write. She had been brought up on a farm at Barlow and spent some years attempting to assist in the household at 'Beechcroft'. My favourite memory of little, broad-faced, smiling Ellen is of seeing her doing acrobatics at the cellarhead in her efforts to reach a far-off jar of jam or cut glass dish of pickled beetroot. In this hair-raising move at the top of the steep steps leading to the semi-subterranean cellar she used a large copper handle which grandad had fastened to the door frame to help in just such operations. I never saw Ellen fall, though she often had cause for alarm as I frequently used to give her a sharp push from behind when she was at full stretch over the void. In exasperation at her lack of imagination my grandmother gave her the nickname 'Cowslip', not the most appropriate of designations for a wholesome but tiresome bumkin! Happily, poor Ellen is still alive, back in her native parish over the hill; still able to recount far-off farm days when she used to drive the flock of sheep from Barlow to Cutthorpe three-quarters of a century ago.

Of all birdsong none is more evocative of those distant, sunlit days than the long, descending note often made by starlings. I first noticed it when I was staying at 'Beechcroft' at the age of 4. It was summer and the bedroom window was left open all night so that early next morning the songs of the birds occupying the tall trees round the house were the first thing I heard. For many years I heard that characteristic descending note without being sure what bird made it. Maybe it was the plentiful house-sparrows, I thought. Whatever made it I knew it as a Hallowes Lane sound and now that it has been identified the starling is always associated in my mind as a Hallowes Lane bird.

The large bay window of the sitting-room occupies a commanding position overlooking Hallowes Lane. It is a fine vantage point from which to watch the passers-by. That sitting-room was both a centre of intelligent conversation and a hive of gossip. On most afternoons and evenings my grandmother's friends would call to discuss up-to-the-minute happenings, scandals, deaths and births. Everyone was made welcome and food and drink were proffered liberally.

"What do you think she said then!" snapped Mrs. Norton, her silver hair flashing in time with her blue-grey eyes.

"See, who is that going up? A stranger; must be going to the club," said another looking into the lane.

"It is nothing short of a scandal! I shall stop them and ask them who they think they are next time I see them together!" declared Miss Outram, her nose curling up in indignation. She always seemed to be indignant to me as I listened quietly from a corner. Once upon a time Miss Outram had been the subject of a local scandal herself, for she was a headmistress with pioneer views on physical education for girls. She was not deterred by such small-mindedness and strode indignantly on, waging war in co-operation with my grandmother wherever she suspected humbug.

So the steady evening light glows down through those beech and elm leaves sheltering Hallowes Lane. It still penetrates the corners of those gardens long since vacated by the people who created them. Quoit Green House and Rhyl Cottage still stand beside Hallowes Lane, with 'Beechcroft' between them. An oboe played far over the hill echoes down those steep fields and is heard still in the 'Croft' where mayblobs once hung so heavily about the arbour. Do they still, I wonder, enfold that favourite seat? At last light a dark figure makes its way up the lane homewards; it could be any one of those many people who live on in the memory. Those memories which made conscious bring both happiness and tears, an inward smile and pain to the heart.

Monsal Head Viaduct and Headstones Tunnel from Putwell Hill

(*above*) A southbound special train, hauled by No. 4472 Flying Scotsman, thunders through Dronfield Station in the autumn of 1968. (*below*) In Haddon Tunnel

THREE

A Conspicuous Derbyshire Hilltop and a Village

Peakland is not notable for the outstanding quality of its hill shapes. It has relatively few conical hills and fewer remarkable topographical profiles. There is, of course, Shutlingsloe on the very western fringe of the Peak District, which must rank as the *pièce de résistance* in this respect, having few rivals nearer than the Wrekin in Salop and Pendle Hill in eastern Lancashire. However, there are several notable Derbyshire heights which are notable in a subtle sort of way; hilltops which impress from several angles because of their interesting shape in a countryside of unremarkable crests and slopes.

Of all the lesser heights of Peakland and its wonderful fringe my favourite is Glasshouse Hill, dominating eminence of the Drone Valley. Its maximum height is 664 feet above sea level so that on the score of altitude alone it cannot claim any distinction. But due to the haphazard forces of weathering it has been left at just that point in relation to the surrounding ridges and valleys where it is most conspicuous, where it assumes a central point of focus in views from almost all angles. Actually it is at its most insignificant when viewed from the north and north-east, from that ground of equal or greater altitude between Apperknowle and Eckington.

For eight years Glasshouse Hill was at the focal point of my view as I walked homewards down Stubley Lane from Gosforth and in that time I came to know intimately the wonderful pattern of fields through every season, and those hilltop trees just 3 miles away across the unseen valley where the Drone winds murkily down from Dronfield towards Sheepbridge. During the autumn each yellow stubble field on that visible north-western flank above and below Windmill Lane turned to brown in turn as each was ploughed. Every spring the exotic pattern of green was renewed as young corn grew to rival the permanent pastures and mow meadows; and as summer comes and goes the colours assume the variety of a patchwork quilt, re-arranged each year. The meadows are mowed and cleared of hay to leave a yellow-brown rectangle, the pastures remain green, the cornfields slowly lose their vivid verdant hue and by late summer shine burnished in the afternoon sunlight. Golden pockets set about by dark green fringes of hedgerow and woodland.

From the upper reaches of the Barlow Vale, Glasshouse Hill peeps over the intervening ridge above Monk Wood, its topmost fields normally set with corn and offering gold to the late summer sky. From this angle, in Unthank Fields close by Rose Wood, the important role played by Grasscroft Wood in the configuration of Glasshouse Hill is clearly seen. The wood grows right across the southern flank between 500 feet and to within a few feet of the summit. The uppermost trees overtop the summit quite considerably so that their profile accentuates the dome-shaped crest, making it seem quite conical. A crook-shaped hill in the true tradition of Peakland profiles, subtle rather than dramatic, suggestive rather than positively accentuated.

From the fields about Old Brampton one has an exceptionally wide view of the southern and western flanks, though from a distance of over 4 miles. The trees smother the top and the particular field pattern seen from Stubley Lane and in the fields between Dronfield and Unstone are almost lost to sight. The name of the wood, Grasscroft, dates from at least the very beginning of the last century—appearing as "Grass Croft Wood" in large-scale maps of 1801 making up part of the Fairbank Collection in Sheffield Public Library. The name appears to have a straightforward meaning and needs no further explanation here. As for the name of the hill itself the words "Glass House" appeared on a plan made in 1769 and referred to the old dwelling of that name which stands at 430 feet above sea level on the south-eastern flank of the hill, on the ancient track leading up from the New Whittington-Handley road.

Richard Dixon came to the district soon after 1730 to found a glassworks. Sand for glass-making was brought by barge up the Chesterfield Canal and unloaded at a wharf at New Whittington, which came to be known as Dixon's Wharf. Little evidence

Glasshouse Hill and the lower Drone Valley from Old Brampton

remains in the vicinity of Glasshouse to show that the place was an important industrial centre. Whittington glass was a lovely product, a glass possessing a pale-blue cast and used to make tumblers, vases and pieces, particularly cruets, in collaboration with the Sheffield Plate trade. Several factors caused the decline of glass manufacture here, and it ceased finally about 1850.

At the time of the Domesday survey Whittington was called 'Witintune'. Three and a half centuries later (1433) it had been corrupted to 'Qwyttyngton'. The name stems from the Old English—'Hwita-ing tun', literally 'Hwita's farm'. Originally it was joined with the Manor of Brimington, William Peverel being lord of the manor. It was granted by King John to a William Briewere and thereafter it passed successively to several notable Derbyshire families, including the notable Foljambes, though the immediate possessors were the ancient family of Whittington from an early date. In 1257 it passed from Simon de Whittington to Robert Dethick. Eventually a portion of the manor was sold in 1813 to John Dixon, one of the glass-makers, and by 1846 the sole lord of the manor was Henry Dixon. This notable industrialist had built Whittington Hall a mile to the north-east of the village in 1822 and he lived there when not at his other residence at Oxford. The original 'big house' of this hillside settlement is

Whittington Hall Farm, a building described by Sir Nikolaus Pevsner as "a handsome sixteenth-century farm-house . . . with gables and three- and four-light low mullioned windows". This building exudes antiquity, mellowed domestic architecture of the finest type; unpretentious in the extreme and shadowing a quieter time now faded in harmony with the well-weathered stones forming its fabric. It is almost certain that the house stood in Elizabethan times, probably built upon the remains of a far older dwelling. Tradition asserts that Dick Whittington once lived here and set forth for London from the crumbling doorway. This is only a tradition—and surely Sir Richard had his roots at Whittington, Shropshire, close to the Welsh border. The old house has been nothing more than a neglected farm dwelling for a long time and today it stands forlorn and neglected overlooking the secluded little approach to the parish church, as nice a close as any I have seen. Looking recently at old photographs it was disturbing to notice that several old cottages which adjoined this square or close have now gone and the place has lost something of its intimacy. Still, here is a fine approach to the quiet of the church and its graveyard and the several tree-shaded alleys or walks.

The Hall Farm stands empty and over it hangs the threat of demolition; and this demolition will not give room for open fields or trees but the development of several bungalows. The argument goes that the cost of repair would be prohibitive; not so high, though, that the planning authority could not afford to help interested parties to see the building and its entire environment revitalized. There are few lovelier buildings in this part of the Peakland fringe but it may well be that by the time that this chapter is read the ancient central feature of the Whittington church approach will have disappeared forever, having taken with it an aura of slower days and longer summers.

At the south-western corner of the graveyard of Whittington Parish Church was built in 1674 the grammar school, founded with £200 left by Peter Webster "to be invested in land for the maintenance of a schoolmaster". In his will this benefactor directed that the sum of 36s. be given annually to "six poor scholars, to buy them books, and the residue of the rents to be distributed to the poor". In early Victorian times the school was moved a short distance to Church Street, largely due to the efforts of the local and well-known Swanwick family. For some reason the ugly, redbrick school at Whittington Moor was later designated the Peter Webster School; though there was a second Peter Webster, who in 1750 gave a charity to be used to assist the local poor. The old grammar school, now at Church Street, has taken the name of Mary Swanwick in honour of one of the best known and loved members of that local family.

The church was built in Victorian times as a replacement for the very old building which may have dated from Norman times. An old etching taken from the *Gentleman's Magazine* shows the original church as it appeared in 1783. It shows a tiny tower and a sharp spire reminiscent of that at Barlow. This building had been added to (enlarged or altered as fashion and parish wealth dictated) at many periods, but by 1862 there developed a dispute which contributed much bitterness to the parish. One group of churchmen desired that the lovely little building should be carefully restored, the other group demanded a new building. The latter faction had their way, the church was demolished and a new one in the modern idiom erected some distance to the north. Among those advocating repair of the old church were the Dixons of glass-making fame. They left the village and never returned. We may well appreciate their sense of helpless anguish as we, a century later, contemplate the final destruction of the nearby Hall Farm.

Some may have looked back thirty years with a knowing sigh when, in 1895, the new church was almost totally destroyed by fire. The chancel and nave were gutted and many of the treasures (including parish registers) were destroyed. Only the tower and spire remained intact.

A decade after the first new church was erected, a 17-year-old girl came to live in the village from the lovely village of her birth, Wragley in Leicestershire. In 1874, the year after her arrival, Emily became a Sunday School teacher and so began a long and deep association with the parish church, an association extending over the offices of six rectors. This Emily Lewin ran a private school in the village, at which she taught a future Governor of Assam and Mamie Parker, later the Duchess of Somerset. In 1889 she married Edward Redfern, organist and choirmaster at the neighbouring St. Barnabas' Church, New Whittington for forty-four years and second Master at New Whittington School until his death in

1920. Though associated with many charitable and church societies her great devotion was to the church organ. When Emily Redfern retired from the post of organist at Old Whittington Parish Church at the age of 79 years she was the oldest church organist in the country. Her memory lingers in the village she served with great love for well over sixty years; only recently a native of the village told me "Whenever I think of your grandmother I am reminded of things, of qualities which have vanished from the world. She epitomizes graceful life, restraint, peace and charity. We shall never see the like of her sort again". It was in March 1938 that my grandmother died, at the age of 82. I have a memory of her as she sat in a high, sunlit bedroom at Church Street, propped up by pillows and wrapped in a mauve and white woollen shawl. That is all, the memory lingers but there is no more to reinforce it.

In an earlier age the parish church of St. Bartholomew had a long association with a notable antiquary. He was the famous Dr. Samuel Pegge, who came as rector in 1751 and died in office in 1796. His studies of the past were legion, but one of his greatest contributions was a history of the church written in 1793. There is sufficient space here to mention only one or two interesting facts. The 'Ting-Tang' bell (or Saint's Bell) hung within a stone frame or tabernacle 'at the top of the church' between the nave and chancel; that is, on the outside of the building. Dr. Pegge notes that;

> it has a remarkable fine shrill tone and is heard, it is said, three or four miles off, if the wind be right. It is very ancient, as appears both from the form of the letters and the name which is that in use before surnames were common. Perhaps it may be as old as the fabric of the church itself, though this is very ancient. The inscription, in Lombardic characters, is as follows:—RICARD: L:E: FTZ: JOHAN.

Dr. Pegge's researches at Whittington established that there was a rectory here as early as 1140 and that there was a rector by the year 1219, though his name has long been forgotten. In 1302 Roger de Mabelthorp became the next rector, to be succeeded by nineteen others before Dr. Samuel Pegge arrived in 1751. During the office of this illustrious cleric, in 1785, the two church bells were weighed and found to total 317 pounds. Subsequently they were sold for 8d. per pound, being badly cracked. A pair of new bells, weighing 413 pounds, were bought at 1s. 4d. per pound from a foundry in Lancashire. The tower of the new church contains one of these 1785 bells and five new ones. Dr. Pegge died at the age of 91 in February 1796, and was buried in the chancel of the original church. The memorial tablet in black marble was situated over the east window and was moved in due course to the new building.

The village is almost without parallel in the number of famous associations with it—events and, more particularly, people of note. A first acquaintance would suggest a typical north-east Derbyshire village at the fringe of Peakland somewhat overwhelmed by industrial development at its edges.

At 'Elm Wood', by the road towards Handley, lived the caricaturist Phil May. He was born in 1864 and worked as artist for the *St. Stephen's Review, Pick-me-up, Pall Mall Budget, The Graphic,* and for *Punch,* where he became so well known as successor to George du Maurier before his early death on 5th August 1903. Subsequently 'Elm Wood' became the home of Henry Brealey when he worked for the large steel manufacturers of Brown Bayley Ltd. of Sheffield. Previously Brealey had worked for Thomas Firth and Sons Ltd. and while so employed had invented stainless steel. It was because of this discovery that the patent for Firth Stainless Steel was procured.

More than a century earlier Joseph Brotherton had been born (in May 1783) at Old Whittington and worked in a nearby factory, working his way to a partnership in the business. After the Battle of Waterloo he became connected with a powerful political party in Manchester and in 1827 was elected first M.P. for Salford. Perhaps his fight against the notorious Corn Laws stands out as the greatest contribution he made in a very active life. To the memory of this life of public service a statue of Brotherton stands in Peel Park, Salford, bearing the following telling words from one of his speeches to Parliament: "My riches consist, not in the extent of my possessions, but in the fewness of my wants".

By strange coincidence there was born at Old Whittington in the same year that Phil May was born in Yorkshire (1864) a child destined to become a great English artist. Joseph Siddall was born into a Whittington family of joiners and undertakers and began work in a Chesterfield solicitor's office. His talents were well known locally and Miss Mary Swanwick, of the notable Whittington family, took the initiative of sponsoring the young Jo.

He studied in London under Sir Hubert von Herkomer, Slade Professor at Oxford 1885–1894. Though Joseph Siddall's work is not now widely known, he created copiously, though much of his work was tragically destroyed during World War II. He designed the Great War memorials at both Old Whittington and Dronfield, and both stand in a sense as memorials to his genius. The memorial at Old Whittington, with its ingenious crosses on all four faces, was executed by Tom Moxon who lived in the village. Jo Siddall died at the age of 78 in 1942.

Less than three months before the dawn of the twentieth century was born at Church Street a boy who was destined to become a foremost engineer of his time. He was Arthur Lewin Redfern, son of Edward and Emily. His elder brother, Rowland, rose to become Managing Director of the Bryan Donkin Company at Chesterfield. Gaining a scholarship to the grammar school at Dronfield Arthur later joined the Royal Navy and served on mine sweepers during World War I. After returning to Whittington he worked at the extensive works of the Sheepbridge Coal and Iron Company close by the murky confluence of the River Drone with the Barlow Brook, and later for Sheepbridge Stokes Ltd. He became well known as a research engineer and inventor, patenting with a fellow engineer a successful method of converting reciprocating motion to rotary motion (or vice versa) by means of gears; and several other original patents were taken out and brought into general use. However, it was as the pioneer of centrifugally-cast cylinder liners that he became best known, most of those now in use in internal combustion engines having been designed by Arthur Lewin Redfern. In later years he became a Consultant Engineer and took most successfully to the design and construction of steel-framed buildings in the modern idiom. Though a notable engineer and technician A.L.R. was most at home in garden, wood and on the high hills for he was at heart a real countryman.

Still living in the village is Wesley Stone a friend and contemporary of Arthur Lewin Redfern. Here is a wonderful example of the local enthusiast, a man passionately devoted to his native habitat, to the soil about him. His great-grandfather came during the thirties of the last century from Ashover to teach in Old Whittington. For most of the time since, the family has lived in Clematis Cottage in Church Street, where Wesley Stone and his wife still reside. He is undoubtedly the greatest authority on the village and the world authority upon the subject of the Great Revolution of 1688.

Samuel Bagshawe's *History Gazeteer and Directory of Derbyshire* published in 1846 states that "there are few places in England equally distinguished in the annals of history with the village of Whittington". What, briefly, was this Great Revolution and in what way is Whittington connected with it?

James II had succeeded his brother, Charles II, in 1685 and his conversion to Roman Catholicism was unpopular. His efforts to emancipate the Catholics led to rebellion. Amongst the powerful noblemen who wished to see James off the throne so that all threats of Catholicism should be removed was the Earl of Devonshire. Two traditions exist concerning the decisive meeting which led to the revolt against the unpopular king. One states that the Earl of Devonshire's harriers were taken to Whittington Moor—then an infertile area of common and river confluence—so that everyone in the district would be following the chase. According to an old account "when the pack were in full cry, and the field in hot pursuit, his lordship and friends drew away from the hunt, and rode to the 'Cock and Pynot' (pynot is the old name for magpie), to deliberate upon the means by which to procure King James' overthrow".

The second tradition is that the Earl of Devonshire and his friends "had agreed to meet in council on the moor, but being inconvenienced by a storm they sought shelter at the inn". Whichever account is the more accurate it is certain that James II was a mediocre king and never understood his subjects. Louis XIV of France repeatedly warned him of the imminent danger but the latter refused any help, relying almost entirely upon the strength of his navy. The little party were ushered into a private parlour—ever afterwards known as the 'Plotting Parlour'—by the landlord. At this meeting to plan the overthrow of the king it is known that there were, besides the Earl of Devonshire, the Earl of Danby, Lord Delamere and John D'Arcy (son and heir of Conyers, Earl of Holderness). It is not certain that another supporter of the proposed revolution, Sir Scroop Howe, was actually present at Whittington on that November day in 1688. Seated in high-backed chairs around a small table the group examined a map of the country and agreed upon the wording of the invitation to the

Prince of Orange to take the throne when James had been expelled. William was a grandson of Charles I and had married James II's daughter, Mary.

It was agreed that the Earl of Danby was to give the signal for the rising in the north of England and Devonshire was to raise an armed force in the Midlands. He was to become the First Duke of Devonshire (created thus by William in 1694), a man of few words and great action who had become the leader of the Opposition four years before the plotting at Whittington.

William landed at Tor Bay on 5th December 1688, and before entering Exeter the Earl of Devonshire had reached Derby with a small group of followers and declared before the mayor his support for William. It was soon clear that William was taking all before him, gathering evermore support as he passed from Bristol to Salisbury and on to London. James fled for France on 10th December but was stopped at Faversham, Kent. However, William decided it wisest to let him go and so he was allowed to 'escape' on 23rd December. This time the king reached France, where Louis XIV gave him security and the seclusion of a house at St. Germain.

William III and his queen, Mary, made successful joint-sovereigns. The early death of Mary in 1694 dealt William a severe blow, though he continued to reign with distinction for another eight years. At this time James was still dreaming of a successful return to the throne. He attempted to fight his way by way of Ireland but was defeated in July 1690, by William at the Boyne, showing the same incompetence as previously. He died a year before William III at St. Germain, having spent his last years as a penitent.

The 'Cock and Pynot' sank into obscurity after 1688. For many years it was the property of the Dukes of Devonshire but was sold in December 1880, to Mansfeldt F. Mills of Tapton Grove, Chesterfield. At this sale the Duke reserved the right in the event of the building being pulled down "to erect and maintain a stone to commemorate the site of the Revolution House". The new owner wrote, some two years after his purchase, that it was his wish to keep "the tottering old fabric together so long as may be practicable, and certainly, I hope, till after the bi-centenary in 1888, when, no doubt, a great gathering of Liberals will again be held on the spot to celebrate the Revolution of 1699".

The centenary of the Revolution was marked by "great festivities" in the area. A service was held in Whittington parish church, conducted by the Rev. Samuel Pegge—later Dr. Pegge—who was celebrating his eighty-fourth birthday on the very same day (5th November 1788). His sermon, later published in pamphlet form, condemned the "ill advised" James II and praised at length the virtues of William III. Regarding the Revolution itself he claimed that "the most High was pleased to approve and bless the measure, as was fully demonstrated by His Hand so evidently appearing in it, by the many favourable circumstances that attended the Prince's Expedition".

Following the service of commemoration the company went down the street in procession "to view the room called the Revolution Parlour, and the Old Arm Chair; and then partook of a cold collation, which was prepared in the new rooms annexed to the cottage". The great procession then formed and moved "in regular order" to Chesterfield, where the rest of the day "was spent with the utmost cordiality and rejoicing". The cavalcade or procession must have constituted an impressive sight for the hundreds of onlookers for it extended a considerable distance, as the detailed Order of Procession below suggests:

Constables with Long Staffs
Mr. Deakin's Club
Mr. Bluett's Club
Mr. Ostiffe's Club
Mr. Barber's Club
Mr. Wilkinson's Club
Mr. Stubb's Club
Mrs. Ollerenshaw's Club
Mr. Masingale's Club
County Clubs if any attend.
N.B.—The members of the club to go four and four.
The Derbyshire Band of Music
The Corporation of Chesterfield in their usual order to join the procession on entering the town of Chesterfield.
The Duke of Devonshire's coach and six.
The Attendants
Other coaches and six in proper order, with their respective attendants.
The coaches and four with their attendants.
The chaises and four in like manner.

The chaises and pair in like manner.
Hack Post Chaises
Gentlemen on Horseback, three and three.
Servants on Horseback, three and three.

This grand parade of county and local dignitaries and their servants in a fine assemblage of wheeled vehicles made its way along Holywell Street, up Saltergate after the sharp, right turn, and so down Glumangate to turn left along the upper side of the Market Place to "Mr. Wilkinson's house" and down past the mayor's house, back westwards along the lower side of the market place to the end of West Bars and "from thence past Dr. Milne's house to the Castle", where the Derbyshire Band of Music left the procession. Dispersal took place finally outside the mayor's house overlooking the eastern side of the market place. Dinner was served to the vast congregation at the three principal inns of the town at four o'clock and two and a half hours later there was a grand display of fireworks, followed by a ball at the Assembly Rooms which went on long into the November night.

A century later the bi-centenary of the Revolution was celebrated in a similar way, a service being conducted at Whittington's new parish church by the rector, the Rev. G. W. Botham. Similar services were held at Newbold and at the Primitive Methodist Chapel at Whittington. After the service at the parish church a great crowd gathered close to the Revolution House to hear long speeches by several dignitaries. The area was decked by triumphal arches, flags and garlands which were on a surprisingly massive scale—as indicated by a pen and ink illustration by W. Fidler in the booklet produced to commemorate the bi-centenary which I am lucky enough to have in my possession. The speeches delivered on that dull, damp autumn day were long and, some, tedious, as shown by the pages which they occupy in the commemorative booklet. There was the chairman of the Celebration Committee, the mayor, Mr. T. D. Bolton M.P., and a Mr. Jeudwine. A procession even longer than the one a hundred years previously now made its way towards Chesterfield.

A detailed list of the people and groups represented in this great crocodile is beyond the scope of this chapter though it did include such diverse interests as:

The Tradesmen of Whittington
Independent Order of Good Templars

Independent Order of Oddfellows
Manchester Unity
Potter's Glory Lodge
Terra Firma Lodge
Miner's Lodge
Ancient Order of Foresters
Court Havelock
Bud of Hope Lodge
Ancient Order of Druids (Sheffield Equalized District)
Drum and Fife Band
Church of England Sunday School
Chesterfield Grammar School boys under the charge of the Headmaster, Mr. A. E. P. Voules, M.A.

Speeches followed in the market place, longer than ever, and a great banquet of eight courses was taken by a great company in the Assembly Room of the Market Hall, at which Lord Edward Cavendish, M.P. gave an address, received with "loud and prolonged applause". Grand firework displays ensued at Whittington and Chesterfield, supplied by Messrs. J. Pain and Son. It is recorded that "owing to the time of the year Messrs. Pain omitted elaborate set pieces which are seldom successful in damp weather, and substituted aerial designs of great beauty, the blending of colours in air, the flights of rockets fired from immense mortars, being specially grand."

A final act of celebration was the provision of a "treat for the poor of the town". About 200 of the aged and poor living in Chesterfield sat down to "an excellent tea" in the Lower Corn Exchange before the fireworks began.

At the time of the Revolution the Cock and Pynot Inn where the secret meeting took place was a long, low building, having six rooms upon the ground floor, the northern end of the row being private quarters. Due to decay and dereliction this northern section was finally demolished, leaving the present squat building with its thatched roof and pretty dormer window. Long ago the licence of the public house was transferred to the newer building behind the Revolution House. This is now the Cock and Magpie Inn and the Revolution House has become a notable public museum run by Chesterfield Corporation and containing a copious collection of relics associated with Whittington and its close connection with the seventeenth-century rebellion. Wesley

Stone is the curator and no better an authority on this village and its past is it possible to imagine, a man of immense learning and feeling for his native soil and stones.

Go up behind the village on a crisp autumn evening, up the fields towards the crouching wood of Grasscroft which crowns the crest of this most conspicuous Derbyshire hill called Glass-house. As the sunset banners unfurl in the west the grey-blue bulk of Grange Hill, Eastmoor beyond and those familiar steeps of home about Monk Wood change to an ever darker solidity, washed with a brush and colours so soft that at times they melt into the haze of the Drone Valley below and into the sky above. It is possible to imagine the inhabitants who lived all their quiet lives just below in the village and who now largely lie in the shadow of the trees and St. Bartholomew's church.

There was the labourer-craftsman called Woodward who lived in a cottage close by Hundall Lane. He was very tall, thin and immensely strong. He spent much time travelling about local farms making and thatching hay- and cornstacks in the summer. In the winter he helped with threshing and a dozen other jobs on several holdings in the district. One hot summer's day a visitor came to the haystack which Woodward was making. The visitor asked the farmer who the tall, thin stack-maker was.

"Oh, him? Woodward—and he's got a brother twice as tall and half as thin!" the farmer replied. Unfortunately the skilled labourer had a limited sense of humour and instantly flew into a rage, threatening to leave the stack and never return.

In old age old Woodward had the frightening habit of walking with his back bent so that he appeared to be a doubled-up little man. Suddenly, to the consternation of strangers and all the village children, he would straighten up to his full height of 6 feet 4 inches as he passed them.

Another long-dead character of the village was a man called Bonser. He was a nightly visitor at the 'Cock and Magpie' and regularly bragged that he had never been frightened of anything in his long life. A group of youths decided to play a practical joke on old Bonser and lay in wait one dark night in the churchyard, armed with sheets. Now it was the old man's habit to walk home up the long, flagged Slack Walk and as he passed by the darker shadows of the churchyard trees on this particular occasion the white-sheeted forms rose from behind the gravestones uttering spine-chilling calls. Old Bonser turned casually towards the apparitions, stopped in his tracks and, pushing his hat back, said, "It's either Resurrection Morning or you've all got up to pass water!" So saying he passed on homewards.

And so with the passing of time the village changes its character. Whittington Hall—once a notable house of the gentry—is now a mental home; a new piece of road by-passes Church Street and the hillside part of the village near to the church and the decaying Hall Farm. Perhaps that is a good thing for it certainly leaves the upper portion of Whittington as a back-water. The redbrick rows of cottages forming the ineptly named Mount Pleasant still stand as reminders of the Victorian and Edwardian colliery and industrial interests of the area. There were several small collieries hereabouts and a great number of village men worked at Sheepbridge Works, a mile and a half below in the Drone Valley. From our viewpoint in the fields beneath the top of Glasshouse Hill it was a really dramatic sight to watch at night as the great blast furnaces at Sheepbridge were tapped. The blackness of winter midnights was suddenly shot through with orange, red and rose. If there were low clouds about they were caught in the glare and reflected one to another the shimmering light, an illumination with satanic overtones and backed up by the distant noise of clashing metal and great activity. That nightly spectacle of the many men-controlled furnaces vanished years ago, to be replaced by the vastly less romantic automatic blast furnaces. Now those, too, have gone and no more is that great night sky resplendent with heat, light and colour.

The compensation, of course, is that greater western vista, up the valleys to the north and west, to the setting sun and its incomparable and never repeated finale of light on cloud and sky.

FOUR

Characters of a Derbyshire High Street

The birds are singing in the trees again, starlings and house-sparrows in the pair of beeches across the front lawn. In the horse chestnut outside my bedroom window a blackbird sings at the end of day. It is a still summer evening and I am 9 years old. There are few sounds outside except those birdsongs and the distant voices of men talking upon the Monument. Every fine day and evening of the year the local men gathered to chat and to prepare a thirst before entering the public house opposite.

Quite suddenly the loud, crackling laughter of 'the Laughing Hyena' breaks in upon the birdsong. Just as suddenly everything is still again. There is the gentle, stifled asthmatic cough of old Mr. Ward, a somehow reassuring sound across the evening air; Mr. Ward stood upon the Monument for many years and told we scrambling boys all manner of thrilling tales of long ago. Of the accidents in local coal mines and of the day the brewery's steam wagon ran away down High Street and demolished one of the stout stone pillars of the Monument. You can still see the new stones which were used to repair the damage. That gentle, stifled asthmatic cough still rings in my ears, reassuringly, across the years.

Another regular upon the Monument steps was Tom Timpson, who lived in one of the cottages incorporated into the substantial Victorian Town Hall lower down the steep street. So very often this old fellow left his black boots undone so that his trouser bottoms became caught in the heels. Next door to the Timpsons lived Tom's aged mother, a tall, lean woman with bony arms and blue veins across the backs of her hands. Now, both houses had a steep flight of steps up to the front door and Tom's mother regularly indulged in breathtaking acrobatics as she traversed delicately above the pavement towards her son's door. On days of heavy rain a row of large, painted pots containing aspidistras were placed out in the High Street gutter by this family and the old lady and her bespectacled daughter-in-law would be seen emptying their teapots into the soil around the dripping plants. On one such day a careless vehicle ran close along the gutter and smashed the precious pots and left the plants in a broken, saddened state with the old lady looking angrily up and down the street for a possible culprit from her step-top perch.

One summer evening—it must have been in July—a friend and I were passing time in the enclosed garden behind our house and we fell upon the annual game of throwing the small, windfall apples which had fallen from our trees. The game developed and we ended by seeing how far each could throw the windfalls over the house roof into the front garden. Some of our missiles went further than expected and very soon the door in our high front wall opened. Tom Timpson strode purposefully to the front door carrying what we guessed must be windfall apples. We vanished into the undergrowth without delay.

"See what we're gettin' on t' Monument", he said, thrusting a handful of small windfalls under my mother's nose, "It's your son and some others. It's not safe to be out on t' street!"

We didn't try throwing the apples quite so far streetwards in subsequent summers.

In the house adjoining Tom's old mother, on the uphill side, lived a family called Gribbs, who caused us no end of amusement over the years. The poor lady of the house ended her days, not surprisingly, in a mental home, for her husband and son drank heavily and regularly turned the house into a 'bear garden'. Their antics weren't confined to the house, either; on one occasion the son returned from a visit to the public house and threw his father into a conveniently placed dustbin in the backyard. Another evening saw the son walking close to the pavement edge on his way up High Street, when opposite his front door he ran sideways with all his might and burst open the door with his shoulder. He played the old upright piano in the front room with equal violence and often have I hesitated in passing the house on a dark, winter's evening to listen to the loud cacophony issuing from within and so reminiscent of a tap room. In later years the virtuoso took to living rough in derelict sheds and cottages, working for short periods between spells of inebriation.

By coincidence the vicinity possessed another musician. He was a cobbler who worked in the little, two-roomed building at the road junction close to the Monument. For several years Len Mitchell lived in a wooden hut with his aged mother on allotments at Meadowhead several miles distant. He would walk along the road each night and return to work each morning. In later years, after the death of his mother, he lived permanently in the backroom of his shop. Len Mitchell was a small, thin man who never looked very clean. He had large eyes which peeped from behind wire-rimmed spectacles and, I recall, as he spoke in that inimitably fast and chattery way a large gathering of saliva would form on his lower lip, below the single front tooth on his upper jaw. Eventually this wet mass would be discharged at the listener, it was simply a matter of waiting, watching and dodging at the critical moment.

On a memorable evening we were invited to enter Len's living quarters beyond that drab hanging blanket. The room beyond was, like the shop, open to the rafters, and in the yellow candlelight black shapes leapt towards the darkness under the blue slates. A fire crackled in the iron grate, but there was a damp chilliness and a bad smell of habitation. Upon the distant bed was thrown a dark blanket and on this sat two ancient, powder-puff dogs.

"That one's eighteen and not too well," Len gleamed through the sad gloom. "This one's sixteen and isn't too good on its legs," he explained attempting to roll the second animal over on its back. I have never seen dogs quite like those since, remnants of fluffy, Victorian lap-dogs. The oldest one had been white and possessed a long, patchy coat not unlike a Pomeranian. They were dream-dogs of the night and terribly frightening in the leaping candlelight. I was ready for flight for Len himself assumed the texture and proportions of a fearful creature in these surroundings of damp, cold and growling dogs at death's door.

"Do you want a tune?" he grinned from behind his spectacles and that single incisor tooth. We nodded. In one corner stood a harmonium and at the centre of the room was an 8-foot grand piano, the lid lifted in readiness for a recital. Len darted to the concert grand and, bending over the yellow-stained keyboard, he began a war-dance. The room was filled with tremendous sound, a sound the like of which I had never heard before and which was fascinating above all else. The instrument was terribly out of tune but wonderful for all that and the tapping of his long finger-nails upon the keys served as a considerable accompaniment. The recital continued, the candlelight flickered up the streaky walls and the ancient dogs blinked and growled. Then he stopped and dashed across to the harmonium in the shadowy corner. Sacred melody succeeded sacred melody as the fire died to a rosy glow.

"There you are!" he grinned as he turned round, "Would you like another tune on the piano?" But we had had enough of the damp cold and the ancient dogs' eyes upon us and said we must be going. We returned quite often to chat with Len, who earned the name of 'Tiptoe' throughout the entire district.

For many years 'Tiptoe' was the organist at little Cowley Mission a couple of miles away over the Finney Fields, and he tramped there twice every Sunday. I often met him on the high pastures which lead Cowleywards, a lean figure bent forward the quicker to cover the remaining distance to his dank cell. It is still amusing to think of the groups of boys who gathered by his shop door on dark evenings and sang together at the top of their voices several lines from "Tiptoe through the Tulips"—until a scuffle within and a thrown-open door sent them racing up through the trees of the Manor House gardens.

One winter our coal supplies became rapidly depleted, and it was suspected that we were having regular nightly visits by a coal thief. My father attached a bell to a length of thread and this was fastened to the middle garden gate, the bell hanging from the bedroom window-sill. For several nights the bell fell loudly to the floor when the thread was broken by the wind or the blowing gate. On the next night the raider came the bell failed to operate for some reason. Finally, however, the mystery was resolved when I was leaving home very early one snowy winter's morning for the farm—an earliness necessitated by the four mile walk through the deep drifts—and 'Tiptoe' came round the corner, bucket in hand. He had been taken unawares and there was nothing he could do but come to the door and inquire of my mother if he could beg a little coal this cold weather as he could not afford to buy any just at that moment. He took a bucketful, but never came, as far as we could make out, for further supplies.

Poor 'Tiptoe' ended his days in hospital, a victim of self-neglect with the slow onset of old age and a weak heart. His two-roomed premises of dark shadow and loud music have long disappeared from that familiar corner of High Street.

From an earlier time comes back in memory the tall, dark silhouette of old Jim Markham, the local sweep. He lived alone in a cottage beneath the Town Hall, a sooty man with bushy, black moustache who never seemed to have washed properly after sweeping his last chimney before retirement. Behind him as he stood in waistcoat, baggy trousers and carpet slippers at his door I can clearly remember the dusty cases of stuffed birds within, apparently imprisoned by glass and layer upon layer of soot brought home, it seemed, by their owner. Once he came to sweep our chimneys and the excitement with which I waited in the garden to see the brush come poking through the chimney pot and revolve rapidly this way and that is well remembered. How remarkable it was that anyone could own such a long brush which reached right to our chimney pots!

High Street seemed to possess a large proportion of peculiar people. Down at the bottom, where it plunged steeply towards the railway line and the river, lived a family of strange characters. They were not natives of the district and did not stay long. The twin daughters were, to our colourful minds, mental and dangerous. One girl, in particular, had a far-away stare in her eyes and was prone to abnormal behaviour when the moon was full. In the castellated cottage built upon an arch over the river and close to the railway lived a woman I always believed to be a witch. Sometimes she would speak, smile and be generally friendly with those she knew, at other times she would cut them dead or scream abuse at them. Living for years within close proximity of the railway she came to know several locomotive drivers and firemen who would regularly throw supplies of coal from the tender and the 'witch' could often be seen at the line-side with a bucket. It is said she rarely needed to purchase coal for the fires in her little castellated cottage above the river. Another so-called 'witch' lived up the slope beyond High Street, a thin old lady with a pointed, red nose. There is little wonder she always had a red nose for she didn't believe in having fires in her villa. Consequently, the interior of the villa always had a temperature several degrees lower than that outside—I cannot recall ever having been inside a building which possessed such a feeling of intense and searching cold.

One of the former features of the steep street was the several 'yards' which led off it and in which were collections of cottages. One such feature was called Chapel Yard—where stands an original chapel now converted to two picturesque cottages. Another is Stoops Yard, a long and narrow passage leading down beside the sixteenth-century inn to a dark haven where once stood rows of cottages. Now it is shaded by elders and willowherb. The inhabitants of Stoops Yard have long since gone and only memories of a few of them linger on. Down this dark alley between the elders and willowherb 'Jobber' Adlington and his son continued to pass for they gardened part of the ground hereabouts, a reminder of far-away times when Stoops Yard echoed with the voices of children and of gardeners arguing on summer evenings. Then there is Ward's Yard, where still live several families in a substantial stone row shaded by tall fruit trees. At the entrance to this particular yard once stood an ancient bow-fronted shop. Mrs. Bennett and her daughter were the last shop-keepers here, selling groceries and sweets. I well recall old Mrs. Bennett clad in black bonnet and shawl sitting behind the broad counter decked with all manner of good things. It was a tragedy that this ancient building was demolished, the flattened site still bare and bleak and contributing considerably to the present patchy appearance of the street. Several old photographs of the street exist and from these it is plain to see the former attractive features which could have been retained by a far-sighted planning authority; retained but modernized within where necessary, making the street capable of a completeness comparable with many better-known High Streets.

One of the very oldest buildings of the street stands at the opposite side of the entrance to this Ward's Yard and for many years has served as a fish and chip shop. The former owner had a completely bald head, a head which shone like burnished gold, caused, I believed, by regular polishing with frying fat. His hard-working wife seemed to enjoy with great relish every portion of fish and every helping of chips she served, pursing her lips tightly as she applied salt and vinegar.

Due to its steepness several accidents occurred through the years upon the High Street. There was a little old man who had come to live nearby from the northern side of Sheffield. He was a wiry, little man in his seventies, a watchmaker and an individual full of purposeful fire, an inveterate arguer and a scooter rider. His high-speed journeys down the street with flying scarf and upturned brim to a big, brown trilby hat were a constant source of amusement to us. Then one day he failed to negotiate the right-hand corner at the bottom of the street and in the altercation with an approaching car his thunderous mount was badly damaged. I believe that ended his high-powered drives in the district, though he is still a very active and exceedingly verbose character of continuing purpose and great age.

One day long ago an upright piano was being conveyed down the street and around that same right-hand bend. Now a second, and even steeper, lane forks off to the left here, and in negotiating the bend the little trailer containing the piano somehow swayed badly with the result that the heavy instrument was flung outwards from it and toppled to the head of the steep lane. It began to career down the fierce gradient end-over-end to the accompaniment of loud chords. People in the vicinity were brought to their doors and windows by the musical explosions as the piano progressed down the hill and several people near its trajectory fled for their lives into convenient gateways.

An old man stood near the point where the piano had parted company with the trailer, puffed his pipe and, as the last notes of the impromptu performance died away somewhere out of sight near the railway, he passed the opinion to the distraught owner that "He'll want tuning afor tha' gets a proper tune out of 'im again!"

At the same place a more spectacular and less amusing accident took place in the long ago. Every Saturday the fruiterer came down the street towards evening from a long round which took him most of the day. A small, wiry, nigger pony pulled his four-wheeled, covered cart. One Saturday evening the pony was startled somewhere up the hill and bolted at full tilt down High Street, the cart swaying violently behind it and the fruiterer chasing both. The pony failed to take the corner at the bottom of the street, careered into the stout stone wall and broke a leg. The cart crashed beside it and overturned. The poor animal had to be shot and dragged away, leaving a scene of almost unbelievable destruction—the cart lay smashed amid heaps of squashed tomatoes, bruised apples and pears, burst lettuce and cabbage.

That night many of the inhabitants of High Street were out with baskets and buckets collecting the unexpected harvest.

Immediately below the Hall is the entrance to the yard of the Hall Farm. One bright morning the octagenarian gardener from the Hall was wheeling a barrow-load of farmyard manure out of this entrance when the doctor who lived at the Hall drove out of his gateway. Proceeding down the street was an octagenarian tailor accompanied by his daughter. One car was a black Rover Fourteen, the other a maroon Triumph Gloria. The doctor came out of his gateway rather smartly, causing the old tailor to swerve across the street and so temporarily lose control of his car. It swung back to its correct side but engaged the barrow-load of farmyard manure. The result was that the gardener was left standing with empty hands and the Triumph Gloria came to a stop bespattered with liberal quantities of manure. In the ensuing argument the doctor took umbrage at the damage done to his wheelbarrow and the delay caused, the tailor at the sudden out-driving of the doctor, and the old gardener at the loss of his valuable load and his wasted effort.

The incidents and the variety of people who inhabited that steep street and adjoining lanes, yards and crofts come back through the passage of time as ghosts and vague half-happenings. They were real people and events right enough but the conditions in which we receive such impressions and experience have passed with the very passage of time itself. It is we, the recallers, who can never live again those precious moments, moments in which their very spontaneity and lack of self-consciousness now remain as part of the valuable heritage everyone possesses to some extent in the deep recesses of the mind. I am forever grateful that such seemingly ordinary events were for me exciting and, therefore, memorable. They will always remain so.

In one of the larger stone cottages near the top of the street lived a large family. Several of the grown-up children lived at home and this large household seemed to us to be in a constant state of turmoil. Argument and bitter strife were the regular order of the day. Sons and daughters took sides and raved nightly, or united in the frequent feuds with their neighbours.

"What about last night? Yes! Now then—what about last night?" one or other would question over and over on a still, summer evening.

There would be a subdued retort from the far side of the wall: "What about last night?"

"Yes! You know! Knocking till all hours."

"There weren't no knockin' last night!"

"Oh no! We heard it. Going on half the night. We've got to get up to work next morning you know!"

"I'm not arguin'."

"No! We've had enough. What about *her*? She's not behind the door. We know all about her!"

And on it would rage, accusation and counter-accusation. One point of argument would be forgotten and another taken up. Dusk came and went. The war of wars continued. And the war of words within the family circle; oh, happy family of united souls. When one of the brothers—in his forties—announced his intention of marrying, his mother wouldn't hear of such a plan and locked him in his bedroom on the wedding morning. He was only able to escape by letting himself down from the window onto the coalhouse roof and so make good his getaway via the back garden. The last brother to live at home finished working as an engineer and took to his bed; he shut himself in his room, counted his savings and relied on his youngest sister to feed him. I was one of the few people to see him being taken away—not so long ago—on a dull summer afternoon. It was one of the last incidents in a long history of such happenings associated with this street of memorable people and days. A policeman, ambulance man, doctor and psychiatrist tussled with the poor, barefoot fellow in the street before he was driven away, never to return. I mention the incident not from a sense of morbid sensationalism but because this sad ending seems to characterize the later spirit of the street—from happy sunlit evenings when the asthmatic cough of Mr. Ward sounded through the bedroom window to the demise of the population hereabouts, typified by the unhappy man's decline and transport from the scenes of his earlier life in a locked ambulance.

Fine gardens can owe their charm and character—qualities essential to make them fine—to a number of basic elements. Water may be the central theme, a moving, lively garden of pools and torrents and noise. Again, the garden may owe its character to an open site, where the garden acts as a foreground to a fine view of land and sky. However, it is the enclosed garden,

The rear of The Cottage, Dronfield. View from the north-west

secreted by high hedges or high walls, which comes closest to the average conception of 'a garden'.

Old town houses often possess such a garden, enclosed by old stone or bricks to keep the place private. Today they provide a haven for birds, animals and man from the bustle of the town without, an oasis in time as well as in place. Frances Hodgson

Burnett's *Secret Garden* was not a town-house garden, set as it was on the edge of the Yorkshire Pennines; but the garden I have in mind is set by the steep High Street, barely a stone's throw from the Monument once frequented by the old men of the neighbourhood.

Lord Byron once owned the property, and this association adds romance to the garden set within its high stone walls and shaded by mature trees. One steps through a door in the wall to leave the High Street rumble and bump behind, in under two fine beech trees overhanging a very old rockery. Here is the relatively small front garden which, being higher than the road, has low walls on two sides over which outsiders are not seen.

I have a photograph taken in this front garden a century ago and in it we see a starched-lace-looking family at the front door. They gaze out over a garden filled with laurel and rhododendrons, the inevitable Monkey Puzzle or Chile Pine conspicuous to one side.

A later tenant cleared this dark and dismal jungle to replace it with a lawn which stretches from house front to the beech trees by the wall. On this lawn fifteen years ago there was a clock golf 'face', but the iron Roman numerals have long since been grown over by the turf.

The back garden is much larger, long and relatively narrow but completely private, as all gardens should be. In early summer the glory of the garden for over a week or so is a very large laburnum tree growing out from the edge of the house—which dates from at least the sixteenth century—and casts a golden light over lawn and house when the afternoon sun gets round to it. The real gem of spring here is the wallflowers—borders of mixed colour beckoning to the visitor to tread ever further down the long, slabbed main path.

Herbaceous borders fill the right-hand (eastern) side as we go down the garden's length. Later spires of delphiniums and lupins point skywards between a pair of sixteen-foot-high cypress trees and the old but well-shaped trees—apples and pears—cast shade on the longest lawn as it slips northwards to the terminal wall that keeps out the coldest wind.

Early July is another highlight here (unseen by all but those lucky enough to be inside the garden), with the Sweet Williams bursting forth in mixed colours. One especially happy combination in this connection is a square block of Sweet Williams planted amongst the fairy blue-mauve of campanulas beneath a Lord Suffield apple tree. In early July, too, foxgloves send up colour in shaded corners and break up lengths of tall walls. All the year round old ivy covers parts of these walls and adds mellowness and a feeling of maturity. Of course, ivy harbours dirt and insects and needs regular pruning but to offset that there is the shelter and food supply—the black berries—it offers to the many welcome feathered inhabitants of such a secluded garden and, maybe, it holds up bulging sections!

Tits, sparrows and starlings, a pair of robins and those most lovely of garden birds—blackbirds and thrushes—are relatively safe herein and nest in the walls, roof and eaves of the old house or in the ivy. Every feeding time sees a mixed flock upon one lawn or another. In return they keep down the population of slugs and snails which haunt the margins of the garden, based as they often are within the cracks of the walls. Domestic animals are safe and happy in an enclosed garden and here a cat reigns as king—never really tolerating the birds—and a tortoise winds his summer way here and there amongst the herbaceous borders, often not seen for a week or more at a time.

Soft fruit took up a large area in one corner of the garden until recent times. Heavy crops of raspberries and blackcurrents were offset by the regular weeding necessary around the canes and bushes and the pruning and propagation required each autumn. One winter day, however, most of these plants were taken up and in the spring a large lawn was laid. At the centre of this new lawn a specimen of Ailanthus altissima—the Tree of Heaven—was planted. This species is a native of northern China and was brought here in 1751. Its Latin name derives from 'Ailanto' which means a 'tree tall enough to reach the skies'. In the years to come this particular specimen will rise above the high walls which now shelter it in its youth; above and out into the open sky and feeding upon the remains of the good dog 'Ferguson', who lies below its roots and has returned to the soil from whence he came.

And the tree will grow strong, to support the many birds of this secret garden, singing away in unconscious thanks for food and shelter. This is another facet of the street I know so well, another gem of memory which adds greater lustre to the coronet of the years.

FIVE

The Railway Age

On a dark winter night of hard frost and flashing stars the slow beating of a class 4F 0-6-0 locomotive built during the late twenties sounded louder and clearer than usual as it climbed the long bank. It must have been hauling a particularly heavy train of coal or iron ore for I remember that the bedroom walls shook as it climbed northwards to the watershed. The throaty barking continued, it seemed, for hours, echoing from beneath Wreakes Lane Bridge and on into the cutting leading ever nearer to the dread blackness of the tunnel-mouth. Up there, a mile away from home, was the sinister, choke-black vault where evil and torment held the day. Wraiths came and went through the briars and willow-herb on sunny afternoons, on black nights it was an area beyond description. Of loud labours, foul air and black-faced, angry gangers. I wouldn't have changed places with the driver of that night goods train for any prize on earth. Indeed, I drew down closer between the sheets and only then, after the familiar whistle followed by the sudden death of noise, did I know that the train had reached the portals of that palace of the demon king and vanished within—never to be heard again.

On any still night, in winter frost or summer dusk, the trains could be heard as they ascended northwards or thundered suddenly into the range of hearing towards the south country. Occasionally a former L.N.W.R. 0-8-0 goods engine (rebuilt in 1912 from an 1892 design by Webb) would haul a night freight up the gradient. Steam was usually very short and the train would be making the slightest progress towards the tunnel. Each beat would sound the very last of which it was capable, but on it would wind its vague way. As often as not such a train was backed onto the colliery sidings to allow a faster one through. Lying in bed on any night of the year I could hear the clashing of buffers as the train came, guard's van first, southwards on the siding opposite the signal-box where we spent so many interesting daylight hours.

On one such shunting operation a goods train was driven back far too heartily upon the siding, and the guard's van and several wagons finished their journey immersed in the river at the foot of the steep bank beyond the buffers marking the end of the line. But it was when frost and snow lay heavily upon the line that the London Midland and Scottish Railway (and later the London Midland Region of British Railways) gave the best value to the night listener. Goods trains would, it seemed, flutter up and down the line, spinning and frothing as wheels sent cascades of sparks over the ballast. A steady rhythm would be gained once more only to be followed by exciting reciprocations and wasted energies; the climb continued in a welter of sparks.

Down to the colliery sidings we would fly if there was any chance of a goods train resting there to allow the passage of a faster passenger express on the northbound line in a column of

The northbound Devonian, hauled by 5XP Jubilee class Straits Settlements, passes beneath Soaper Lane Bridge, Dronfield in 1950

grey-black smoke and steam and sounding steel. Though we were able to gain the footplate of so many parked trains the experience never lost an indescribable thrill as we were asked aboard and climbed the greasy steps to the wonderful alcove between fiery furnace and heaped coals; where the all-pervading aroma of steam and oil transported me upon a magic carpet of delight to dreamlands of far-away and unknown main lines where really exotic machinery belched fire into the night sky and columns of grey-black cloud into the blue. One hot Friday afternoon I was stung by a wasp on the back of the ear while inspecting the footplate of a Stainer Class Five, but there were more important things to occupy us than for me to worry about or mention such a triviality as a sting and from that day it seems that that is the best attitude to adopt over small physical discomfort—always more to thrill the mind and keep one occupied than to bother about wet feet, cuts, bruises and stings. Another day remains as memorable for on that occasion we were invited aboard none less than No. 5654 Hood, one of the great Jubilee 5XP 4-6-0s introduced by Stanier prior to World War II. They, the Class Fives, were the motive power which hauled almost all express trains on this line and for some reason unknown to us here was Hood on ignominous duties in front of coal wagons! I remember, even at this distance in time, that the driver was a particularly benign man and allowed me to pull the regulator and set this great locomotive upon its way out of the siding and on the gradient towards the tunnel. Before reaching the stone road bridge over the line we were set down and waved farewell with proud and thumping hearts.

The North Midland Railway Company opened its line between Derby and Rotherham on 11th May 1840. The route followed the Rother Valley northwards from Chesterfield, passing through Staveley and Beighton. At Masborough, close to Rotherham, there was a junction with the Sheffield and Rotherham railway line which ran the 4 miles up the Don Valley to the Wicker Station on the northern side of the town. During the next quarter of a century mounting pressure was brought to bear from influential sources in and around Sheffield for a better railway link for this expanding industrial centre. The small station at the Wicker became totally inadequate and improvements were virtually impossible as it was "jammed in between principal streets of the town, and bounded by numerous vast and costly works". During 1863 one works alone used 100,000 tons of coal and 45,000 tons of pig-iron. A large quantity of this coal had come up the Rother Valley line and so via Masborough up the Don Valley from collieries in Clay Cross and south-east Derbyshire. A meeting of interested parties was held in Sheffield on 5th December 1863. The outcome was a proposal that a new line should be driven from Chesterfield to Sheffield, to be the main line and so cause the town at last to stand astride a convenient and efficient railway route. The 1864 Act of Parliament authorized this direct route after much opposition and plans for a competitive line to go to Baslow, Bakewell, Winster, Ashbourne and Stafford and for a branch to run from near Sheffield directly to Chesterfield. This plan was rejected by a House of Commons Committee and the practical problems involved in the construction of the direct line between Chesterfield and Sheffield were faced.

A mile north of Chesterfield station the new route was planned to leave the existing line at a place which has come to be known as Tapton Junction. Upon the top of the steep rise to the east stands tree-girt Tapton House where George Stephenson came to live in the prosperous years before his death in 1848. The new route follows the valley drained by the River Drone for several miles, ascending towards the high ridge which forms the major obstacle. It was this high land which had turned Stephenson up the Rother Valley in the first place.

Great embankments carry the line above the flood plain of the meandering Drone by Sheepbridge Station and Sheepbridge Works. A mile and a half north of Tapton Junction, on the steadily ascending incline, the contractors were forced to construct a tunnel 88 yards long as a condition of permission to cross land here. The landowner insisted that a right of way across the line must be given by the Midland Railway by means of a wide belt of land for the passage of farm animals and local inhabitants. This 88-yard-long tunnel was the costly result of the railway company's compliance with this condition. It was called Broomhouse Tunnel, taking its name from the landowner's house nearby. In August 1969 this tunnel was removed by British Rail as maintenance costs were proving prohibitive. The line now runs through a wide cutting where a century ago the railway contractors found and marketed coal during tunnelling operations.

Less than a mile to the north the River Drone comes down through a narrowing of the valley, an impressive gorge is seen from some viewpoints. The railway had here to cross the valley narrowing and gain the far bank in order to maintain a direct course. The answer to the problem was the erection of Unstone Viaduct. It is an impressive structure of seven graceful arches in mellow stone, best seen from the banks of the river where one sees it in true scale *vis-à-vis* the hill slopes and curve of the valley. Immediately to the south of the viaduct the Midland Railway Company constructed about 1878 a branch line which wound about to the east of the main line to serve the several collieries which were then being worked. The tall, brick winding-house of one of these still rears through the woods near Dronfield as a forgotten turret where, in childhood, brave knights came to rescue imprisoned maidens. The branch swung into the main line immediately to the south of Dronfield station.

The main line has steepened to a gradient of 1 in 90 from Unstone and from the platforms at Dronfield it was always a thrill to watch steam-hauled trains approaching up the long, straight line. A great column of creamy smoke and steam would rise into the clear sky on a frosty morning as a heavy freight train came northwards; the lower line of exhaust and rocking front of a fast-climbing express would be more exciting. We always tried to reach the down platform in time to watch the high-speed passing of the Glasgow-bound Thames-Clyde Express at 12.30 p.m. Sometimes we were late out of school and heard its close-approaching rhythmic roar but usually managed a mad scramble onto the platform to watch the majestic passing of the double-header. A Jubilee 5XP was usually piloted by a 4-4-0 Fowler 2P or 4-4-0 3 Cylinder Compound 4P. It always seemed the fastest down train of the day. Of course, the sudden and explosive appearance of a London-bound express on the up line, into sight round the curve beneath the Stone Bridge at the northern end of the station, was very impressive, but the greater speed and shorter time they were in view made the impression less memorable.

In 1794 Messrs. S. & J. Lucas took out a patent for the manufacture of small castings by melting pig-iron in crucibles and running it into moulds. A mill pond stood where Dronfield Station was constructed, the water being impounded by a large

Alfred Hyghe (*right*) and his father at Deepwood Old Hall, around 1920

(*above*) Miss Hannah Smith o her 109th birthday. (*left*) Fre Kitchen at Bolsover in July 196

dam and running to turn the mill by the River Drone near the present Mill Lane. The coming of the railway destroyed the picturesque valley-bottom at Dronfield but it brought to local industry a most useful life-line for the transport of raw materials and manufactured products. The demands of the Sheffield industrialists also brought benefits to others; however, the prophecy of Frederick S. Williams in 1878 that the whole district from Sheepbridge to Dronfield "before long will probably form an unbroken series of works" has happily not proved accurate. At this time the population of Dronfield was 3,000 and after the opening of the new railway route this figure steadily increased with the expansion of the collieries and of associated industry.

One mile north of the town the line entered an ever-deepening cutting into the high ridge forming the watershed between the upper reaches of the Drone and the Sheaf. It had deterred Stephenson thirty years before but now work was started on the tunnel. It is Bradway Tunnel and measures 1 mile 267 yards in length, largely through millstone grit. Eight shafts were sunk to facilitate tunnelling operations on eighteen headings. The great problem was water, and 16,000 gallons per hour flowed from the workings. All this had to be pumped from the headings by engines erected at each of the eight shafts. The great civil engineer John Crossley reported that as soon as all headings had been joined to form a 'pioneer tunnel' the water caused little more trouble as it drained away and was "of such purity" that it was taken by pipes to Sheffield to form 'an unfailing supply for all station purposes'.

The eight shafts have been retained to form blue-brick smoke shafts for exhaust purposes, though the familiar plumes of black coal smoke no longer drift over Middle Birchitt and Bradway golf course.

The difficulties experienced with this later construction of the line caused delays so that on 12th July 1869 the Midland Railway Act was passed for an extension of time to complete the new route. Now when proposals were first being put forward for the direct route between Chesterfield and Sheffield it had been suggested that the line should go by way of Sheepbridge up the Barlow Vale and so by a tunnel from Millthorpe beneath the high ridge supporting the village of Holmesfield and so down the Sheaf Valley towards Sheffield. The tunnel would have been very long and difficult to construct; the plan was changed and the Drone Valley used. Dronfield got its greatly desired railway and Barlow and its lovely valley remained unsullied—or almost so. The Midland Railway Act of 12th July 1869 also allowed for the construction of the Sheepbridge Branch. A line came from the old main route near Tapton Junction, through Sheepbridge Works and forked near the confluence of the Sud Brook with the Barlow Brook. One line wound up for over a mile and a half to Engine Hollow, near Barlow village; the other line ran for almost a mile into the lower reaches of Monk Wood. Both lines served the several small collieries developed at that time in these quiet hollows. The rusting lines and white-painted crossing gates remained until quite recently, a silent track winding mysteriously out of sight between hazel and willows. The track waited breathlessly for some 0-6-0 tank engine of old to come churning along the line but none came, and a level trackway, like a forgotten Roman road, is all now remaining to remind of the activity which once enlivened these woods.

The northern portal of Bradway Tunnel is set in a very deep cutting through sandstone and shale. The line shortly swings into the Sheaf Valley and in four miles reaches the Midland Station, built at the same time, to be Sheffield's major railway station. In 1894, incidentally, the Midland Railway completed their route from Sheffield to Manchester via the Hope Valley. To gain access to this Peakland valley the line reaches the head of the Sheaf Valley—near to the northern portal of Bradway Tunnel—and goes beneath Totley Moss by way of the famous Totley Tunnel, the second longest main line railway tunnel in Britain. It leaves the Hope Valley by way of the Vale of Edale and thence through deep Cowburn Tunnel to Chinley and so on towards Manchester.

One of the most memorable characters known to me was Rowland Hill, who died recently at the age of 94. Even in great age he looked like a Viking warrior—tall, broad-shouldered, a great hook nose, flowing white mane and matching walrus moustache. Old Hill, for that is what everyone called him, was almost as active in his early nineties as he was as a young 70. He came out of Lincolnshire at the age of 10 and found work with the Midland Railway soon afterwards, in the hills of north Derbyshire, and that naturally led to work in the numerous tunnels there. Besides a strong constitution Old Hill retained a sharp mind and his memories were interesting, varied and very numerous.

"Yes, I worked in 'em all," he said proudly, standing back from the patch of ground he had dug. "Yes, bein' a gang foreman in them tunnels was no easy job, du y'u understand? No easy job!"

Cowburn, Totley, Bradway, Clay Cross. He had worked in them all, in the smoky darkness of all north Derbyshire's longest railway tunnels.

"In wintertime I used to have to walk down t'middle, between t'tracks, with a long 'ickling pole held up t'roof and fastened in a belt round mi waist to support some o' weight—that were to knock off ice and some o' them icicles used to rattle down and clout y'u on t'head!" He grinned as he reminisced and recalled that a mate held a paraffin lamp up towards the roof so that he could see the icicles which had to be dislodged before the trains could be allowed to pass through.

"Your 'ands very near dropped off wi'cold in them days," he explained, "By gum! It were cold for that job."

After retiring from the railway Old Hill worked as a jobbing gardener in the countryside near his well-loved tunnels. He developed something of a reputation as a tree-feller and until his eighty-eighth birthday still claimed to "love a bit o'swarmin' ".

Swarmin' consisted of climbing the tree to be felled, no matter how tall, and fastening a rope to the selected branch to ensure that the tree fell in the desired place.

"Y'u can't drop a tree in t'right spot without a bit o' swarmin' and I've always managed that," he often said when remembering his lumbering activities. Perhaps his proudest moment came when he was invited to cut down a tall and dangerous Lombardy Poplar close to the main road at Unstone.

"The police were there, tha' knows, and they stopped all traffic while I swarmed up, fastened mi rope an' came back down and helped our Pete to saw through trunk near to t'ground."

"I 'ad to drop mi tree in a tight corner and if I'd made a mistake I'd ha' fetched a row o' cottages down!" But Old Hill had calculated accurately and the tree fell in the correct place. He had help to cut up the trunk and eventually the traffic flowed again, no longer menaced by the leaning tree.

Even at 90 my 'swarmin' ' friend was still strong and when he was 88 I saw him pushing his 'cratch' up Farwater Lane, with a gradient of 1 in 6. In the hand-cart were at least two-hundredweights of beech logs that he had just sawn up from a fallen tree. I offered to help him up the hill but was told that "there's nowt in this load, y'u should have seen the last one!"

As the days passed the catalogue of my friend's tales became bigger, and it is hard to remember all the amusing and outstanding events recalled by him. However, another incident stands out as worth recording here.

On a dull autumn day some years ago he stood up from pruning the raspberry canes, straightened himself to his full 6 feet 2 inches and asked: "Do y'u remember 'owd Haslam, 'im as got buried in t'ballast near Bradway tunnel-mouth?" then, without waiting for an answer, he continued eagerly, "I was 'im as found 'im! Ay, a light engine came up and bowled him o'er before any on us saw it". He grinned impishly as he concluded, "And best of it were—he were t'horn blower for our gang!"

For some time before the new direct route between Chesterfield and Sheffield was officially opened a peculiar vehicle travelled the line. It was something like a stage-coach, and, writing in 1878, Frederick S. Williams states that it "may still be seen, apparently turned out to grass and rottenness, in a field at Dronfield".

The official opening of the line was carried out on 2nd February 1870, without any particular ceremony. An eye-witness at the arrival of the first down train at Sheffield Midland Station reported that he "had witnessed far more fuss and ceremony over the opening of a drinking fountain or the inauguration of a new parish fire-escape". It is also recorded that ". . . some enterprising country people at Dronfield left their beds at an undesirable hour in a February morning, in order that they might be able to say that they saw the up Leeds express pass at 4.7. . . ."

Dronfield station never saw its centenary for it, together with all other stations along the direct route, has been closed. It is true to say that far more ceremony attended the closure of this station on 31st December 1966 than had been the case when it was opened almost ninety-seven years earlier.

In 1846 a scheme had been drawn up to join Ambergate, on the Derby-Chesterfield line built earlier by Stephenson, to Cheadle on the edge of Manchester with a railway which would pass through the heart of the limestone valleys of Peakland. It had the grand name of the Manchester, Buxton, Matlock and Midland Junction. The southernmost section was soon completed, from Ambergate to Rowsley, where there was a very fine station and where visitors to Chatsworth House alighted to complete their journey by coach and horses.

On 25th May 1860 the Midland Railway Company gave authority for the railway to be extended for 15 miles to Buxton. Now Rowsley stands at approximately 325 feet above sea level while Buxton is at 1,000 feet. A rise of 675 feet in this short distance represents a considerable average gradient for a railway, and then there was the problem of the descent on the western side to Manchester. As far back as 1845 proposals had been made to cross Peakland by railway. One route came to be called the 'Bilberry and Besom Line' as it was projected to cross the Baslow Moors (part of Eastmoor) where there was a very small population and little to be transported by a railway. Another route had been suggested via Eyam, Chapel en le Frith and beneath the gritstone moors of the High Peak. It would have entailed a fantastic amount of tunnelling so came to be known as the 'Flute Line'. At this time permission had been granted by the Duke of Devonshire to take the railway northwards from Rowsley, through Chatsworth Park to Baslow, providing that the line was covered throughout its entire length through Chatsworth Park. By 1860, when the line was ready to be extended beyond Rowsley, the Duke of Devonshire was dead and the new Duke refused to entertain such a proposal. An alternative route must be found—and the only feasible one was to go up the Wye Valley to Bakewell. This meant going through the grounds of Haddon Hall, a mile above Rowsley. Negotiations with the Duke of Rutland commenced and finally it was arranged that the line would pass through Haddon Hall Park, behind the Hall, provided that no trees were felled or lopped and that the line was hidden for its entire passage through the park in a tunnel.

Keepers were set to watch the grounds, to prevent and report on any damage done by the contractors and their navvies. One of the principal objects of this exercise was, of course, to prevent the taking of game. The line was excavated from the hillside, partly by a cutting and partly by tunnelling. The cutting was then arched over with masonry and filled in with rock and soil to form a continuous tunnel—the present Haddon Tunnel—of 1,058 yards length. It is most interesting to walk through this strange corridor of blackened masonry, lit here and there by light shafting down from the amazingly short ventilators. It is also strange to emerge from one end or the other into a wooded landscape where, as often as not, pheasants strut across the lines.

To the north of Haddon Hall the line contours high above the flood plain of the Wye and passes to the east of Bakewell. To satisfy the insistent demands of influential local inhabitants stations were built at both Bakewell and Hassop—though the latter is some distance from the village of that name. It was one of the first stations to be closed in this part of England some years ago. The line climbs steadily through the limestone countryside about Longstone; the memory of freight trains being assisted from the rear by a barking engine stationed at Rowsley Sidings is quite clear.

Since this line was closed to traffic in July 1968 I have walked the most dramatic section of the route on several occasions, examining details of construction and of scenery *en route*. A deep cutting through dark-grey limestone leads one to the southern portal of Headstones Tunnel. Walking towards the north the line curves round to the right, so cutting out any sight of the other end until one is well advanced along the tunnel's 533 yards length. Ahead is one of the most dramatic points on any British railway, where the lines emerge from Headstones' northern portal and almost immediately cross the arches of Monsal Dale Viaduct. Had this line been projected today I am quite certain that permission would not be given for such an intrusion upon the green slopes of Monsal Dale. Ruskin was outraged but his was a voice crying in the wilderness of Victorian 'railway mania'. Anyhow the line crosses the dale and is thereafter virtually hidden by another long, deep cutting in the limestone. Probably the best viewpoint of the viaduct and the tunnel is from the slopes of Putwell Hill, as shown by E. Hector Kyme's remarkable photograph herein. The only feature missing is a steam-hauled train emerging from the depths of Headstones Hill but that could not be contrived as the line had been closed for over a year when he took this picture!

Beyond this the line passes through limestone spurs above the River Wye by means of Cressbrook Tunnel (471 yards) and

Litton Tunnel (515 yards), again good fun if negotiated on foot. On the approach to Miller's Dale Station the railway was constructed over the river again, by means of Miller's Dale Viaduct. This time it is a structure with three arches, each of 90 feet span and carrying the lines almost 100 feet above the river and the road. Then comes the difficult passage of beautiful and intricate Chee Dale, involving the negotiation of three tunnels and sudden downward glimpses to the dale of woods and white limestone outcrops. The work involved at this point was excessive. The railway traveller had a most interesting ride, with ever-changing glimpses of a typical limestone dale close at hand on either side of the carriage alternately. After the opening of this line it was described as carrying "the traveller through perhaps the most interesting series of railway works to be found in England".

Where the branch line wound up to the west, along Ashwood Dale to Buxton, was situated Blackwell Halt, which had the distinction of being the smallest British railway station. The main line was driven on up the dry limestone valley called Great Rocks Dale at a gradient of 1 in 90. The summit is reached 2 miles up this incline, 1,000 feet above sea level at the southern portal of Dove Holes Tunnel (2,860 yards long). Today this valley is heavily industrialized—the longest quarry face in Europe stands back above the railway on the western side—and kilns belch smoke and fumes day and night. The tunnel itself caused considerable consternation to the contractors during construction because of subterranean drainage water from the Black Brook.

The line then descends by way of Chapel en le Frith to Buxworth. Here, late in 1866, 16 acres of clay and shale land slipped bodily down the slope and damaged the railway construction works, followed by severe damage to the new five-arch viaduct. Even so the line was finally completed and opened to passenger traffic in February 1867—three years before the direct route between Chesterfield and Sheffield.

There has been much speculation as to what will happen to this recently abandoned route between Ambergate and Manchester. At the time of writing a diesel railcar service still operates between Derby and Matlock—largely to cater for the many employees of the Derbyshire County Council working at the County Offices at Matlock. How long this section of the line will remain open is not known. Likewise mineral trains still use the line southwards from Manchester, through Dove Holes Tunnel and along the Buxton branch line. Again, for how long these will continue to run is a matter for conjecture.

Several proposals have been put forward for sections of the line north of Rowsley, the most attractive part of the route. A road by-pass for the congested centre of Bakewell, a rambling and pony trekking route through the heart of the limestone kingdom of central Peakland, or private use by a railway preservation society using steam locomotives to haul trains packed at weekends with visitors and enthusiasts—after the pattern of the successful Keighley and Worth Valley Railway in the West Riding. Whatever happens to the route we may be sure that the direct route between Chesterfield and Sheffield will continue as busy as ever for most of the trains which formerly used the Ambergate-Manchester line have been diverted through Chesterfield and Dronfield, turning onto the Hope Valley line near Dore and Totley Station.

The romance has gone, the red glow and the sparks and the slipping wheels of the night. The laboured bellowing of a midnight freight as it climbed towards Bradway Tunnel's southern portal; rides on the footplate at Dronfield Colliery Sidings with the friendly men; pulling the levers in the signal-box while Mr. Whitmore drank his tea from an enamel mug; racing the down Thames-Clyde express to Dronfield Station on the way home from school. The line is still busy, the spirit has gone.

SIX

Countrymen Gone By

It was by way of W. H. Hudson's classic of the English countryside *A Shepherd's Life* that I first became fully aware of the wonderful vein of character running through most true countrymen. People ranging from the sinister and miserly Elijah Raven to the wholesome simplicity of Caleb Bawcombe and his father, Isaac, seemed far more like fictitious creations than real men who had lived and worked in the Wiltshire countryside of the last century. Quite soon, though, I came to realize that such people were still to be found about my own countryside—from humorous pig-men whose old-world turn of phrase caused me no end of amusement to old eccentrics whose habits and habitations were as fascinating as they were frightening.

Such people still exist in the hills and valleys of Peakland. I could fill a book with reminiscences of remarkable countrymen and women, stories both amusing and tragic. Below I describe four such rural characters; two have died within the last three years and two are still living at the time of writing. In the next chapter I have set down the perfectly true story of another old friend of mine, a story which warrants an entire chapter for the telling.

The old lane winds up from the village of Carlow in north Derbyshire, and eventually reaches the moors. By tradition it is a Roman Road and has the name Rumbling Street—which can be traced back to the 'Romlingstreete' of 1630—presumably from the noise of passing traffic.

The first farm up the lane from the village stands down a slope towards the brook and is sheltered from the north and west by tall trees. Ivy covers the front of the house and adds picturesqueness. Here live the brothers Bundy, both octogenarians and bachelors who have farmed in the district all their lives.

Nowadays the yard in front of the farm-house is empty of implements, weeds grow between the cobble-stones, and a few hens wander here and there in search of the grain which no longer falls from buckets, sacks and stacks. In fact, the little stackyard beyond the empty cowsheds and barn is deep with nettles and rosebay willowherb in late summer and autumn.

Brother John does most of the housework and keeps the stone flagstones on the floor of the living-room scrubbed, the paraffin lamps filled and the windows clean. He wears a black sou'wester on his head and clogs on his feet at all times, indoors and out, summer and winter. The first time I saw him at close quarters his white moustache and sea-salt headgear immediately reminded me of a well-known advertisement for a brand of fishpaste—though here at Carlow one could hardly be farther from the sea. His elder brother Archie goes shopping with a bag made from scraps of brightly-coloured cloth, now severely faded. In late years he has become much bent and the walk up the lane from Carlow takes him a long time. Brother Archie is known locally as 'Uncle Arch' and his main interest in life is the collection of rents from his several widely scattered properties in and near the big town 4 miles distant beyond Carlow.

The story goes that 'Uncle Arch' had once worked in a solicitor's office and "knows the law from A to Z". Brother John was formerly a chemist and had been dismissed ignominiously for surreptitiously drinking the medicinal wine. In any event the brothers Bundy have farmed their little holding below Rumbling Street for many, many years. Their methods of husbandry were known in the district for flamboyance. At one time they owned an ex-circus horse which proved to have a mind of its own and literally made clowns of its owners. 'Uncle Arch' took charge of the ploughing, and everyone in the neighbourhood knew when he was turning a furrow for his voice roared instructions and oaths at the ex-circus horse. Such thunder and lightning had little or no effect upon the exotic steed, which wound its self-selected route across the field, paying little attention to the tugs on the ploughing lines attached to its bit. As often as not he would slow-time poor 'Uncle Arch' and the latter's calls (verging, it is said by those who heard him from afar, upon pleading) were repetitions of "Get along there! Get on with you! Get along there!". The results of these highly vocal ploughing contests between man and horse were usually highly amusing to local farmers and their men.

"Let's go and see what patterns Uncle Arch has ploughed today," they would say, jokingly, and make off across the fields to inspect the day's play. The furrows generally snaked wildly to and fro' across the field. Headlands widened here and narrowed there, ridges twisted and were lost beneath subsequent runs of the plough. "It looks as though that horse 'as been ploughing on his own agin!" they would joke as they went home.

Then one morning not long ago 'Uncle Arch' made his way up the yard to the lane at great speed and crossed to the neighbouring farm where he arrived and breathlessly announced that "John's gone! He's gone!"

"Where to?" inquired the mystified lady of the house, for John never goes anywhere beyond the yard and nearby fields.

"He's gone! Come and have a look at him", said 'Uncle Arch', clearly upset. So across the lane and down the yard they went. "It's unlike him not to be down in the kitchen soon after dawn and now it's after nine o'clock—and a bright morning!" he declared, as they entered the house. The farmer's wife was sent upstairs to investigate.

The bedroom floor was bare except for two rectangles of sacking. The room was almost bare, too, and beneath one wall stood the bed in which Brother John lay motionless. The farmer's wife slowly went closer and saw that, at least, he was still breathing. Suddenly the occupant awoke and shot bolt upright, his white hair awry in the absence of the sou'wester. It was obvious that he had overlain.

"What's the time? Goodness me, the sun's high and the cock's long since stopped crowing!" he declared. As far as I am aware Brother John has not slept on since then.

One summer not long ago I was given an old photograph showing the local hunt at the Kennels and I set out to identify all the people in it. Someone suggested that I try the brothers Bundy as they had lived in the district for a very long time. On a warm, sunny evening I went down their yard to the front door overhung with ivy. Brother John appeared, clogs and sou'wester in their normal positions. He is rather deaf but at least I was able to explain the reason for my visit.

"Oh, you must see my elder brother. He knows about such things", he said. I asked if I could see his brother, to which he exclaimed "At this hour? Why, it's half-past seven. He's long been in bed. You will have to call at a reasonable hour during day-time! Night's not the time to come!"

I returned one afternoon not long afterwards and 'Uncle Arch' came out to the yard as I went down from the lane. He wore a gay tam-o'-shanter on his head and glasses at the end of his nose.

"No, no, no", he declared as he looked at each face in the photograph I had brought with me. "No, I don't know any of these people. You see, we don't come from these parts—we were born at Butthorpe." The village of Butthorpe is all of 3 miles distant over the hill.

A mile and a half distant to the north-east, beyond Sweetingsick Wood and the winding lane of Johnnygate, stands a valley-bottom hamlet.

Uncle Ben was 66 when I first met him. It was a mellow September day, and the gnats were still biting. I remember that because he had a knotted handkerchief on his head in a valiant effort to keep those tiresome insects at bay. Having come to my new job on the farm that very morning things were rather strange, but the farmer was friendly, and after drawing a trailer up between two manure heaps with the tractor, he had suggested that I didn't take too much notice of Uncle Ben who was to load-up on the other side.

The old man was thin and angular, his face acquiline, and he walked with a bad limp caused by a hip injury sustained when he was young. He was very, very deaf into the bargain, and this affliction, too, had been with him since youth. The result was that Uncle Ben was a sour old thing who had lived and worked on his brother's farm all his life. Until one got to know him well—perhaps until he got to know you well would be more accurate—any communication was difficult, to say the least. He was not given to showing interest in anyone, but was quick to point out faults and grievances in sudden outbursts of undulating sound, caused largely because his deafness denied him tone and volume control.

"Naw! Naw! Chuck it on 'trailer", he screamed over the load of manure on that first morning long ago, when I threw a forkful too energetically, causing it to clear the trailer and land upon the floor at his feet. The gnats and this raw youth were certainly testing his patience. Mugs of steaming coffee came out at eleven o'clock, but Uncle Ben ignored such time-wasting hindrances so I stole quick gulps from my mug while he wasn't looking. He was always like that; a cup of tea brought up the fields to where he was creosoting a hen-house would be left until stone-cold, unless he thought no one was watching and then he would consume it quickly. I never discovered whether it was obtuseness or virtuous example-setting.

In earlier days, long before I knew him, he was the horse-man on the farm and managed, despite lameness, to cart manure up the lane to some outlying land two miles away high above the valley; and in summer he carted the hay and corn down to the farm. These climbs and descents were normally accomplished at full speed, Uncle Ben attempting to control the horses from a seated position at the back of the shafts. His roars and screams were well known to the people living along his route to the top of the lane. Once, a pair of particularly lively mares threw him from his precarious perch below a load of manure and he lay in the hedge-bottom until the careering horses were seen by a farmer's wife farther up the hill, and he was subsequently rescued screaming oaths at his vanished team. Autumn ploughing must have presented the ageing cripple with severe problems, though he was able to walk with his short leg on the 'land' and his good leg in the furrow. In still weather his commands at the headlands could be heard from a considerable distance, but his horses worked well on the whole and the work was completed in a surprisingly short time.

By the time that I got to know him his bad hip regularly caused severe pain and he had a day or two in bed every week. His bedroom overlooked the farmyard, and on those mornings when he had not risen I could hear his agonized groans through the open window as he attempted to turn over. To a stranger these sounds would have been most disturbing, but we knew that the noises were far more dramatic than the pain which caused them to be uttered. At dinner-time Uncle Ben's place at the table was vacant and a bowl of cold rice pudding or 'pobs' (bread and milk) was taken upstairs to him. Now it so happened that his bedroom was directly over the kitchen where we ate, and I tried not to choke as he was helped to sit up in bed amid a cacophony of groans and roars. The worst part for me was that no one else around the table took the slightest notice of the vocal exhibition overhead. Things were just as embarrassing for me when he took his midday meal with us. The meat course would be taken away and his niece would ask in raised voice if he wanted some rhubarb pie or rice pudding, or whatever the sweet consisted of, her spoon poised for immediate action. Uncle Ben would contemplate the dishes for some time while his niece's patience was smartly dissipated and finally he condescended with great benevolence—always with those same words: "Go on, then, I'll try a bit". Needless to say he rarely refused a second helping. On the few occasions when he did refuse he replied with contempt, "No! I don't want no more".

Of all the jobs on the farm his chief preoccupation in later years was that of cleaning out the large free-range poultry breeding houses that dotted several fields around the holding. Some of these were almost a century old and needed regular attention, so every summer saw Uncle Ben groaning on sticks across the fields and carrying brushes and buckets and stirrup-pump, armed with creosote to do battle with rot and red spider. After a couple of hours at this task he usually looked very much like an Indian village headsman, particularly if a strong wind was blowing. On such days a return to the farm-house for dinner was out of the question so a tray would be sent across the fields to the battleground. I never discovered where Uncle Ben took dinner when out in the fields, until one memorable day when I happened to go into a large hen-house that stood in an elevated position and was called 'the Knob'. Upwards of 200 Rhode Island Red fowls made their home here, and at least half that number were gathered in the house on that day. There seemed to be no trace of the warrior as I entered, but after a few seconds he came into sight between an interested group of hens. He was seated on a pellet box in the far corner surrounded by the quietly clucking flock. One hen stood on the dropping board by his shoulder, seeming to whisper in his ear; another perched on his head and looked down into the bowl of rice pudding.

Every week he did a complete round of the hen-houses to clean them out, using a cut-down draw hoe and a dustpan to scrape the dropping boards and fill the sacks. These he left outside and it was my duty to collect these sack-loads up in a manure spreader afterwards. It was a revelation to see Uncle Ben's deft action with draw hoe and dust pan as he cleaned up the droppings, sometimes resorting to the use of fingers to pick up obstinate bits.

The threshing contractor maintained his traction engine in perfect condition. At regular intervals during the day's thresh he would go to it and polish up any brass or paintwork which had gone dull. Care was exercised in re-fuelling so that no coaldust spoiled the look of the pressure and water gauges. The shining boiler and brightly painted wheels were a joy to behold as the fearsome locomotive moved the threshing implements—drum, trusser and, later, stationary baler—from farm to farm throughout the winter months. It was rather ironical that such a pristine machine had such a dirty task as threshing to perform.

In due course steam gave way to the diesel engine and the tall, blue tractor did all that the belching locomotive had done previously, though with less need for care and attention—and less romance. The stackyard of the farm where I worked lay at a steep angle and the stacks of corn were built with care and not a little skill on great baulks of timber, their roofs and eaves being horizontal so that one end of each stack stood higher than the other. It took considerable time and effort for the thresher-men to manoeuvre the threshing drum and stationary baler into position for these had to be perfectly level so that the drum could thresh out the grain properly. The fact that they arrived towards dusk on a winter's evening didn't help, having just completed a thresh on some farm not far distant.

Uncle Ben would eye the ceremony of drum levelling on this difficult ground. Was he thinking how much better he could have done the job had he been asked? Or was he brooding about the thought of hard work on the following day? Whatever thoughts passed through his mind at such times he never aired them; and if seen spying on the stackyard manoeuvres he would quickly get on with business far more important—sorting corn sacks, picking up hen manure with his dutch hoe and dustpan or cleaning a creosote brush. Such tasks were, of course, made more difficult for the industrious and very deaf Uncle Ben because of a diseased hip. Bending or walking with the help of a stick resulted in a series of groans and terrible gasps, often exaggerated to show what a brave fellow he really was.

At last the drum would be chocked up with wooden blocks and wedged into a level position below the corn stack, the baler pushed into position behind it and the contractors would get on their tall, blue tractor and go homewards in the darkness. We were at work early next morning. I had the milking finished a good half-hour earlier than usual and did the yard jobs more quickly than was normal; in the meantime the contractors arrived and un-sheeted the drum and baler, attached the several driving belts and went round with grease-gun and oil-can. During their preparations Uncle Ben would as likely as not be dragging sackfuls of empty corn bags to the grain delivery spouts at the back of the drum. He always made sure that there were several large, loosely woven sacks by the chaff outlet for his job was to bag as much chaff as possible for use later in the poultry houses. A good layer of chaff on the floor of a free-range poultry house made a good base for a shallower layer of straw.

With a whine the belts would begin to turn and soon the drum was humming. Work began. The contractor climbed the ladder to the top of the drum, kneeled on the platform and began to feed the first sheaves from the roof of the stack. Upon the stack were a couple of men who had previously removed the neat thatch of wheat straw—it always seemed a shame that the time and energy used in thatching the stack was undone in a matter of moments when the threshing set arrived. These two stack-men now maintained a steady flow of sheaves, cast carefully to the contractor on his platform. At the rear of the drum the farmer and his younger brother saw to the bagging of the grain and had the heavy job of carrying the two-hundredweight bags up the stone steps to the corn chamber perched above the little cowshed at the top of the yard. The contractor's son saw to the wiring of the straw bales and my job as often as not was the carrying and stacking of these bales. Uncle Ben took up his position at the chaff spout between the drumside and the end of the stack.

Now, the speed with which the sheaves of corn were fed into the drum by the contractor naturally dictated the speed at which the rest of the team had to work. If the grain and straw was dry and the stack-men fed the sheaves to the drum smartly the corn-carriers and the men on the straw baler had to work quickly to keep up. This applied equally well to Uncle Ben in the dark and dusty confines at the side of the machine. When he had filled most of the bags with chaff and these stood about him, their necks tied with twine, he used the few remaining bags in rotation to fill the empty space at the rear of a large, wooden shed called the 'Food

Mr J. Smith ploughing with a team at Nether Birchitt Farm, Dronfield.

Mr 'Ned' Morgan's outfit threshing at Over Newbold Farm during World War II

The ruins of Eastwood Old Hall, Ashover

Room' where all the poultry foods were stored. His problem was that by the time he had dragged a voluminous bag behind him up the stackyard, emptied it in the 'Food Room' and returned to the scene of activities the next bag would be full. It only needed a slight delay on one of these slow and apparently painful journeys for the chaff to build up in the feeding shute and jam the chaff fan and riddle. Many were the times that Uncle Ben could be seen ripping the over-filled bag off the attachment hooks and attempting to free the blockage by pushing his arm up the shute. A sleeve-full of dust and chaff was inevitably the result. Once I saw him poke his indispensable walking-stick up the shute; there was a sharp crack and the handle of the stick was withdrawn without the shaft! Over the passage of the hours the pile of loose chaff which had evaded Uncle Ben's efforts to capture grew about his feet and threatened to bury him. His temper decreased proportionately to the increase of loose chaff.

The welcome mid-morning break saw us sitting below the stack, glad to have five minutes quiet and rest. The valiant chaff bagger sat on a full bag, his face and clothing grey with dust and filth. As often as not his cap lay awry at this stage and he instructed me to "Fetch a few bags from cart shed afor' we start agin!" His aim was to avoid a repetition of the near-rout just suffered and only saved by the appearance of his niece with the tray of mugs and that familiar steaming earthernware jug.

The drum was soon humming again and the baler clacking rhythmically as the straw was rammed tight. Having filled all available storage space with chaff Uncle Ben now began the longer pilgrimage down the stackyard, across the road and into the brookside pasture field where the excess chaff was burned, along with the riddlings raked from under the drum at intervals. Someone helped him now by changing the great, loosely-woven bags on the chaff spout when they were full. As the day wore on and the chaff expert grew weary the assistant carried the bags into the field where Uncle Ben was firmly established, stick in hand and controlling the conflagration. "Naw, naw! Chuck it right on top o' fire!" he screeched in a voice hoarse with the dust of the day.

And when the day's thresh was completed and the contractor had cleaned down his tackle and moved away into the dusk, and when I had done the belated afternoon milking, Uncle Ben could still be seen tending the great yellow heap in the pasture field, a tall, white plume of smoke curling into the frosty sky, tinged pink with the dying sun as it set beyond Burrs Wood.

In his late seventies less and less time was spent outside and more and more was spent in bed. In the winter it was common for him to take to his bed for two weeks or more, then emerge to sit washed and shaven by the kitchen fire. His long, white hair and drooping moustache lent him a dignified appearance, and a stranger could easily have taken him for a member of the aristocracy. His long, clean hands belied the work they had done—the ploughing, the creosoting and the mucking-out.

Great age naturally generates veneration, and in the memories and character of those attaining extreme old age I have always had particular interest. It is a well-known fact, often lost sight of, that a very few retrospective generations takes one back a surprising period of time. My great-grandfather, for instance, was born in 1830 and would know in youth old men who had been born in the mid-eighteenth century.

I knew a remarkable old lady who died only recently. She was born in the last year of the Crimean War and her grandfather was born before the dawn of the nineteenth century. Her name was Miss Hannah Smith and she lived on the western edge of Chesterfield in old age. She was for me the epitome of all that is fascinating and remarkable in great age and in our conversations I was fortunate that she was an intelligent, well-travelled and alert individual who had to a surprising degree maintained her faculties.

My first meeting with her, I remember, was on a balmy August evening in 1962. Hannah Smith was then 106 years old and virtually self-sufficient, living alone and caring for her own needs. She sat in an easy chair with her back to the garden window so that the lowering sun shone upon me; a mauve shawl was draped about her shoulders and a large ivory brooch was clasped at her throat.

In recalling her earliest days Hannah Smith was at her most remarkable for she was able to recount at first-hand things which no other living person could do. Her childhood was spent in Salford.

"I was lucky, of course, for I went to school until I was 15," she said, on that first meeting. "I had a half-hour walk to school and the same back in the afternoon, though I generally ran all the way."

At the age of 15—in 1871—young Hannah went to Manchester Technical School, the first educational establishment of its kind in the country. For a long time she had nurtured the desire to become a wood-carver. "It was thought unsuitable, however, for a young lady of ninety-one years ago to become so practical a person as a carver in wood, so I forgot the idea and learned needlework, though I have always loved wood and the working of timber." In 1886 the River Irwell flooded and the Smith family took to their first floor and watched the rising floodwaters swirl by, carrying drowned pigs and reaching the middle bar of the kitchen fireplace.

Five years later came a milestone in Hannah Smith's life, a turning point. She obtained the post of travelling needlework instructress for Derbyshire County Council. For a few years previous to this appointment she had been living with her younger sister, a headmistress, in Clay Cross. She continued to live in this colliery village to the south of Chesterfield until the turn of the century when she came to Ashgate Road, where she lived until the age of 107. Her work naturally took her to many parts of Peakland and in our conversations it was the clear memories of remote corners of her territory that were intriguing above all others.

"I went first of all to North Wingfield—not far from Clay Cross—and then to Tupton," she recounted, "and you must realize that most of the people I taught were not girls but ladies. The fee was £1 a lesson, out of which I had to provide my own transport. A number of times I went to Derby and two or three times to Ashbourne. Yes, I took the express to Derby then hopped onto the Ashbourne train. But in later years I used the bus from Derby to Ashbourne and got quite friendly with the conductor on one occasion. I told him there ought to be a bus running between Clay Cross and Chesterfield. And, do you know, very soon there *was* a bus service inaugurated between the two places and the people became so excited in Clay Cross that there were as many people standing and sitting on the open top as there were inside. Yes, I rode on that bus—the first woman in history to ride by bus between Clay Cross and Chesterfield!"

When her classes were far from home Miss Smith was accommodated at the house of the squire or vicar. On two occasions she stayed with the Fitzherberts at Yeldersley Hall while taking classes at Ashbourne.

"The Fitzherberts sent a horse and gig down to Ashbourne to fetch me and on one occasion I was sent back to Ashbourne with a very fresh horse. Mrs. Fitzherbert seemed very frightened for me saying that it had been out to grass and was very lively. Anyhow I jumped up and the groom did too. But would that horse move?

"The groom coaxed and pulled—but he dare not use his whip. Anyhow, in the end we set off and at the top of a very steep hill we could look down to the brook, and, being Shrove Tuesday, the men were having the Shrovetide football match. The groom jumped down and telling me not to touch the reins for fear the fresh horse should take off, he joined in the game. I needn't say that I never went near those reins, and was glad when the groom got back on the gig."

Those days were busy and happy ones and many a summer's day was ended with a 10-mile walk through the fields to Hardwick Hall and back.

Most of the needlework classes were held in the winter evenings and the one thing Miss Smith disliked was having to travel in the dark. When Hannah Smith came to Clay Cross the railway between Chesterfield and Nottingham was a single track and she well remembered the change-over to double track. Work often took her down that Nottingham line, though her best-loved memories were of travels to the west, to Miller's Dale, Calver and Edensor.

One severe winter's day before the turn of the century Miss Smith alighted at Miller's Dale station.

"I had to reach a house some way up the hill beyond the railway station—you know that steep road up past the station," she told me—remembering every detail clearly though she had not been there for sixty years.

"The snowfall had been so much that a snowplough had to be sent for. The horse team had a big job getting the track opened up for me but I got there before nightfall.

"The next day the train home wasn't able to run so I had to hire a horse to take me to Chapel-en-le-Frith and there I managed to catch a train for Sheffield."

And then there were her visits to Edensor, which ended with

the gift to her of an umbrella by one of the daughters of the eighth Duke of Devonshire. It had an ebony handle with a solid silver top engraved with the date.

During the severe winter in early 1963 Hannah Smith fell heavily and to recover fully she went to a private nursing home, little thinking that she would stay there for the rest of her life. She was now officially recognized as the oldest inhabitant in Britain. Her sight was the only faculty to seriously deteriorate, so that by the age of 108 years she was virtually blind.

Still, though, the spirit lingered on and the Matron often remarked at the marvellous sense of humour which made everyone in her new home laugh daily. I often used to think with pleasure of the sudden instructions she would give me after a conversation.

"You had better be going now—I've a lot to do. Won't be in bed before midnight and there's a meal to cook and eat between now and then!" she would announce, slapping the arms of her chair. Determination and an active mind prevented the days from dragging intolerably by. She used to remark how quickly each day seemed to slip by, apparently stealing valuable time from her, time she could ill afford to lose.

Her 110th birthday came on Friday 7th January 1966. The tenth annual greetings telegram was delivered by the postmaster, bringing memories of six eventful reigns. The customary birthday glass of sherry awaited her guests as Hannah Smith prepared to greet them. But tragically she became ill on that very day. Though able to sip a glass of champagne and drink a little turkey soup her condition slowly deteriorated, and two days later she died peacefully. This great milestone reached, was it possibly the excitement or the lack of a further goal upon the horizon of the future which caused this grand old lady to loosen her sharp grip on life's treasures?

My lasting memory of her is of a gay face beaming in the evening sunlight of her sittingroom overlooking the quiet garden beneath tall trees.

"Oh, the summers seemed so much hotter in those far-off days. Those lovely summer days—I used to run down the street towards home so fast. In fact, I really used to fly. But that is more than a century ago," she said, and as she did her smile became indescribably sad.

SEVEN

Alfred Hyghe of Deepwood Old Hall

I first heard of Deepwood Old Hall and its enigmatic occupants when I was a child, of the strange family who refused to farm their land as directed by the local War Agricultural Committee during World War II and of their struggles with the law concerning a dispute over a boundary fence. The latter conflict led to numerous open scuffles with the police when hand-to-hand fighting took place and shotguns were brought down from their resting places among oak beams.

The ancient house stands close by a sunken lane as it climbs the steep slope out of a pretty Derbyshire valley, and in later years I passed the place on my motor cycle each evening on my way home from the valley-bottom farm where I worked. I was greatly fascinated by the place, all the more so on account of its neglected appearance and its eventful recent past and the old man who sometimes crossed the lane from the Old Hall to a barn on the other side. In time he began to nod to me as I passed.

Here, at Deepwood Old Hall, was a true piece of a rural England that has all but gone. In still later years I came back to walk along the footpaths above the valley and often stopped on the grassy banks near the old farmstead.

The yard was overgrown with nettles and brambles. The pair of very old cottages which adjoin the great stone cowshed and barn had holes in the roof where the beams had rotted and broken under the weight of the stone slates. The mullioned windows of the Old Hall itself were cobweb festooned and dark.

On my wanderings I sometimes saw the same old man scything grass in the fields nearby. We first got into conversation, I remember, when I asked if I could take a photograph of his home from the field by the lane where he was collecting the scythed grass.

This, then, was Alfred Hyghe, last of a generation of Hyghes who had come to Deepwood in 1817 from Brampton, near Chesterfield. He was the second youngest of a family of five (four boys and a girl) brought up here to an old-world life of farming, books and church. Their father, Samuel, had been a God-fearing farmer educated at a private school in Chesterfield, and only one of his sons had married and left home to farm on his own account. Alfred, his two elder brothers and sister remained at Deepwood in close contact with the soil all their lives. Now only Alfred remained, living in seclusion and carrying the grass he scythed each day to the cow and heifer he kept fastened up in their stalls summer and winter. The only other stock that remained were the old Shire horse, Prince, and four very old hens who had made their roost in one of the empty cottages in the yard.

On one memorable day Alfred Hyghe invited me inside his home. We entered the large, low-ceilinged kitchen on an afternoon of fitful sunshine, into another world of dust, cobwebs and accumulated furnishings. On the large, oak table in the middle of the room were piled hundreds of newspapers; under the long mullioned windows was a large settee on which was a mattress and blankets where I later learned that the owner of Deepwood slept with his cats.

The Yorkshire range contained a small fire and upon the shelf above the flue was a great pile of eggshells. Around the hearth were accumulated heaps of ashes which had been raked out and left where they lay. Odd piles of sacks and logs lay in various positions on the stone-flagged floor—it was obvious that Alfred Hyghe did not believe in wasting things which one day might be useful again.

A plain, wooden kitchen chair stood to the left of the Yorkshire range and this was where he always sat and rested, reading or looking through the cobwebs festooning the mullioned windows across the room.

Subsequent explorations of the old buildings surrounding two sides of the yard revealed many relics of agricultural practice no longer common. Hanging from a beam just inside the great barn were three heavy horse nose-bags made of coconut matting. One had a circular wooden base, the others were of leather. Alfred once explained to me that years before there had been so many accidents to passers-by at Chesterfield market when feeding horses swung their nose-bags to reach the last of their oats that a ruling was made that no more nose-bags with wooden bases could be used in the market, so leather was substituted. Up in the loft I found a chaff-cutter of considerable antiquity, of much more primitive design than the common type still sometimes found at work where there are horses. There were also numerous mummified hens complete with feathers hanging where they had been placed after slaughter decades previously.

I got into the habit of visiting Deepwood Old Hall quite regularly and my brightest memories are of winter nights when I knocked on the heavy kitchen door and was invited from afar to "Come in." Going into the yellow candlelight I would see Alfred Hyghe sitting amongst his tumbled kingdom by his temperamental fire. He was full of tales of long ago and it is my regret that I didn't record more of them on paper, soon after the telling, when the details were still clear in my mind.

On a chilly morning at the turn of the century Alfred and an elder brother rode by trap up Fox Lane and onto the moor towards Baslow. Suddenly, from the hawthorns to one side, a ruffian jumped out and demanded any money they might have. Alfred recalled that quick wit allowed him to drop his purse into the heap of sacks behind him and the vagrant had at last to let them go their way without a 'haul'. Close by the spot where this took place is an eroded stone cross erected by an order of monks in the Middle Ages to guide travellers over the "howling wilderness". On one side are carved the words "Here lies Godfrey", and many are the ramblers who have decided that the cross marks the grave of a long-forgotten celebrity. Alfred Hyghe remembered the man who carved the inscription in the last years of the nineteenth century, a youth called Godfrey Silcock who lived lower down the lane and emigrated to New Zealand; but before departing he carved the words here to denote that his spirit was left behind in the lovely, lonely hills of his birth.

Then there was mole-catcher Gregory who came over the moors from Curbar and stayed in the Hyghe's barn alongside the lane; a hardy character dressed in corduroy who regularly slept in his wet clothes amongst the straw after a long day trapping moles. His unusual hobby was the carving of Bible texts in the large millstone-grit boulders by the steep lane above his home, texts which are still in a good state of preservation.

At the outbreak of the Great War Alfred joined the army,

together with his brother Andrew. His hatred of those four years was still evident almost half a century later; especially hated was the forced divorce from home, the land, and all that he loved so well. I believe that it was largely due to his memory of the Somme and 'Hell Fire Corner' that caused him to stay at Deepwood for the rest of his life, amid Nature and a sensible order of things. He recalled being in charge of a gun crew in the deep mud near 'Hell Fire Corner', and every time the gun was fired his pocket-watch stopped so in the end he got into the habit of taking it from his pocket and hanging it upon a convenient nail in a nearby tree until the end of his particular duties. On one occasion he forgot to collect the watch and when he returned all the trees around had been blown down except for the tree carrying his watch!

Those were not his only 'battles', though. When a neighbour, the M.F.H. of a local pack, wished to purchase a field belonging to the Hyghes to facilitate easier access to fox coverts and better hunting, Alfred refused and there was much angry argument, terminating in a feud which lasted until the M.F.H. died. Until Alfred's death no foxes were hunted upon Deepwood land.

At the lowest point of the Deepwood land, where it reaches the floor of the valley, a cart-road gives access from the valley road to that lowest lying field. It had always been a useful entrance as it allowed farm implements to be brought down from the farm by way of the road and so to the lower land by way of the cart-road rather than by crossing inconveniently to higher fields. Now in 1938 the owners of the land adjoining the cart-road, Mr. and Mrs Gribbs, decided to erect a new cleft chestnut fence. Tragically, as events later proved, they presumptuously had the fence erected on a new alignment so that it took in part of the cart-road belonging to Deepwood Old Hall. The Hyghe brothers were naturally outraged at this trespass, and maybe unwisely, demolished part of the offending fence.

Alfred and Arthur Hyghe were found guilty of doing this damage at Chesterfield County Court and ordered to pay a total of £83 7s. 1d. They were further ordered to refrain from "further demolishing a cleft chestnut paling fence erected along the western boundary of the Plaintiff's land and premises". Judge Shortson decreed that Mrs. Madge Gribbs could, in fact, erect a fence between 4 and 5 feet west of the stream which the Hyghes had always understood to be the legal boundary of their property.

So it was that Mr. Gribbs proceeded with the work of re-erecting the fencing. Alfred Hyghe later described the operation in his written evidence as follows:

> On April 25th 1939, Gribbs and two workmen took complete possession of our cart-road that we own, and with posts and boards resting on garage shown on plan, they had picks, large iron bars and spades, and were making large holes four feet deep to put the posts in. We tried to stop them. Mrs. Gribbs, who holds County Court Injunction over us for chestnut fencing sent for the police. Police Sergeant Copse and P.C. Thomson came and when they saw what Gribbs and workmen were doing they asked me who did we pay our rent to for the farm. I told them "We don't pay any rent, we are the owners!" Police Sergeant Copse advised me to summon Mr. Gribbs and instructed P.C. Thomson to take their names. We told him it is a County Court case and we cannot take it to a Police Court. The Police told me to order them off in their presence. I did, and Gribbs and his men collected posts, boards and tools and went back over the stream, but they returned later and continued to dig out the foundation of our cart-road and erected the post and close-board fence as shown on the sketch by C. Potter, F.R.S.A. Our drays, carts and farm implements glide into the boards and the wheels sink in where Gribbs have dug out and left our land sloping towards the boards. There are farm implements wider than the space they have left us to go through. Mr. Gribbs measured across our cart-road and told us they had left plenty of room to get through. Now it is the cause of damage to our crops as it is not safe to go through the gateway now with the binder or the corn drill. The horse rake scraped both sides and finally had to be pushed through without the horse. We have had to go nearly two miles out of our way with wide implements, so wasting time.

It was obvious that the situation was coming to a head, and on 25th July 1940 the fence was accidentally damaged when a load of hay caught it. Alfred Hyghe continued in his written evidence:

> Gribbs sent for the police and P.C. Maris came while we were picking the hay up that the fence had pulled off our dray. He asked what had happened, we tried to explain about the County Court Injunction and Maris said he was a man of the Law and would have me put in my place. Later he brought a Summons for me to appear at the Police Court.

At the Police Court it was explained that the case was already at County Court level. Later, on 5th September 1940 at Renishaw Police Court it was definitely proved that the disputed fence had not been erected by Mr. and Mrs. Gribbs on their own land. However, after four hours deliberation the magistrates decided that Mr. and Mrs. Gribbs had done the right thing in coming farther onto the Hyghe land with the fence, which was a different one to the one specified by the County Court Injunction. Subsequently Alfred Hyghe appealed to the Quarter Sessions at Derby. Due to the complex nature of the case (involving both Police and County Courts as it did) his appeal was dismissed.

Alfred Hyghe continues:

> P.C. Maris came several times asking for the Renishaw Police Court costs, he told me if I did not pay I should be sent to prison. On December 9th 1940 I was arrested by Police Sergeant Beaver and P.C. Maris and taken to sign the Bail Book. I was told I must appear on December 18th when I should be released. Lord Grey de Ruthyn said on that date at the hearing that I must go to prison for one month. The clerk told him "In this case, sir, we must give him longer to think about it."
>
> The Chairman replied, "He has had long enough to think about it—he must go to prison for one month!" The Doctor at Lincoln Prison told me something had gone wrong. He said I ought not to have been sent to prison. Many times I asked the magistrates that Mr. and Mrs Gribbs should claim her Quarter Sessions appeal costs in the County Court, where we have a chance to get a wrong put right.

With the approach of Spring 1941 the bitter strife had still not been resolved and on 21st April Police Sergeant Beaver and P.C. Maris arrived at Deepwood Old Hall about 8.0 a.m. with a warrant for the arrest of Alfred Hyghe and to seize all bank-books and documents relating to the farm.

Alfred Hyghe describes the events as his evidence continues:

> They said "we have given you time to get them (the documents), you must produce them, we have come for them NOW!" The two police officers ill-used me and dragged me out of our house. Police Sergeant Beaver, with truncheon drawn over me, said they had orders to break in and take me and the documents. I told them they didn't know what they were talking about. My two brothers, John and Edmund, came to my assistance, we got clear of the police, but they returned later.

And in returning later the police literally took the law into their own hands. Had the following events taken place today—witnessed as they were by others—the misdeeds of the so-called law-keepers would have caused headline news in all national newspapers, a scandal of the first order committed against an innocent, simple family who had minds of their own and who were not willing to bend to bullying and bureaucracy for the sake of peace and quiet. Let the evidence of witnesses speak for itself.

John Arthur Hyghe was directly involved and in written evidence described the events of the morning of 21st April 1941:

> I saw my brother Samuel Edmund Hyghe, who has suffered epileptic fits, down on the side of the road. I saw P.C. Mapleton with truncheon and Police Sergeant Beaver and P.C. Maris putting handcuffs on my brother and I went to his assistance. P.C. Mapleton met me and hit me on the left temple with his truncheon, knocking me down helpless. He hit me a second blow and injured my mouth and loosened a tooth, cutting the upper lip – scar to be seen.
>
> P.C. Mapleton knelt on my legs and Police Sergeant Beaver handcuffed me and dragged me to the motor.

Handcuffed, injured and bleeding badly from lip and mouth John Hyghe was dragged up the road and thrown into the vehicle. All this happened to a man nearly 60 years of age who had simply gone to the assistance of his brother, an epileptic who had simply supported his younger brother Alfred in this boundary dispute and who had been quite unnecessarily roughly treated by offensive policemen. As luck would have it an old tenant of the Hyghes who lived in one of the ancient cottages overlooking the farmyard was an eye-witness of this disturbance. He later signed the following account of what he saw:

> On the 21st day of April I was in the farmyard of Mr. Hyghe and heard a bit of disturbance and I went to investigate and then I saw that the police was pulling Mr. Samuel Edmund Hyghe across the yard to the car which was in the lane. And the police was trying to handcuff him. When his brother Mr. John Arthur came up and went to his brother's assistance the policeman pulled him away and cracked him on the head with his truncheon and knocked him silly and then the police got him into the car and drove away. He (Mr. John Arthur Hyghe) never assaulted the police in any way, I swear.

Ever after that serious head injury John Arthur Hyghe was a

semi-invalid, suffering almost continually from head pains. In further evidence he recorded:

> Since I was injured I have suffered from severe pains in the head and dizziness and sharp pricking pains in the left eye, the sight is very dim. I had very good eyesight before. Now I am unable to bend to help with the planting of root crops or climb onto loads of hay and corn on account of dizziness. The brain specialist has told me that I must not take more than 1½ pints of fluid per day. I am still unable to do any usual work and the ridge is still to be seen and felt in my head.

The next chapter was written a month later when, on 17th May 1941, Alfred Hyghe was arrested as he got off a bus which had brought him from Chesterfield to within a mile of Deepwood. He was taken to Dronfield Police Station and locked up from Saturday until Monday. Alfred Hyghe describes the experience thus:

> I had a wooden bed and wooden pillow and I was very cold. I asked Police Sergeant Beaver for another blanket or two; he told me I could not have any more. On the Monday morning, May 19th, I told a constable, he said they had plenty of blankets—I could have had more. I had Trench Fever in the Great War and still suffer from the effects of it. Police Sergeant knows I do but he said he should do his worst and his very worst for me.

Three weeks later, on 5th June 1941, the Magistrates sitting at Renishaw Police Court sent Alfred Hyghe to prison again. This time for a period of one month for failing to pay the Gribb's Derby County Court costs. A solicitor who visited him in prison told Hyghe that "if someone has put a fence on a cart-road making it narrower than it has ever been before, you ought not to be here."

The new Superintendent of Police at Renishaw was a tall, dignified but kindly man called James Brailsford. From the beginning he had wanted the case removing from the Police Court so that there could be a final and just settlement for the Hyghe family.

So it was that Alfred Hyghe produced his written evidence in an appeal made through "the poor man's solicitor" which opened its doors from time to time for those unable to pay for the professional services they often desperately needed. This evidence was addressed to the presiding County Court judge and dated 8th December 1941. Alfred Hyghe had been out of prison five months, and there were some large trees which the family wished to sell. He explained:

> We know what will happen to Gribb's fence if these trees are felled and I am tired of going to prison. I have not been one inch off our own land. May we please, your Honour, apply at your Court in the near future to ask for Mr. and Mrs. Gribb's fence to be removed from land which has definitely been proved in the Police Court not to be theirs? I never touched P.C. Maris on April 21st 1941 but was fined five pounds by the Magistrates, and five pounds for Police Sergeant Weaver. I have the demand that ten pounds be paid on or before June 26th 1941, but I was arrested and cast into Lincoln Prison on June 5th 1941.

The final outcome was that the County Court found Mr. and Mrs. Gribbs guilty of trespass and ordered that the cleft chestnut fencing be removed from land which was undoubtedly owned by the Hyghe family. Throughout the whole story there ran the theme of injustice and even the rightful outcome was charged with irony for the fence was quietly re-aligned by workmen employed by the guilty party; the local newspapers which had borne headlines about the recluse-like and stubborn farming family who were causing the police force so much unnecessary work in "breaking the law" now ignored the fact that justice had finally been done! And, perhaps worst of all, many of the local people continued to ignore the Hyghes; there were few congratulations from neighbouring farmers and valley folk. Everyone kept to their own fireside, the story and the excitement was over. But the Hyghes had memories.

Not very long afterwards Samuel Edmund Hyghe dropped dead by the side of the lane; John Arthur died suddenly in the cow-shed one day, and his brother Alfred was certain that both deaths were the direct result of the physical and mental violence suffered during those eventful three years.

Some years later Alfred's only sister became cancer-ridden and died a painful, lingering death on a sofa in the great kitchen at Deepwood. Now the eldest brother was alone, and in the years before his death he fought another legal battle, a battle of words and ill-feeling which undoubtedly accelerated his end. It was a fight over the purchase of the now-empty farm cottages in his farmyard. But that is another story.

As time went on Alfred Hyghe became crippled with rheumatism and lack of proper care. His kitchen became more of a 'kennel' than ever and the chimney smoked to such an extent that on some evenings when I arrived it was not possible to see across the room to where he sat with a blackened face.

One winter's day news came that he had had a stroke and that night I set out through deep snow on my bicycle to see what could be done. Half-way down Deepwood Lane I encountered deep drifts and had to abandon the bicycle. Soon I was walking over the roof of a neighbouring farmer's abandoned car. All was still when I reached the Old Hall, a half moon and stars shone frostily upon the pure drifts which had piled against the house. The whole valley below was illuminated by that pale moon. A tawny owl's hoot sounded suddenly from the ancient horse chestnut behind the house, and I went into the kitchen.

Alfred Hyghe lay upon his sofa by the fire, his long, white hair trailing on a dirty pillow. He looked at least 100 years old in the half-light but recognized me and rallied enough strength to ask what the weather was like. The old man was nearing his end amid the squalor and solitude which had gradually collected about him; an independent in the true sense of the word, stubborn yet shot through with a life of misfortune and the wrong side of the coin.

How the smoke and dust and the gathering pain must have contrasted with the merry winter evenings he had once recounted to me, when there had been music and singing beneath the ancient rafters. One brother had played a violin, another the piano, another had sung with his mother and sister—good, old, happy, golden days he had remembered with not a little nostalgia.

A few days later Alfred Hyghe died, and now the Old Hall is empty and derelict, left as it was. There is still an aura of mystery about the place as one stands in the overgrown yard, the threadbare curtains flap in the broken windows as the wind passes through.

The butcher who delivered the meat every Saturday afternoon for many years still sometimes says with a nostalgic smile, "Alf was just mending the fire when I went by this afternoon, there wasn't half some smoke in the lane—but I didn't seen him at the gate, I wonder what he's doing now?"

But the spirit of Deepwood has almost gone for Alfred was the spirit of the place, the last of the Hyghes; a lonely yet, I believe, a contented man, despite that wrong side of the coin.

EIGHT

An Artist in Barlow Vale

Alfred Hyghe of Deepwood once gave me an old, framed photograph of the Barlow Hounds, showing them grouped before the Kennels near Horsleygate Hall. It was quite a large photograph, and upon it were several people looking out, it seemed, through the glass at me from a bygone age. Who were they? What sort of lives had they lived? Where had they lived? These, and several other questions occurred to me but they were not fully answered for some years.

One or two persons were identified almost immediately, and this identification was verified by Alfred Hyghe. The most imposing figure was William Wilson, Master of the Barlow at the time the photograph was taken (about 1898). He lived with his family at Beauchief Hall on the south-western fringe of Sheffield a matter of 4 miles distant from the ivy-clad Kennels. Next to him, on a smaller horse, sat his eldest child, Winifred, who was then a young woman not quite 20. Beyond her a groom sat on a hunter which stood probably sixteen hands, and to his left sat young William Wilson, younger brother of Winifred and destined to become Major Wilson of Horsleygate, last Master of the Barlow. Grouped in front of the seated riders are the hounds, twenty couples of them in the full control of their Master and the Huntsman. Between the horses and behind them are standing several men typically attired in corduroys, tweeds and hunting jackets.

In my search for their identity I first went to see Samuel Revill, the retired postman and cobbler at Holmesfield. He sat by a roaring fire amid a great collection of shining brasses—kettles, bells, horse brasses and candlesticks—which gleamed down from shelves, mantelpiece and dresser to enliven the dreary winter day. 'Sammy' had travelled the surrounding hills and vales on a bicycle, and later on his well-known motorcycle combination delivering the post for untold years but now was well into his eighth decade and still cobbling shoes in the little green shed alongside the house.

"Well, that's owd Bill Holmes of Moorhall," he pointed out as he took the photograph from me. "He was the gamekeeper and kennelman at this time—fond on 'is ale!" he remembered with a smile beneath a well-trimmed moustache.

"Aye, and behind Miss Winifred there, t'owd chap with grey whiskers is 'Taffy' Hill," said Sammy with another smile and then he went on to recall the other members of that family. They lived at Tanyard Farm, Millthorpe, a mile down the valley from Horsleygate. There was 'Taffy', Sammy who worked at home on the farm, Bill who worked as a joiner, and Pim who had one eye and had worked on the construction of Barbrook Reservoir on Big Moor. These brothers were bachelors and were looked after by their spinster sister Elizabeth. In later years they moved from Millthorpe to a smallholding near Fox Lane which has now been rebuilt into something of a 'stately home'. Standing between the horses of the groom and the young William Wilson is a proud, middle-aged man clad in a tall felt hat. His left hand rests across his chest, the thumb thrust into the armhole. Long, grey side-whiskers meet beneath his chin. The identity of this man remained in doubt until my old friend Mr. Isaac Biggin of Unthank recognized him as Bill Hill, the joiner brother to 'Taffy' and Sammy and Pim. This same source identified the venerable, tweed-clad man with white whiskers meeting beneath his chin and standing well back in the group as Bill Booker, one-time woodman to the Duke of Rutland in this district. Beside the young William Wilson stands the Huntsman of the Barlow, William Haslam. He always hunted on foot and was landlord of 'The Royal Oak' at Millthorpe. As a matter of interest he was the father of Kate Webster, who took over the licence of 'The Royal Oak' and became one of Peakland's best-known landladies. At the right side of the photograph stands Jack Haslam of Barlow, brother of the Huntsman and a general assistant and fox handler to the Hunt. A man clad in riding cap, tail coat and jodhpurs; a man notorious for his fondness of ale. Between these two brothers is a stout, middle-aged man with a cloth cap and corduroy breeches. He carries a horn-handled stick. Alfred Hyghe had originally told me that he believed this to be William Haslam, the Huntsman's son who worked with his father at the Kennels and later became landlord of the Chequer's Inn, Coal Aston. This I now doubt, as the William Haslam I remember, who delivered meat for a Dronfield butcher and later took the licence of the Chequers Inn could not have been a man of 50 or so at the end of the last century when my photograph was taken. The other argument against this man being William Haslam is that it looks impossible that such a grey-haired, middle-aged man could be the son of the Huntsman standing close by his side. It seems far more likely that it is Harry Helliwell of Bank Green, father of the well-known Helliwells who still inhabit this lovely countryside. He was gamekeeper for the Wilsons and lived in the ancient farm-house upon its conspicuous knoll and now regrettably in ruins above Fox Lane.

But there were still gaps in my knowledge so I decided to visit the only person on the photograph who was still alive.

Miss Winifred Wilson left the old family home of Beauchief Hall in the thirties and settled at Highlightley in the equally lovely Vale of Barlow. On a quiet summer Sunday afternoon I recall walking up the red ash drive between rhododendrons and a line of fruit trees, ahead stood the mellow stone front of the farm-house. At the far end of the drive the lawn opened out to overlook the little valley with the murmuring Dunston Brook, girt by alders and ash and oak. At the far side of the green sweep of lawn was the arresting vermilion splash of Californian poppies in full bloom; that simple contrast of green and red was Miss Wilson's creation, and how it worked; a touch of genius.

Taking a turn at the edge of the lawn was the old lady of the house, clad in a maroon suit and wide-brimmed hat. Her small, bent frame contrasted with the generous bulk of her factotum, called Haggerstone, who walked at her side. Through that afternoon I was shown some of the considerable work done by Miss Wilson in three-quarters of a century spent in painting the beautiful countryside and animals which have been in all, her life. Her oils possess that powerful, direct application of colour and a realism which marks them as stemming directly from the same school to which such eminent artists as Sir George Claussen belonged; a simplification only to a degree of allowing the work a character marking it as the work of one artist interpreting what was seen in a readily appreciated form.

Her most arresting canvas is the large, summer scene executed in the garden at Highlightley before World War II. It shows the mellow south front of the house soon after Miss Wilson had had it rebuilt with larger windows. There is a Scots pine growing by the front door, and one can still see its stump close to the terrace heavy with scent of Rose of Sharon in August. The entire foreground of the composition is filled with a variety of herbaceous

Highlightley Farm from the bank of Dunston Brook

plants in bloom, great white lilies predominating. The composition dominates an entire wall of the studio and sets going the hazy music of long-ago summers, and the smell of hay drifts over the high wall from the meadows which rise one way towards Cartledge and along the other towards Barlow and the beckoning woods beyond.

Then there is a small painting done in the grounds of Beauchief Hall perhaps half a century ago; we are looking up a flight of stone steps set in a grassy bank, steps which lead into the trees beyond and flanking the weathered steps are the magic yellow heads of daffodils. It is spring and there is a stirring in the air—my instant thought every time I have seen this composition is of first spring heat, the initial pulse of the sun's rays which never lessen their life-giving thrill as each succeeding awakening of the year slips into view beyond the silver birches of the mind. Where are those particular steps? I have often wondered if they still exist.

Also painted at Beauchief is a much bigger work. Two children, a boy and a girl, are astride a pair of ponies and appear momentarily between tall drifts of rhododendrons. The background trees stand guard over the track down which the riders have come and a blue sky is glimpsed beyond. The colouring of those great piles of rhododendron blooms shows a remarkable control. The whole makes an arresting painting which is both accurate and tremendously exciting. Then there is her "Hunters at Grass" completed during the Great War and first exhibited in 1919 and subsequently at Newcastle, 1920, Liverpool, 1921 and one-man shows in 1931 and 1946. It has been described by an art critic as "the equal of Sir Alfred Munnings". But this is only one of literally scores of Miss Wilson's paintings which have been exhibited all over the country. "In Great Brind Wood" was painted about 1942, and here we are looking out across the vale above the artist's home, to piled cumulus clouds approaching over Moorhall and Barlow Grange and soon to cast dark shadow across the ploughlands by Johnnygate Lane. The lane is glimpsed too, through the nearby trees of the wood which belongs to Miss Wilson; one of the dominant pair of trees is a silver birch, the other is a young oak. I had little difficulty in locating the place from which the picture was painted. The vista has not altered in any dramatic way; the under-shrubs have grown taller and so have the young oak and silver birch. But there is still the atmosphere of Brahms in Great Brind Wood—literally 'the burnt wood'—which suggests the production of charcoal in former times or the scene of a great woodland fire prior to 1457, the year in which the name is first known to have been used.

Perhaps the finest work done by Miss Winifred Wilson is her group of British Friesian cows sheltering in the deep shade of a great oak. It is hot and dry, the cows are alive and the entire composition complete. But one comes to the conclusion that the artist's greatest joy has been in the painting of intimate commonplace everyday animal scenes—groups of mixed poultry, a field full of pit ponies having a well-earned holiday at Highlightley, and grey cart-horses at work, drinking or idling beneath those summer trees.

As for the Barlow Hunt photograph she recalled it being taken quite clearly. Not only could she verify the identity of those already recognized but she could readily point out John Risley upon a pony beside William Wilson senior, a groom and kennelman who had come from Bedford. The long skirts and white apron of Nell, his wife, are visible between the front legs of the Master's horse, while their daughter, Jessie, stands behind Bill

Hill the joiner, her sailor's hat, long hair and black boots marking her as a well-turned-out young girl of the period. Instantly, despite the passage of almost sixty years, Miss Wilson was able to identify the horses in my photograph.

"My father is riding Gull, a particularly good horse which was his favourite mount for many years", she explained. "The horse I am riding was called Ramrod—a real flyer—and the big horse ridden by the groom next to me was Double X and because of that we often called the groom by the same name. My brother is mounted on a very friendly animal we knew as Twinkle which had not a speck of grey on his coat."

The young William Wilson of the photograph became Major Wilson, Master of the Barlow in succession to his father. His twin sisters May, and the late Violet were Joint Masters of the Woodland and Pytchley and of the High Peak Harriers. Miss Winifred, the eldest, enjoyed almost eighty hunting seasons for she never missed one season after reaching her sixth birthday. Of late, however, her failing sight and hearing made long days in the hunting field something of an endurance test. When her last animal Star died she resigned the horse but still takes a very active interest in hunting, following the hounds on foot. No more shall we see that familiar side-saddle figure riding the lanes at dawn and jumping from stubble field to stubble field. The grey drophead Lanchester is still to be seen in narrow lanes and along the road to town, but no longer is it driven by its owner. On an autumn day of lingering tea-time sunlight, when the dying damson leaves reflected the last, warm gold, I watched a field of barley stubble being turned to brown by a distant plough. The shorthorn herd were still grazing an adjoining pasture and through the middle of these animals moved a small frail figure clad in russet and grey tweeds. The artist of the vale was making her way to see how the cultivations were proceeding close beside her Great Brind Wood.

NINE

The Farm Animals of Derbyshire

The regional specialization of farm animal breeds in the past—of the Large White Pig in the West Riding of Yorkshire and the Shorthorn cow in County Durham—is well known and many carry the name of their county of origin. The passage of time has tended to reduce the number of important breeds and a rather dull uniformity prevails. Efficient performance is certainly an important criterion, but the ubiquitous Friesian which is seen in ever-increasing numbers means that the day may dawn not too far distantly when the red and white and blue-roaned Dairy Shorthorn and the pretty Ayrshire will be as rare a sight as is the Shire horse today.

Regionality is giving way to overall uniformity and, what is after all the point of agriculture, efficiency. But before all memory of well-loved things perishes with those who knew them it is worth hesitating and looking at the contribution made over the centuries by Derbyshire to the kaleidoscope of farm animal breeds. Today it is easy to overlook this contribution for the county never produced a breed of cow or sheep or pig which became of really widespread importance; nevertheless, the county has had a share in shaping as wide a range of breeds as any in Britain—sheep, fowl, horse and cow. Only two of these breeds remain at all important in a world of agriculture notable for its increasing lack of former colour; they are a horse and a hill sheep.

Within the confines of Peakland several breeds of sheep were developed long ago. Among these were the Penistone, a breed of hardy hill animals with its vague origins lost in the mists of time which shroud much of the wide uplands which form northernmost Peakland. This breed resembled the Westmorland Limestone, now another 'lost' breed. To my knowledge no pure Penistone sheep exist today, but the breed will long be remembered for the remarkable feat which two animals performed at the beginning of the last century. A few were taken to a farm in Kent, three soon disappeared and two eventually re-appeared at home on the moors! Their horns hung for a long time in Hope parish church.

A very old breed of sheep which does remain, though in very few numbers, is the White-faced Woodland. As I described this lovely old hill breed in some detail in a previous book, it is sufficient to say here that it can be traced back to the Middle Ages in the highest Peak District. A century and a half ago there were eighty or more breeders with some very large flocks. I have seen old photographs of flocks of these big, heavy animals with grey faces and large, spiral horns. Crossing with other hill breeds, notably the Swaledale, and a general decline in popularity has resulted in this colourful breed nearing extinction, though the Elliotts of Ashopton and the Shirts of Nether Booth, Edale, still possess small flocks.

A breed which is still represented by an active breed society and which appears regularly in sheep classes at local shows is the Derbyshire Gritstone, formerly known as the Dale o' Goyt after the western hollow of its origin. As I have also made reference to this breed in a previous book there is room here simply to state that pure-bred flocks have been kept here for more than a century and that the breed became popular in the hills of north-eastern Cheshire, south-eastern Lancashire and south Yorkshire. The Duke of Devenshire became the first President of the Derbyshire Gritstone Sheepbreeders' Society when it was founded on 15th October 1906. There were about thirty members at this time, but now the number has more than trebled. It has a pretty, speckled face, but one of the reasons that it lost favour over the years was that it did not maintain the age-old rule "polled for grass, horned for heather". The breed is polled (hornless), and this was often thought of as being a bad point, a bias based on tradition for the Derbyshire Gritstone has a rugged constitution. It is a stubborn resister of disease. One of the foremost breeders today is Mr. J. J. Brocklehurst of Fernilee Hall Farm, overlooking the Dale of Goyt where the breed originated.

One other breed of sheep associated with the county is the Portland. It probably originated in south-western England, but for a long time there has been a pure-bred flock kept in the lovely wooded grounds of Calke Abbey on the very boundary with northern Leicestershire. Here, in the undulating parkland with its several lakes, Mr. C. R. Harpur-Crewe's flock thrives as a relic breed which reminds us of the extinction which has overtaken so many sheep in the last fifty years.

It was about 100 years ago that A. F. Wragg, the school-teacher at Edensor (the 'model' village in Chatsworth Park) developed the first specimens of the Redcap breed of poultry, a breed which has been linked with Derbyshire ever since.

Mr. Wragg crossed a Golden Spangled cockerel—then named Moonies and originally imported from Hamburg—with a hen of the well-known fighting breed of Old English Game. For the last ninety years the Fox family of Matlock have been closely associated with Redcaps.

Mr. Harry Fox of Smedley Street, Matlock, handled and bred Redcaps for seventy years, and he was acknowledged as the leading authority on this now rare breed. A poultry expert and judge of international repute, he was resident in Italy for a number of years between the wars as adviser to the Italian Government on the scientific breeding and management of poultry. For many years Harry Fox owned a large poultry farm in his native Matlock, but in his later years he conducted much of his business by post, buying, selling and advising in all fields of the feathered world, especially in connection with rare and ornamental breeds. Much time was occupied by judging poultry classes at shows up and down the country, and in 1962 he featured in and advised on the making of a film for the Nuffield Foundation called *The Evolution of the Modern Pigeon*. He had been chairman of Bakewell Show Society's Poultry and Pigeon Committee for almost two decades, and show manager of the poultry section.

The Redcap breed was kept initially in the neighbouring Peak District villages of Birchover and Elton, but its popularity spread throughout the county and later to most parts of Britain. A great fault in the breeding of the Redcap was white ear lobes, a disqualifying feature for the breed. There were so many white-lobed birds at one time that 'throw-outs' developed as a separate breed known as Old English Pheasant Fowl.

In appearance the Redcap is a light breed, not unlike a Leghorn. Its plumage is brown and black, and its outstanding characteristic is the roseate comb, a usual and readily recognizable feature. In the days when the breed was more popular it was used for both egg production and table purposes, since it possessed a surprising amount of meat on the breast. A good pullet will average 200 eggs per annum on free-range, and under such management the eggs are particularly rich in albumoids.

Redcap Cockerels are still in some demand for crossing with other breeds to improve the quality of breast meat and eggs. The pugnacious character of these cocks has led to their popularity in certain parts of the world for fighting purposes; they are capable of making a good showing against fighting game-cocks.

What of the future of the breed? Harry Fox pointed out shortly before his death (early in 1965) that this breed is no longer of great economic importance, having lost ground in favour of the Rhode Island Red, Light Sussex and the Leghorns. Its place today is on the show bench and as a 'hobby' fowl in the hen-run of the fancier. There are birds of the breed in many parts of this country and abroad—from Devon and Cornwall to Lancashire, in the U.S.A. and Canada.

As one would expect, this leading expert on the breed knew the whereabouts of most of the existing flocks, and a few Redcaps are still kept in the Derbyshire villages of Youlgreave, Longstone, Bradwell and Tideswell. Many of these birds were his; as he said, "It's easier for me to own hens and let others look after them."

Beyond the world of pigeons and poultry, Mr. Fox had considerable knowledge of exotic birds too. He advised on wildfowl at Slimbridge and recently on the stocking of a private bird collection at Calver—which includes flamingoes—being instrumental in the obtaining of many rare specimens. More recently, he obtained a pair of Australian black swans for the National Fauna Reserve at Riber Castle, Matlock, on the hilltop above the farm where he was born in 1890.

It was a slight friendship with Harry Fox that set me on the road to becoming a fancier of the breed. As all owners of this hardy breed with its picturesque red rose comb have found, the hatchability of the fine white eggs is rather low. With my very first sitting of eggs, bought from a fancier near Great Longstone, there were bright prospects of a large flock of Redcaps in a short time. Eleven eggs hatched from the thirteen set, seven of the chicks proving to be pullets. I was able to sell the surplus cockerels and introduced a fine male bird bred by one of the best breeders still practising, Mr. Ron Bradwell of Smalldale, Bradwell. Success with hatching has been limited of late, one of the major problems being the procuring of unrelated animals for breeding and the avoidance of crossing close relatives; this is a common problem when one is working with any breed of animal near to extinction and it can quickly lead to loss of vigour in the strain.

The late Sir James A. Scott Watson wrote that an average medieval knight protected by plate armour "and carrying his normal accoutrements, had difficulty in making a riding weight of less than twenty-eight stone". Hence, the medieval war horse, the Great Horse of England of fable and reality, had to be powerful—of great endurance and weight-carrying type. It was Cromwell and the new thinkers of Commonwealth times who directed this type of animal from the battlefield to the farm field. Their armour and weapons were light, and they no longer required a heavyweight charger. The Great Horse began a peaceful career which only now stands condemned, though not quite. Actually the reign of the heavy horse—as typified by the Shire—has been a comparatively short one. Only after a long struggle did it oust the ox as the paramount draught animal at the beginning of the eighteenth century, for the latter could live successfully without the valuable corn needed by humans for their own bellies. By 1950 the heavy horse was fast disappearing as the numbers of tractor increased. No one in his right mind would wish the complete return of the heavy horse, for the tractor has made for lighter, speedier working on the farm. The long and arduous life of the horseman on a large farm even thirty years ago is largely forgotten by the majority these easy days. Old Jim Shepherd was the last horseman at Broomfield, near Derby. He was one of the last of the traditional breed of horsemen in this part of the country. I well remember his short, wiry silhouette in the muddy yard of Lime Farm on wet December mornings at six a.m. His paraffin lamp swung across the yard to the brick-arched stable doorway and sent long, frightening shadows slipping around that big and draughty yard. We lads unloaded the frosted kale from a cart with bare hands for the cowman to fork to the dairy herd and if we got in old Jim's way at that short-tempered time he would snarl and bark and disappear inside the stable. The yellow light reflected warmly off the straw and made the smooth contours of those three proud animals flow like liquid silver. No matter how angry he had been with the ignoramuses in the mucky yard beyond the warm glow of his lantern he rarely had a hard word for his charges within. With soft sounds and a special language understood by both parties he quickly had them groomed, fed and harnessed up for the morning's work.

We took them out to water them at the trough under the cowshed wall and then they came back for their oats. Old Jim had the typical temperament of a professional farm horseman, working quietly and steadily; uttering firm orders to his animals, chewing tobacco and punctuating it with pauses while he spit upon the ground to one side. The horses finally went from Broomfield, and their going nearly broke old Jim's heart; very soon he had joined the long line of colleagues who had gone before him.

The Suffolk Punch, the Clydesdale and the Shire are the heavy horses native to this country and it is the last breed—the most notable and oldest—with which Derbyshire claims the closest affinity. Just as the Shorthorn is the national cattle breed of England, so the Shire is the national heavy horse. It originated in times beyond the scope of detailed history, for Queen Boadicea beat the Romans because of the superior British horses which were the ancestors of the Great Horse and the quiet Shire of recent times. This modern breed was largely developed in the north Midlands, in the Shires, and it is possible to claim south Derbyshire as the headquarters of Shire Horse country. Here, in the Ashbourne district, the biggest success of everyday farmers in the breeding of good strains of the horse was seen. As has been written, it is here "where the sound limestone land seems to give the fullest expression to the inborn qualities that go to the making of a good Shire". As evidence of this fact let it be remembered that here the greatest Shire Horse stallion, the famous Harold, was bred, an animal which did as much for the breed as any other in former or subsequent times.

There is still an important annual show and sale of Shires here at Derby, and the heavy-horse classes are still well supported—albeit by breeders and farmers who use their animals far less for purely utilitarian purposes than previously. Farmers like the Widdowson family of Handley, near Eckington, in north-east Derbyshire still use, breed and show the Shire. The sight of a pair of Shires drawing a single-furrow plough across old pasture, ley or stubble is now rare, and the last farmer to use horses regularly for this task was Mr. Jim Smith of Lower Birchitt Farm, in the upper Drone Valley. Now his horses have gone and the old plough lies rusting.

So to the cow. The only breed of importance which has come cleanly out of the county is the Blue Albion. This, like several of the sheep breeds mentioned earlier, is now virtually extinct. The blue and blue-and-white animal has long been common in the breeding of the Dairy Shorthorn. But it was not until this century that a herd society was formed for such dairy cattle. Known as the Blue Albion Cattle Society, most of the members resided and farmed in south Derbyshire and over the county boundaries in each direction. In the bye-laws and regulations of the society made and passed by the council on 24th April 1924 the permissable colours for Blue Albion cattle were: "Blue, Blue and White, White and Blue, Blue Roan, or Blue Roan and White". The problem of colour was the greatest encountered by the breed. Mendelian laws dictate that the expectation from a cross between two blue animals would be in the proportion of one black: one white: two blue offspring. This meant that the Blue Albion did not necessarily breed true to colour. Another problem was that no one possessed a really first-class bull.

The best Blue Albion herd about 1925 was the one owned by John Seals of Snelston, near Ashbourne, and formerly of the pretty village of Bradbourne. He was an accepted authority on the breed up to the time of his death many years ago. Another name closely associated with the breed—one of its founders—was Trafford of Newlands, Parwich, who came to the Home Farm, Yeldersley, about 1920.

Because of its inability to breed completely true to colour, the animal slowly lost favour and World War II accelerated its decline. By 1949 Sidney Rogerson was able to write that its numbers were so few that "it will be a rare sight outside the stock-pens of one of the bigger agricultural shows". By 1957 the last herd had been dispersed, and during 1964 all activities in connection with the Blue Albion Cattle Society were wound up. There are, of course, blue and white and blue roan animals to be seen, particularly on the limestone uplands of the west; these are not pure Blue Albions but are the type of animal from which the breed developed. So that though it is broadly true to say that the Blue Albion is extinct, there will continue to be animals of the same type and marking while the versatile Dairy Shorthorn remains as a viable breed.

TEN

Threshing Days

John Morgan was born at Holmesfield in 1846. He eventually married a daughter of the family of Wolstenholme, who lived at Horsleygate in the same parish. They lived at Little Chatsworth, cottages standing end-on to the lane which winds down from Holmesfield to the Barlow Vale at Millthorpe. The Wolstenholmes had threshed their own corn by machine for some time and young John Morgan became interested in this skilled activity of the farming year. He obtained a threshing drum about 1869, and a team of horses drew it and a portable steam-engine from farm to farm in the district. As early as 1839 William Howden's portable steam-engine was exhibited at the Royal Agricultural Society's first show at Oxford.

On 26th September 1882 John Morgan bought his first traction engine. It was a brand new 6-horse-power single-cylinder Fowler, No. 4267. The engine was delivered by train to Sheffield Midland Station. A test driver came with the engine from the Leeds works, the new owner providing board and lodging for this man for one week while he showed Morgan how to drive, maintain and carry out any simple repairs. Each traction engine was different, and its ways had to be learnt with the passage of time. A new engine like No. 4267 had also to be run-in carefully. The test driver brought the engine to the Morgan's new home at Newgate Farm, near Barlow.

This traction engine hauled and drove John Morgan's threshing implements for many years; it did other jobs, too. On three occasions it was used to boil the water for special teas in Barlow. In 1911, for instance, it stood in the yard at Elm Tree Farm to boil water for the celebration tea to mark the coronation of King George V. A storm had blown down the marquee erected for the tea in the field across the lane so the tables and forms were moved close beneath the high, roadside hedge to protect everyone from the strong wind. Water was taken direct from the boiler to mash the tea in large urns.

Soon after No. 4267 had been delivered to John Morgan in the autumn of 1882 the threshing outfit was descending the steep and winding Millthorpe Lane when, just below Little Chatsworth cottages, he changed to a lower gear to slow the engine down. The key holding tight the gear-change mechanism came out and the engine began to free-wheel. Speed was building up as they turned the left-hand corner below the cottages so John Morgan turned the engine into the high wall at an oblique angle. The run-away came quickly to a halt, the only damage done being a broken hub cap on the nearside driving wheel. A search along the lane revealed the lost key which had come out of the rack and pinion gear-change mechanism. It was rubbed in road dust and knocked back into the key-way. The remarkable thing was that the key never came adrift again up to the time the engine was scrapped fifty years later.

This fine old engine was kept by the Morgan family until 1926. It then went to Newbold and was used to pull coal out of a drift-mine. After the General Strike it was used at a gannister mine at Upper Loads, above Holymoorside, before returning to Newbold to be used on another farm to haul coal out of a drift mine in the stackyard. Before World War II it was cut up for scrap. As a tribute to the Victorian traction engine builders No. 4267 was a good example for it was really built to work at a steam pressure of 120 pounds per square inch; however, late in its working life the safety valve had been regularly screwed down so that it worked at a pressure of 140 pounds per square inch in order to drive the straw-chopper.

The Morgan family was a large one, and all the brothers and half-brothers were involved in the threshing business. My good friend Mr. E. (Ned) Morgan of Ashgate was the last of this long line of threshing contractors. He is one of the younger members of John Morgan's family. About 1900 Ned's eldest half-brother obtained a second-hand traction engine to do contracting work on his own account, mainly in the Staveley district. It was a 8-horse-power single-cylinder Fowler, No. 6772 and had been bought new by a colliery owner at Spennymoor, County Durham. Fowlers had fetched the engine back to Leeds as it could not be paid for, and so it came to Newgate, Barlow.

In 1907 John Morgan was threshing corn stacks at Grove Farm, Old Brampton when the Midland Railway delivered the great metal valve for the third (and last) reservoir then being built at Linacre in the valley below Grove Farm. This big piece of machinery controls the flow of water out of the reservoir into the main waterpipe. The driver refused to take his dray hauled by a team of heavy horses across the fields beyond the farm. John Morgan was asked if he would attempt to haul the valve down into the valley. He agreed and the engine was slowly eased across the steeply-angled fields towards the site of the dam works. Where necessary a chain was secured around the driving wheel on the uphill side to prevent the engine from slewing round and going down the slope out of control. This was before the trees surrounding the middle reservoir had been planted and the entire journey was over open fields, a journey which was broken while an official Water Board photograph was taken to show the valve being drawn by No. 4267.

In 1916 the Government commandeered this engine so that it could be used to provide power for baling hay for army horses. The bales produced were extremely well made, being bound with five wires instead of the normal two. Mr. Ned Morgan recalled that even if one wire snapped after baling the bale was broken open and put through a second time. No. 4267 was kept on this special work for three years so a second-hand engine was obtained by the Morgans to take its place. Ned Morgan's eldest half-brother usually drove it; within a year (in 1917) a new firebox was required, for the new acquisition hadn't been well maintained by its previous owner. It was used in later years to thresh at farms in the Newbold, Old Brampton, Holymoorside and Walton districts. It was also used to boil water for celebration teas at Barlow to commemorate the Silver Jubilee of King George V in 1935 and the coronation of King George VI in May 1937.

The commandeered engine was returned in 1919 to Clay Cross Station after having done much work in the South Wingfield district. It had not been well-maintained during those three years of war service and a considerable amount of repair work was needed before the Morgans were satisfied that it was ready for normal threshing and haulage work. Its first job, in September 1919, was hauling felled timber in Kitchenflat Wood near Linacre

House between Cutthorpe and Old Brampton. The trees had been purchased by Joseph Green of Old Whittington, of the well-known family of timber merchants and industrialists. The traction engine hauled whole trees with a steel cable to the hard trackway where horses could pull the timber away on wagons. It is quite likely, on reflection, that my father was in the woods watching No. 4267 timber-hauling, for as a young man he travelled about in his spare time with the Greens and learned much about the timber business. The scene is quite clear in my mind—the "tufter, tufter, tufter" of the engine as it hauled the heavy trunks along the dry, autumn woodland floor and the distant rasping of cross-cut saws and horses jingling their harness beyond the edge of the trees—though I never saw a traction engine at work in Kitchenflat Wood.

In December 1919 Ned Morgan, who was 26 years old, started contract threshing on his own account with No. 4267. His father was now 73 years old. He began these independent operations in the upper part of the Barlow Vale. He remembers how he set up his threshing drum at the side of Horsleygate Lane in order to thresh Mr. Frank Lowe's stacks at the Middle Farm. They finished threshing there, and at 4.30 p.m. (as the light was failing) they set off down the lane and so to the foot of Fox Lane. A long, steep haul now faced them to reach Fox Lane Farm at the edge of the moor. Ned Morgan decided that his engine could make the ascent with all the tackle behind and so save a lot of time and trouble. He had not reckoned with the soft nature of the rubble forming the surface of this lane, for when they drew level with Adamfield Farm the engine stalled, its driving wheels spinning, the exhaust bellowing beneath the tall trees and the wheels digging deeply into the soft ruts. One of the men jumped down and came back to report that the leading axle of one of the trailing implements had come to rest on the lane, its wheels having sunk deeply. There was no alternative but to chock up the tackle and winch each implement slowly in turn to easier ground farther up the lane. That wasn't the end of the problem, either. On the final, steep pull to Fox Lane Farm the same tactics had to be resorted to again, and it was ten o'clock on that midwinter night as they covered up the engine and machines with tarpaulins. Then, of course, there was a long way to walk home. The Morgans travelled over a wide area of the countryside and almost always they had to walk home to Newgate after a long day's threshing. On this particular dark December night Ned Morgan had a walk of at least 3 miles as measured in a straight line on the map. Such a route would have been quite impracticable, though the threshing Morgans were well known for their cross-country walking to and from work in winter darkness. Ned Morgan refers to these routes as being by "hedge and dyke". Often they finished in a deep, wet ditch but always managed to reach home for a meal and a few hours sleep before getting up very early next day to reach the farm in good time to set the machinery up and get steam up. On that December night one of the thresher men had to walk a mile beyond Newgate as he lived at Cutthorpe—and he was carrying a large chaff-carrying bag of holly collected on the way up Fox Lane!

On 26th September 1924 Ned Morgan took delivery of a new traction engine. It was a 7-horse-power single-cylinder Burrell and cost £959. This utterly reliable machine was used until May 1948, when a tractor took its place. It never cost a penny in repairs and up to the present time (1970) has never had a bearing reduced. This engine worked at a steam pressure of 200 pounds per square inch and was fantastically economical to run. Just before Christmas 1924 the engine was driven with the threshing machinery from Newgate to Bowling Green Farm, close by Haddon Hall, a distance of 13 miles. They arrived at dusk with very little coal left in the engine's bunker. The farmer apologized that he only had 25 hundredweight of coal in his shed and imagined a lot more would be required as there was four days work on the farm. Ned Morgan said that that amount would be ample. The farmer was dubious. For two and a half days corn was threshed and the straw chopped and for a further two days corn was threshed and the straw tied in 'bottles' for subsequent thatching of stacks. At the end of those four and a half days hard work the engine's bunker was filled and a sack was also filled for fuel for the journey home. There was still 3 hundredweight of coal left in the astonished farmer's shed! On average that Burrell engine had a fuel consumption of 6 hundredweight good-quality coal per day of eight threshing hours.

In 1941 a second engine was obtained so that a second threshing set could be run. It was a 7-horse-power compound Fowler built by Fowlers for the Ministry of Munitions in 1917. It weighed over

13 tons. Ned Morgan had an ex-amusement arcade man to run this second outfit. Though this man was completely illiterate his former employer remembers him as a wonderful 'steam man' who treated the Fowler as if he had owned it.

At the outset, however, this engine proved a great headache. They fetched it from Loughborough on Boxing Day 1941, but after completing 9 miles it ran out of steam, and by the end of that first day water could not be induced to enter the boiler because of inadequate cleaning-out over a long period. They stayed overnight with a threshing contractor north of Loughborough, and they were able to wash the boiler and water tank out before setting off next morning. That evening they reached the entrance to Newstead Abbey and left it in the darkness to catch several buses home. The following weekend they crawled to Heath, south-east of Chesterfield, and on the next day arrived at Newgate, Barlow. On every hill bottom gear had to be engaged, and Ned Morgan's disgust with this new purchase can be imagined. On arrival in the yard it was covered up and left for five months! In the following May, the threshing season over, the cylinder was stripped down and rebuilt. It subsequently proved to be a very good engine, able "to make steam out of anything you gave it". As threshing work declined sufficient work for this second threshing set was hard to find, and in 1946 this engine was sold.

At one time five threshing sets and engines stood in the steep yard at Newgate, Barlow. There was only one level place in the yard where an engine could be overhauled or a wheel taken off with safety, and Ned Morgan well remembers the shunting and manoeuvring often necessary there.

But the combine harvester was coming on to the agricultural scene increasingly after World War II, and the internal combustion engine was seriously threatening the steam traction engine. Soon after the war a TVO Standard Fordson had been obtained for hay baling, and in May 1948 Ned Morgan took delivery of a TVO Fordson Major. In October 1949 the famous Perkins diesel-powered Fordson arrived, and the well-loved 1924 Burrell engine was sold to an enthusiast. Its former owner recalls that a lot of the best traction engines and showman's engines were scrapped about this time, before preservation of such wonderful machinery was seriously considered by many people. He knew of four showman's engines standing in one yard and sold for scrap for £90 each. In

1924 his Burrell cost £959, and today it would change hands for a figure in excess of £3,000. Some good examples of showman's engines are sold today for over £7,000.

Mr. Ned Morgan is still a steam enthusiast. He is one of that now rare breed of countrymen-engineers who worked with traction engines for most of his life, who treated them with feeling and respect and who understood to a remarkable extent the peculiar life force of steam and the machinery which it drove in the service of agriculture. Ned (born in 1893) and his brothers and their employees walked hundreds of miles each year by "hedge and dyke", and subsequently he took to cycling, for in 1935 he and his wife went to live at Ashgate, entailing longer distances to and from the farms.

In September 1955 he decided quite suddenly to wind up his threshing business, and the last thresh took place in the first days of October when Ned was 62 years old. For many years he had averaged 100 hilly miles on his bicycle every week. Sometimes the journey was a long one—over Puddingpie Hill to Foolow or Stoney Middleton—and after a day's hard physical work it seemed much longer home to Ashgate. That shining green bicycle is maintained, even today, as was 'Dolly' long ago. That was the name given to the 1924 Burrell engine when it arrived at Newgate in honour of Barlow-born Dolly Margerison, a life-long friend of the Morgan family who spent most of her spare time as a girl at Newgate. Old John Morgan would not start tea on a Sunday afternoon until young Dolly had arrived. It was typical of Ned Morgan that he should name his new machine after their jolly family friend. Happily 'Dolly' never went to the scrapyard and runs resplendent in the hands of an enthusiast in the south of England.

Though I don't recall seeing that famous Burrell engine in the days of her prime, I did thresh with the Morgans on several farms in the years immediately prior to October 1955, when diesel power had replaced steam. Though Ned Morgan no longer wheels his shining, green bicycle out of the stackyard to ride off along the lane after a dusty day's work feeding the drum, that very drum (built in 1893, the year of his birth) stands at a farm at Barlow Grange. Several farms hereabouts still possess and use threshing drums, but the threshing contractor has passed. The distant "tufter, tufter, tufter" sounds ghostly beyond the darkened wood, and there, at a turn in the lane, I seem to see the red glow of the firebox between the hedgerows. A dense, irregular procession moves out in silhouette against the night sky—drum, baler and straw-chopper—at its head the proud engine of childhood dreams, sparks glow across the blackness towards the stars entangled in the winter treetops.

ELEVEN

Carpenter and Kitchen

During 1883 there came to live in the pastoral calm of Barlow Vale a man of letters who had decided to change his way of life. He found and purchased three fields at Millthorpe and built himself a cottage and buildings. That man was Edward Carpenter, the once-famous scholar who believed that "mankind should make more effort to be worthy of the world they have been given". That his life and works are not generally known today is not really very surprising, for many of the things advocated by him all that time ago have now come to pass. He never sought publicity for himself and claimed that most literary people had too high an opinion of themselves anyway.

But the story begins in 1844. Edward Carpenter was born on 29th August in that year at Brighton, into a wealthy, middle-class family. He had six sisters and two brothers. His love for the countryside began in childhood, on the South Downs inland from his home. From Brighton College he went to Trinity, Cambridge and graduated a 10th Wrangler in 1868; in 1869 he was ordained into the Church of England. But the life of a Victorian curate to a Cambridge church was not satisfactory to Carpenter; he saw it as a somewhat artificial way to spend one's time, and after reading Walt Whitman's works (particularly the book *Leaves of Grass*) he developed a strong desire to live a life "in conformity with Nature". After a holiday in Greece he decided what course he would take and resigned his curacy.

To the industrial centres of the North he came, a great change from the quiet environment which had thus far been his. He filled the post as an extra-mural lecturer and travelled about the towns and cities on both sides of the Pennines delivering lectures on astronomy. He developed a fondness for the people he met in Sheffield, the working folk and Socialist leaders. As he said much later, he was finding fulfilment in the cause of Socialism. About 1877 he came to lodge more or less permanently in the suburbs of Sheffield. He wrote many poems at this time, but they were not readily received and Edward Carpenter is not best remembered as a poet.

Some time after that he moved farther out of Sheffield, lodging with the Fearnehough family at Bradway. At that time it was a small village quite separate from Sheffield and looking out over the Sheaf Valley to the high moors of Peakland, towards Totley Moss, Burbage Moor and the Hallam Moors. To the south lay the pastoral country about Dronfield and Holmesfield. The direct railway route between Chesterfield and Sheffield had been driven under the village by means of Bradway Tunnel only a few years before and the very long Totley Tunnel had not then been constructed to take the new line from Sheffield to Manchester via the Hope Valley. Bradway was still a peaceful village but possessed the convenience of being quite near to Sheffield. Because he had a small private income Edward Carpenter was able to give up lecturing to turn his attention to writing. He planned and constructed a long poem on the subject of true socialism. It was to be called "Towards Democracy". His enthusiasm for socialist ideas was not motivated by politics. He had no time for this "time-wasting and often corrupted sphere". His was a socialism of the William Morris School based upon a revolution in industrial, family and social life. From this standpoint much of what he advocated has become reality—some for the good but much has been realized with a less happy outcome.

In the garden at Bradway he constructed a retreat or summer-house where much of "Towards Democracy" was written. After the death of his father he found himself comparatively wealthy. He had walked from Bradway southwards into the pastoral country of north Derbyshire on many occasions, and now he looked for a place of his own, a holding where he could live in the way which appealed to him most of all—"in conformity with Nature". It so happened that he discovered those three fields at Millthorpe, and they were for sale. He bought them and began building his smallholding. At that time Carpenter was able to rejoice over the fact that the Barlow Vale had no tyrannical squire living at a Big House "nor even a single villa". Later a squire of the typical sort came to live in this "happy valley" and after Carpenter had gone away a few 'villas' were built in and on the slopes of the valley. One such monstrosity was, ironically enough, erected in a field almost opposite his smallholding though he never saw it. His "Towards Democracy" was published in 1883, soon after his arrival at Millthorpe. It was more successful than his previous work though not on any large scale.

It is possible to see a close similarity in the ideas and way of life of Carpenter and the older Walt Whitman, whose works had so influenced the former in earlier days. Like Carpenter the American produced much verse but his best-known prose is "Democratic Vistas", published in 1871. In 1884, having organized himself at Millthorpe (the Fearnehoughs moved with him from Bradway) he visited the United States, particularly to see the 65-year-old Whitman. During his stay he met many modern thinkers who had an influence on shaping and crystallizing many of his philosophies.

After his return to the idyllic rural scene of the Barlow Vale—a peace which is still present if one gets away from the roads—life went on as he had planned it, with hard work and dignity. His major philosophy was based upon the theory of 'one acre and a cow'; he believed that smallholding for the vast majority of the population was the correct way of life, with the most benefits to the mind, body, soul and to the soil. It was a very sound idea but impracticable on a large scale in Victorian England. He was a vegetarian and believer in life in the open air and became well known locally for long walks in all weathers, his feet usually clad in the leather sandals of his own making which he advocated to all his friends.

The vegetables he grew were far in excess of home requirements, and the surplus Edward Carpenter sold from a stall which he had in Chesterfield market. He also produced handicrafts, in the vogue of fellow-thinker and poet William Morris—who was ten years older than Carpenter. In 1893 the Fearnehoughs left Millthorpe and were replaced by the Adams family who stayed until 1898. George Merrill became the handyman-gardener-companion after this and shared to a remarkable extent his employer's outlook. During the passing of the years at Millthorpe more and more people of note came to know Edward Carpenter through his writings. In 1902 the fourth edition of *England's Ideal and other*

Papers on Social Subjects was published; in 1903 a new edition of *Adam's Peak to Elephanta* appeared, being a collection of prose sketches describing former travels in Ceylon and India. Two years later appeared his inquiry into the causes and treatment of crime and criminals entitled *Prisons, Police and Punishment*, and so the list of titles could go on. Such a recital of facts has no place here, though another work published in 1906 is worthy of note, for it was on a different sort of subject from those which had gone before. Called *Love's Coming of Age*, it was a series of papers on the relationship of the sexes. It was well written and remarkably modern in outlook for its era. Carpenter came to know all styles and manner of men, and in 1914 'an address' was presented to him as a mark of respect upon his attaining 70 years. Among the signatories of this document were John Galsworthy, Laurence Housman, George Bernard Shaw, H. G. Wells and W. B. Yeats.

Through the years a wide variety of notables walked the countryside of Barlow Vale as Carpenter's guests. His small house could not accommodate everyone, and the farming family of Key of Cordwell Farm, just along the lane from Millthorpe, took his overflow from time to time. They recall an interesting trickle of guests at that period, among whom the fine figure of Captain Lawrence Edward Grace Oates is memorable. Oates had served in the Boer War and been severely wounded. He came in his twenties to see Carpenter and stayed in the ancient farm-house at Cordwell not long before joining Scott's last Antarctic Expedition. He never returned to the Barlow Vale, for on the long and arduous return from the South Pole (to which Roald Amundsen had beaten them by a narrow margin), Oates became crippled by frostbite and on 17th March 1912, rather than being a burden to his three starving companions, he walked out into the blizzard to die alone. Ever since, the epitaph "a brave and gallant gentleman" has been associated with Oates.

It was obvious that in the unchanging close-knit community of a rural North Derbyshire valley in late Victorian and Edwardian times such a man as Carpenter must attract a great quantity of attention. By some he was labelled a crank, by others a madman; to those with sufficient intelligence and interest to get to know him well Edward Carpenter became a trusted friend. With the late William Key of Cordwell Farm he built up a close acquaintance, as he did with the late Isaac Biggin of Woodseats

Hall, a house standing on elevated ground half a mile to the south of Millthorpe. In 1920, at the age of 33, Isaac Biggin moved to Unthank Lane Farm and he recalled for me before he died in October 1968 how Carpenter—then aged 76—used to come up to the farm and talk on all manner of subjects. "He was a very fine man", remembered Isaac Biggin, "when you got to know him. Some of his ideas were unusual at that time but today he would be considered a perfectly normal and very clever man." His *Sketches from Life* and the second edition of *The Healing of Nations* (first published in March 1915) lie before me as I write. The first is inscribed:

"Ike" Biggin
from his friend
Edwd. Carpenter.
Nov. 1913.

Towards those who became his friends, like William Key and Isaac Biggin, there existed a great warmth. It was once written that "a look from his calm, kindly face is a benediction". His youthful appearance and great physical fitness, even in great age, was a living advertisement for his philosophy of the simple, open-air life. He was one of the real pioneers of the cult of the great outdoors, for it was an extension of his doctrines which led directly to the foundation of such movements as the Youth Hostels Association, to cycling, to rambling and so on. The latter had one of its true sources in this very district. 'The King of Ramblers' was the usual name given to the late G. H. B. Ward. As a young man he came under the Carpenter spell of Christian socialism. In 1900 G.H.B.W. formed the Sheffield Clarion Ramblers, which still exists as a thriving club of men and women keen on the countryside and on the expenditure of physical energy in the pursuit of its exploration.

In the book *Sketches from Life* is a chapter in the typical manner of the author. He takes a simple subject—weeds—and discusses it in an interesting and informed way; from groundsel to bindweed and wild vetches. But he then associates the subject with humanity, with the types of 'weeds' found in human society; how some plants have made themselves useful in the service of others—man or animals—and how the 'weeds' of society can justify their existence only if they follow this example. His last book of note was an autobiography in which he gives contemporary glimpses of many notables of his times. The book is called *My Days and Dreams* and was published in 1916.

Six years later he left Millthorpe and went to live at Guildford, Surrey. In 1929, at the age of 85, he died. For years an annual pilgrimage took place in his memory. People from all over the country came to Millthorpe for the meeting which was held in the field by the Millthorpe Brook. His house has changed hands several times since 1922 and has been altered and enlarged but to this day bears the name Carpenter House.

At Edwinstowe, at the heart of the remnants of Sherwood Forest, was born in 1891 a boy called Fred, who was to rise to fame in an unsually humble and wholesome sort of manner. Within a very short time of his birth the Kitchen family moved northwards to the village of Maltby. This place stands in that peculiar, arable part of the West Riding which few people visit for pleasure. It is 9 miles from the place where the north-eastern corner of Derbyshire meets the western border of Nottinghamshire and that surprising southern dip in the southern boundary of the West Riding. It was, eighty years ago, a land of large corn and potato farms with collieries developing in the arable and wooded landscape as the shallower coal-seams to the west were worked out. Fred Kitchen's father earned 17s. a week as cowman on a farm belonging to a big estate adjoining the village. This was supplemented by a free cottage and garden and two pints of milk a day. Before Fred was 12 his father died of diabetes and the really hard struggle of his life began. At school he proved a bright and eager pupil, but with the death of his father the chance of an apprenticeship vanished. A bright future faded. The family were forced to leave their cottage but were housed in another close by, on the estate, and his mother found work for two days a week in the Big House, though this entailed a 2-mile walk each way, morning and night.

In March 1904 Fred was at last old enough to leave school, and he obtained a post on a local farm for 1s. 3d. per day, a working day which started at 6.30 a.m. and ended at 5.30 p.m. Before he was 14 he moved to another farm, where he lived out. Though he took in his wooden chest the books he had won as prizes at school, he never had time to open and read them for he was either working or too tired to think of reading. Work on that farm he recalled in later years as being very hard. He rose at 5 a.m. (6 a.m. on Sundays) and worked until well into the evening. Other farm jobs followed, and then in 1912—when he was 20—he got work in a nearby colliery. He was soon promoted to working in the attached sulphate house, and in 1915, earning £2 per week, he married the beloved Helen. One luxury of that first year of married life was the purchase of Dickens' Library, and a pleasure shared therafter was for Fred to read aloud to Helen.

In the spring of 1920 Helen died and left Fred with a young family to look after. The following years were lonely, unhappy ones during which he read a great deal from the classics. He married Elizabeth and in January 1925 returned to the land, being set on as a farm labourer near Sheffield. It was a dairy farm and the work was hard. One of his duties as time went by was to deliver milk to the suburban houses of parts of the city, and this he generally enjoyed for it allowed him to meet all sorts of people.

Then in February 1927 the Kitchens moved close to Worksop, Nottinghamshire. He had obtained a position on a farm with a good and educated farmer, and through this man he came to appreciate good music, going with his employer to the opera in Sheffield. Three years after arriving at Worksop he had to move again, for his employer moved himself to Kilton Forest Farm, Worksop. Fred Kitchen went with him.

A turning point came in 1933 for in that year he joined the Workers' Educational Association, and subsequently he studied in his spare time subjects so widely varied as literature, music and economics. His written English possessed a simplicity and beauty from the beginning, and his tutor suggested sending short stories and other creative work to several magazines. Many regretful refusals from editors followed but he did not despair. Then one day his wife suggested that he write a book. Now, to my knowledge, no farm labourer had ever successfully told the simple tale of his life in book form before. Fred Kitchen, though dubious of the result, thought the unique idea a good one and set to work in his limited spare time. It was his autobiography and he told the story in simple, everyday language, with chapter titles ranging from "Early Pastures" and "The Day-Lad" to "The Farm in the Wood" and "Sunshine and Shadow."

In the end a notable London publishing house accepted his book —no one was more surprised than the author—and it was first published in 1940, entitled *Brother to the Ox*. Looking back upon things Fred Kitchen was the first to admit that it could not have been published at a better time, when serving troops and those remaining at home soon after the outbreak of World War II welcomed in a variety of ways such a down-to-earth book about a simple, honest and meaningful way of life—some as an escape from the turmoil about them and some nostalgically as representing a way of life which had suddenly disappeared (and which—though this was unknown at the time—was never to return). The book quickly proved to be a best seller and Fred Kitchen won the Foyles Literary Prize. Letters came from all parts of the world and the author was overwhelmed, though his financial reward was pitifully small. The farmer for whom he worked was a tenant of the Duke of Portland and His Grace had agreed to write a preface to the book. So well was it received that it was reprinted in 1944, 1945 and 1947. Encouraged by such success Fred Kitchen had had three more books published by 1947—*Life on the Land, The Farming Front* and *Jessie and His Friends*—and these were successful, but not to the extent of his first.

He recalled much later how he had been invited to a Foyles Literary Luncheon and on arriving realized that he would have to speak to the assembled company. Such an ordeal terrified him, but he stood up at the appropriate moment, thanked everyone for reading his book but said he didn't know why anyone had bothered to buy it, let alone read it! He sat down to loud cheering and applause.

In the meantime he desired to be his own master and the opportunity came. He became the tenant of a county council smallholding at the Oxcroft Settlement, on the crest of the limestone escarpment between Bolsover and Clowne. There he continued to work the soil and to write. Later he moved to a bungalow in Bolsover and, a widower for the second time, he lived with an unmarried daughter. Religion played an important part in his life, and for twelve years he was a preacher of the Methodist Church Circuit. Some of his later works were written specifically for children and, being countryside-based and beautifully simple of language, they were most popular. The last book published during his lifetime was the story of a village of reality though called enigmatically *Nettleworth Parva*.

And so it was that I came to know Fred Kitchen in his old age.

That was in August 1967. We walked his long, productive garden into the orchard, where stood a poultry house. Not long before he had disposed of the birds for they didn't seem to be worth the trouble. We drove, I recall, on a sunny evening, to look over the ruins of Sutton Scarsdale Hall and then into the hills about Ashover.

"It's grand to get out of your own little world for a bit", he smiled as we motored along the quiet lanes near Milltown, "and see how the other half live. If I'd had the money I reckon a car would have come in useful for seeing more of God's good earth. But then—I might never have had the contentment to write books." And that sort of simple, philosophical statement was typical of the man; it drifted recognizably through his created work. In *Brother to the Ox,* for instance, he recalls that as a boy gardening for that first, fatherless season he had had "as good a show of weeds as any one in the village".

The following summer—it was a June evening—I went to see Fred Kitchen again. He was now 77 years old and scything the long grass in his orchard. He was pleased to see me and we talked about his blackcurrants and carrots. While I was there he autographed a copy of *Nettleworth Parva* and told me about the book he was planning. *Brother to the Ox* came up again, and Fred recalled the pleasure that had come his way when the book was used as a standard study for G.C.E. 'O' level English Literature. He had made a lot of pen-friends as a result, for many pupils had written to him during that particular year.

How often are our intentions thwarted by the quick passage of time. I had invited Fred Kitchen to tea but we never finalized the arrangements, and the next time we met was on the last day of July 1969. With my good friend, E. Hector Kyme, I called at 'Pleasant View' during an expedition when taking photographs for this book.

The sun shone in the early afternoon and the conservatory door stood open. The little dog came bouncing out, barking and tail wagging. I knocked and there was a distant movement inside the kitchen; Fred Kitchen emerged from his after-lunch snooze and was most pleased to see us. He readily agreed to the request that my friend be allowed to take his photograph.

And so it was that the illustration herein was taken in the usual, masterly way by E. Hector Kyme. We got on very well together during that short visit, I remember. We were grateful for his permission to photograph him and he for our company. He walked to the gate with us, "Yes, a call like that passes the time on very nicely," he grinned. He waved farewell and his little dog bounced at his feet. We promised him a large print of his photograph; but it was not to be. A month later Fred Kitchen took ill and a fortnight later he died. He never gained great monetary wealth from his wonderful, creative life, and it is sad to realize that, despite the pleasure he had given to countless folk, his old age should come to a close quite lonely on his eastern hilltop.

TWELVE

The Civil War in Peakland

Derbyshire and its close environs has nothing to compare with Naseby or Edgehill, no great encounter between the forces of Cromwell and the King's men which lives on in national history and so links the region with seventeenth-century strife on the grand scale. That is not to say that the troubles of the Civil War passed by and left the sleeping countryside unscathed. The subject of the great struggle for ultimate victory in these parts is rarely brought to light these days. It is a fitting subject for the intelligent Peakland explorer, and the following, I trust, will be of some interest, though it is not intended as an exhaustive study of the progress of the Civil War in these parts.

There are the well known, maybe partly traditional stories: of the Royalist Sir Christopher Fulwood who rallied over 1,000 men from the lead mines of the limestone plateau in order to put up a fight against the Roundheads. He lived at Middleton-by-Youlgreave, and when Parliamentary forces came upon the scene unexpectedly he was forced to hide in a cave in nearby Bradford Dale. Here he was discovered and killed, and the cave—known rather strangely as Cromwell's Cave—remains unaltered. In the roof of the house now known as Royal Cottage beside the road crossing Axe Edge between Buxton and Leek tradition has it that Charles I lay in hiding while his Roundhead enemies passed by.

Thomas Hobbes lived with Cavendish family—the forebears of the Dukes of Devonshire—for seventy years as a tutor and "master mind considerably in advance of his time". He wrote a comprehensive history of the Civil War called *Behemoth* (the animal described in the Book of Job and probably a hippopotamus; at all events "a huge and terrible thing"). It was published posthumously sometime after 1679, the year of Hobbes's death at the age of 91. This, of all accounts of that time, gives an accurate picture of those frightening days as experienced by a man resident in Peakland.

The family name of Gell of Hopton, near Wirksworth, is synonymous with the events of the Civil War in this region of England. Early in the thirteenth century the family of De Hopton owned most of the property in this south-facing hollow between Wirksworth and Carsington, a hollow drained by the Scow Brook and looked upon downstream by Hognaston. Sir John Gell became a baronet in 1642 and rose to the position of chief Parliamentarian in the region during the conflict with Charles I. Hopton never played an important part in the strife—though the Royalists did plunder the Hall—and gets its fame solely from the fact that it was the home of Sir John Gell. He took Lichfield for the Roundheads and on several occasions received the public thanks of Parliament for his services in and about the county of Derby. Writing prior to 1846, Samuel Bagshawe states (in his *History, Gazetteer and Directory of Derbyshire*) that Sir John Gell's leather doublet, weighing 11 pounds, "is still preserved. In the neck of this doublet is a flaw, made, it is supposed, by a ball with which he was wounded, but when is not known, but supposed to have been near the termination of the war, and after Newark, the last fortress in this part of the country, had capitulated". At the end of the Civil War he let it be known that, in all, he had spent more than £5,000 (plus the damage caused to Hopton Hall during Royalist plunder) and had received the paltry remuneration of £64 from the Parliamentarians. Despite his long and ardent services, Sir John was condemned in 1650 by the High Court of Justice to life imprisonment and confiscation of his properties. This was largely due to his forthright speech and actions. Nevertheless this former hero was liberated after two years.

In November 1642 the Earl of Chesterfield decided to fortify his home—the Manor at Bretby, a village 3 miles east of Burton-upon-Trent and less than 2 miles to the south of that wide major river. The Earl garrisoned sixty horse and forty musketeers to protect the place; but soon Sir John Gell got word of what this Royalist had done and sent a party of dragoons and 400 foot-soldiers under a Major Molanus. The battle was short for the Earl of Chesterfield saw that his position was hopeless. He took to his heels with his troops and made directly for Lichfield. The Countess of Chesterfield (a daughter of the notable Royalist Sir

John Packington) remained at Bretby, refusing to pay any money to prevent plunder by the invaders. Plunder indeed took place, but it is recorded that Major Molanus and his officers saved the chamber of this lady "together with all her goods".

Six miles to the north-east of Bretby is the very old riverside settlement of Swarkeston. It is but 3 miles from this village, where the Melbourne road crosses the Trent, to the built-up southern side of Derby. Here stood once a great castle and banqueting house. The ruins remain, but the main building besides the church of St. James' is Swarkeston Hall, a large stone house dating from about 1630 and which is today a substantial farm-house. Early in 1643 this house, the home of Sir John Harpur, was fortified by the Royalist Colonel Hastings. At the same time the notable bridge over the Trent was fortified. In usual fashion a party of Parliamentarians under Sir John Gell came on 5th January to do away with such fortification. A relatively long engagement ensued because the Royalists put up a better defence of the bridge than anticipated. At length Sir John Gell won the day, and that particular pocket of resistance was put down before he rode away once more.

This incident must have been a particularly distasteful affair to local people, for they had proclaimed themselves true to the King in a letter addressed to the Aldermen "and other inhabitants of the Towne of Derby" one year earlier:

> Whereas the County of Derby hath enjoyed the happiness of peace ever since the beginning of these great distractions, and have not endured the miseries and calamities which follow the best governed armyes, so with greate blessing we retourne our most humble and hearty thanks to Almighty God. Yet we cannot but take notice of the forces lately raised by Sir John Gell, Baronet, who have theyre residence within the towne of Derby; and from thence issue into divers partes of this county to the greate suffering of manie, and to the terror and affrightment of others; as is in particular the greate prejudice donne to the Earle of Chesterfield at Bretby, to the value of many thousand pounds; and since taken from Mr. Sacheverell of Morley £3,000 in money, beside horses and other goodes; and from Mr. Gilbert of Lockse to the value of £200; and from many of us, and our neighbors' horses coming to the markett, which caused divers to throw off theyre sacks of corn upon the way and returne home; so that we dare not come to your markett to sell our commodities nor can we assure ourselves of safetie at home. . . .

The letter continues at length to thank the Aldermen of Derby and to the King for their "princelie care" of the people of the county by sending Colonel Hastings to protect them against the "greate oppressions" of Sir John Gell. The document concludes by assuring the dignitaries of Derby that:

> . . . we shall be ready to joyne with you in the preservation of the general peace of this county–
>
> The inhabitants of Melbourne and Newton, Ticknall and Stanton, Repton and Barrowe, Swarkeston and Chelliston, Thurlston and Elvaston, Wildon and Shardlowe, Aston and Weston.
>
> Swarkeston, the 2nd of January, 1642.

At the beginning of April 1643 Lord Deincourt started the fortification of his house at Sutton in the Dale, now known as Sutton Scarsdale (see Chapter 13). The hall was then less grand than in relatively recent times but the defences had been substantial, so that when Colonel Thomas Gell—brother of Sir John—arrived with 500 men and three pieces of ordnance, Lord Deincourt felt secure enough and refused to surrender himself or his property to the Roundheads. The fortifications withstood attack for some time, but at last the attackers took the house, taking Lord Deincourt and his men into custody. Then, after promising to report to the Parliamentarians at Derby within eight days and having seen his fortifications dismantled, he was set free. But he did not keep his word; his failure to report at Derby enraging the Roundheads. Unfortunately this was not the end of the affair because when Bolsover Castle fell into the hands of Parliament some time later, troops crossed the Doe Lea Valley to Sutton and plundered the house. Lord Deincourt was created Earl of Scarsdale in 1645 because of his loyalty to the Royalists. Thereafter Sutton became Sutton Scarsdale. At the close of the Civil War the newly created Earl of Scarsdale had his estates confiscated and later sold, because of his "exertions in the royal cause" which made him "very obnoxious" to the victorious Parliamentarians. Much of the property was brought back to the family through the earl's son, who managed to arrange that personal friends were the purchasers, to the tune of £18,000.

Beautiful Bolsover Castle, of pale magnesian limestone atop its tree-girt ridge and barely scarred by the nearby industrialization, was involved slightly in the great struggle. The great keep was rebuilt in 1613 on the ruins of the Norman Keep, and the magnificent palace crowning the grand terrace—which today stands roofless—was probably completed before the start of the Civil War. In 1633 the first Duke of Newcastle—elder son of Sir Charles Cavendish—entertained King Charles I and Queen Henrietta Maria on their progress to Scotland. The hospitality extended to the royal visitors may well have been the most lavish to have taken place in this country at any time. The cost of the formal dinner alone ran to £4,000! Ben Johnson was engaged to provide "such speeches and scenes as he could best devise", the result being the masque *Love's Welcome*. A decade later Newcastle was Commander-in-Chief of Royalist forces in the North and Midlands. He placed Colonel Mushcamp as Governor of the garrison at Bolsover Castle. By August 1644 the castle had been taken by the Parliamentary forces without any great struggle. Later it was planned to sell Bolsover, together with Newcastle's other great house at Welbeck in Nottinghamshire. An attempt was made by the friends of the Duke to save his properties, but it failed and Bolsover was sold to a speculator who intended to demolish it and sell the stone and furnishings. Some of it was pulled down, but then Sir Charles Cavendish was able to re-purchase it and preserve many of the treasures; part was finally restored but the great east-facing palace remained a ruin.

The third Earl of Devonshire was an ardent Royalist and supplied Charles I with money during the progress of the Civil War. To avoid inevitable persecution from Parliament he went abroad, but this didn't prevent confiscation of his estates. However, Chatsworth was not to suffer any great physical attack at this time. The earl's brother, Charles, was killed before the battle at Gainsborough in July 1643, during an engagement with Cromwell. While his horse floundered in a quagmire the Roundheads attacked him. He was buried thereafter at Newark and taken later to the family vault at Derby. Several miles to the west is Wingerworth, a former village on a rising ridge and clothed liberally with trees. It is today largely ruined as an independent settlement by a great rash of suburban development. Here stood Wingerworth Hall, seat of the ancient family of Hunloke. Henry Hunloke was a zealous Royalist and at his own expense raised a troop of horse to fight with Colonel Frecheville's regiment. As lieutenant-colonel of this regiment, Henry Hunloke performed outstandingly at the

Battle of Edgehill and was knighted on the battlefield. In 1743 the Roundheads took and garrisoned Wingerworth Hall. Luckily the Parliamentary Officer Colonel Michel prevented the property from being badly damaged—a very logical thing to do, for this man later married Sir Henry Hunloke's widow after the latter's death in 1648. Wingerworth Hall was demolished two and a half centuries later.

Hassop Hall, between Calver and Bakewell, was the seat of the notable Eyres. At this time it was the home of a fighting Colonel Eyre who distinguished himself at the siege of Newark. In December 1643 he garrisoned the Hall in the interests of the King, and it remained a Royalist outpost of Peakland for a long time.

Two months later, on 15th February 1644, an engagement took place between the opposing parties at Barton Blount, 11 miles to the west of Derby. In those days a village stood here upon the fertile, rolling lands which slide down to the Vale of Trent. The village is no more, but the manor house—Barton Blount Hall, formerly the seat of the Blounts, Bradshaws and other notable families—stands, beautifully girt by deciduous trees, a good distance from the nearest road. The castellated building stands today the result of much addition and re-modelling during following centuries. At the Domesday Survey in 1086 the population must have been close to 150 souls. By the year 1789 there were less than half a dozen houses here. The village disappeared for the same general reason as did the large crofting communities of the north-western Highlands—the land was more profitably farmed by changing from arable crops (with its high labour requirements) to the grazing of grassland (with its relatively small labour needs). The population was moved and the village fell into decay and ruin. Now it so happened that a Royalist army captain owned Barton Blount Hall at the time of the Civil War, and he had been at nearby Tutbury Castle as part of the garrison there when it was besieged by the Cromwellian forces. Barton Blount Hall was thereafter taken by these Parliamentarian troops (on 15th February 1644) and several farm buildings and the rectory were demolished. The Royalists attempted to secretly maintain a flow of supplies to the besieged garrison within Tutbury Castle, but the Roundheads, using their new base at Barton Blount Hall, intercepted this flow. One such interception which was recorded in some detail reports that 500 Roundhead horse attacked a relieving Royalist party close to Barton Blount, and in the skirmish there were many injuries and several killed on both sides. For more than two years this attack and counter-attack continued in the vicinity, the Royalist garrison at Tutbury finally agreeing to surrender after a three-week siege if certain conditions were complied with by their adversaries. One of these conditions was that the owner of Barton Blount was allowed to re-possess his home. The Hall had been damaged by fire, the rectory and buildings demolished and "the church defamed".

A month after Barton Blount fell to the Roundheads a battle took place 5 miles to the south-east on Eggington Heath. Sir John Gell's superiority was again demonstrated for the Parliamentary troops drove the Royalists down and across the River Trent where they turned and moved off.

During 1644 a skirmish took place near Ashbourne. The Parliamentarians shot cannon-balls at the west front of the parish church of St. Oswald, the marks still being visible. Three of these cannon-balls are preserved in the church. Some time later (in August 1645) King Charles came through the town from Ludlow *en route* for Doncaster, and as it was Sunday he worshipped in the church and signed the parish register. Unfortunately this register was stolen during the nineteenth century. It is interesting to note in passing that King Charles's great-grandson, Charles Edward, marched here from Cheshire, occupying Ashbourne Hall before moving on to Derby. Three days later he was back in Ashbourne from his proposed march on London, having been turned back by his opponents at Swarkestone Bridge crossing the River Trent. This proved to be the farthest south the Young Pretender ever reached in his bid to gain the throne.

Only 3 miles to the north-east of Chesterfield is the now dirty and busy little town of Staveley, overlooking lower ground drained by the Poolsbrook. The family of Frecheville were long lords of the manor here, and Sir John Frecheville was described as "a most active royalist". The old Hall was garrisoned, and even after it had become the much altered rectory in Victorian times the great iron hinges for the defensive window shutters were still in place on the outside of the building. In August 1644 the Hall was captured by a Parliamentary party under Major-General Crawford, despite the fact that twelve pieces of ordnance and 230 muskets were found within. Sir John was later created Lord

Frecheville of Staveley, and in 1681 he sold the manor and estate to the Earl of Devonshire, the first Duke of Devonshire.

The greatest story of this troubled time within Peakland and its fringes relates to the events connected with beautiful and sad South Wingfield Manor. This large and finely-sited building was erected about 1440 by Ralph, Lord Cromwell, who was Lord Treasurer to King Henry VI. Later it came into the hands of the Earls of Shrewsbury, and because of this connection we find that Mary Queen of Scots spent some years in confinement there prior to 1585, when she was moved to Tutbury Castle. At the commencement of hostilities during the period of the Civil War the manor was taken and garrisoned by the Parliamentarians. Then in 1643 the Royalists successfully attacked and re-took it under the command of the Marquis of Newcastle. Sir John Gell was not a man to let this victory go unchallenged for long and soon a storming party of Roundheads were again attacking. They "shattered the walls with artillery from the neighbouring heights". The Royalist Governor of the manor, a Colonel Dalby, attempted to conceal his identity by dressing as a member of the ranks. A deserter from his garrison recognized him and shot him in the face. His loss to the Royalist cause was a great blow. After the Battle of Naseby in 1645 King Charles retreated northwards with about 3,000 horse—the remnant of his army—and met and defeated Sir John Gell at Sudbury and Ashbourne. Though now a Roundhead stronghold, South Wingfield Manor was the scene of frequent skirmishes until the middle of 1646. By the spring of 1646 most of the Royalist troops were needed in Ireland to quell the troubles developing there. While they were out of the country the Parliamentarians decided that all possible hide-outs should be destroyed before they returned. On 23rd June 1646 the order was given for the destruction of South Wingfield Manor.

It is easy to agree with Bemroses' *Guide to Derbyshire*, published during the last century, when we read that "the ancient Manor House must have been a very stately edifice in the days of its original magnificence. It is said to have been one of the earliest examples of those noble quadrangular mansions which succeeded the irregular piles of mixed construction that were the first deviations from the gloomy castles of a former age." The wrecking of this massive building is the best piece of "knocking about" done by Cromwell in this part of England. When this mission had been accomplished and the manor lay in tottering ruins on its hilly knoll above the River Amber, instructions were given for the destruction of Eastwood Hall, Ashover, 6 miles to the north up the Amber Valley.

Originally called New Hall, Eastwood Hall stands close under the sheltering escarpment clothed with East Wood and was in the possession of the Lincolnshire family of Reresby from 1282 until 1623, when the Rector of Ashover, the Reverend Emanuel Bourne, bought the property. An old employee of the Reverend Bourne overheard the order for the march to Eastwood being given close by the smouldering walls at South Wingfield. Word was immediately sent, and the Reverend Bourne got together several horses and carts and removed as much furniture as possible before a company of dragoons in the charge of a Muster Master Smedley arrived the next day.

Possession was demanded in the name of the High Court of Parliament. The owner agreed but said, no doubt bitterly, that he had "never done any mischief" against Parliament, and he would report the outrage to Fairfax or Colonel Hutchinson. That the whole affair passed off in a relatively cordial atmosphere is apparent when we read a contemporary account of how the troops offered to help to remove the remainder of the Hall's contents before demolition commenced.

When all was made ready three pieces of ordnance were taken to the top of Freebrick, the wooded escarpment a little to the east and high above the Hall. These were discharged in rotation, but the only damage that seems to have been done by these small cannons was to break the windows on one side of the house and knock off some wall-corners. This action, proving almost fruitless, was followed by the despatching of pioneers who climbed the walls and commenced to dismantle the chimney-stacks. However, the Hall was to prove more than a match for the pioneers as well, for they soon descended from the roof with little accomplished. A barrel of gunpowder was now brought forward and set in the centrally placed tower. The troops withdrew and soon a violent report rocked the whole Ashover district. When the dust clouds had cleared it was seen that half the Hall had been destroyed and the remainder lay in ruins.

The troops assembled and sang a psalm. After this they marched the half mile to Ashover church and listened to a sermon by Muster Master Smedley on the evils of popery and kingcraft. When the sermon was finished the Parliamentarians mounted their waiting horses and were not seen again in the Amber Valley. Before leaving the troops caused a disturbance at the Crispin Inn close to the church, abusing the illustrious publican. The story is set out on a board on this old building.

The Reverend Bourne was naturally greatly upset by the events of the day and soon afterwards wrote a long lctter to a relative living in the south. He said that he believed that he would never recover from the shock he had sustained at the Roundheads' hands. He also reported that his clerk, a man by the name of Wheatcroft who seems to have been something of a poet, had written a verse to commemorate the sad event. It is quoted in full:

The Roundheads came down upon Eastwood Old Hall,
And they tried it with mattock and tried it with ball,
And they tore up the leadwork and splintered the wood,
But as firmly as ever the battlements stood;
Till a barrel of powder at last did the thing,
And then they sung psalms for the fall of the Kyng.

The Hall remained in the Bourne family until 1762 but was never repaired. Today it is a picturesque ruin partly covered by ivy and is the haunt of jackdaws. It is one of those small but attractive ruins which add an indescribable element to the atmosphere of our countryside, something almost permanent and perhaps best described as typically English.

A mile and a half away across the Amber Valley to the west and at a higher elevation stands lonely, lovely and historic Eddlestow Hall Farm. This was considered the hall of one of the four manors of the Ashover district, called Musters' Manor. It was garrisoned during the Civil War by the Roundheads, though no great number of troops were based here.

Now for what can only be claimed as a tradition, though the story may be quite true. Close by the northern bank of the River Trent, between Swarkeston and Willington, is the little village of Twyford with its short spired church and wide views of the flat river flood plain stretching away under Midland skies. Half a mile to the eastward lies what is known as the Round Hill, a large tumulus or burial mound. Here it is said were buried the bodies of those slain during a Civil War encounter. It should be remembered that Eggington Heath, or Common, lies but 3 miles to the west.

Finally a mention of the way in which the growing town of Sheffield was involved in the struggle between King and Parliament. There was, it must be realized, a strong Parliamentary party in Sheffield at this time, and in the summer of 1642 they joined with Colonel Sir John Gell to storm Sheffield Castle. The attack was successful, and the castle—now the property of the Howards since passing by marriage out of the hands of the Earls of Shrewsbury in 1654—was garrisoned. Earthworks were thrown up around the castle and the town in readiness for a Royalist attack.

The Earl of Newcastle, with 8,000 troops, marched southwards through Yorkshire in the name of Charles I, taking Leeds, Wakefield and Rotherham in April 1643. He then marched upon Sheffield and, according to an old account, "the Earl's prowess at Rotherham had struck panic into the undisciplined forces at Sheffield Castle; and when they heard of Newcastle's approach they fled into Derbyshire". The Earl of Newcastle re-took the castle and fortified it, leaving a garrison under the command of Sir William Savile.

Attack did not come immediately but on 4th August 1644 a cavalry regiment and 1,200 foot soldiers were placed against the castle by the Roundheads. It was to be expected that the small Royalist force of 200 infantry and a troop of horse within could not hold out for long, but the fortifications were very strong. There was a moat filled with 18 feet of water, a "strong palisaded breastwork" and a 6-foot-thick wall. The Roundhead commander decided to attempt a breach of the walls by the use of cannons. He built two batteries 60 yards from the outworks of the castle, and from these he began to hammer the walls with the three guns he had to hand. After meeting with no success after a twenty-four-hour onslaught he sent to Lord Fairfax for extra equipment, namely ordnance which he referred to as "the Queen's pocket pistol and a whole culverin". The latter was an 18-pounder long cannon or hand-gun. Now it was a short task to form a break in the walls. Before entering he offered the Royalists within the chance of coming out "with all the honours of war" and without any of them being taken prisoner. This they readily agreed to. And so ended the King's supporters' stronghold in Sheffield.

The surrounding estates were confiscated by Parliament, but by 1648 they had been restored to the Earl of Arundel upon payment of £6,000.

But the last real encounter of any significance in or near Peakland came with the destruction of South Wingfield Manor and Eastwood Hall, Ashover in 1646, a matter of two and a half years before the execution of Charles I, when the Roundheads overcame all obstacles to ruling England as they saw fit. Away from the midsummer greens of the Amber Valley they rode in 1646, over the hills and far away; to leave the inhabitants of Peakland to their age-old devices of farm-craft and trading and squabbling and peace.

THIRTEEN

Ruins West and East

If you stand upon the northern end of Axe Edge or on the side of the road which winds down from Congleton and Macclesfield towards the east, the hill-encircled town of Buxton—Aquae Arnemetiae of the Romans who found the subterranean spa waters valuable in the restoration of health—lies in full view a long way below, situated at more than 1,000 feet above sea level. Many of the imposing buildings of the town are recognizable, even from this distance—the great dome of the Devonshire hospital which was formerly the stables of the fifth Duke of Devonshire and one of the largest domes in the world; the proud façade of the Palace Hotel; and, until recently, the great, grey mass of an enigmatic building standing alone, tree girt and little known. This was the great Empire Hotel.

My first close acquaintance with the 'Empire' was many years ago. We had walked, I remember, up a quiet residential road near the park, and, seeing a dense tangle of bushes and trees on the left, we found an opening which led through the undergrowth where we had to stoop low; then we were out on a broken concrete forecourt and high above us rose the great bulk of the biggest ruin I had ever seen!

There was very little glass in any of the windows, though the remains of curtains blew out on the wind. Some of the stucco had broken off on this front of the building, revealing red bricks. Ivy hung precariously to one wall, obscuring many windows. When a jackdaw cawed as it flew from an upper window, and a door crashed to somewhere within, we had had quite enough, took to the encircling vegetation and didn't stop until the quiet road was reached again!

That was my first encounter with the Empire Hotel at Buxton, but I have been back many times since, back to explore more fully this 'fairy palace', seemingly forgotten and slowly being invaded by ivy and privet, by jackdaws and field mice.

But to discover the reason why this mysterious and romantic building should have stood so long as a ruin we must go back to the beginning of the present century.

The western fringe of Buxton was spreading out on to the wooded slopes beneath the crags of Corbar Hill as the town grew as a watering place. It was here, at 1,100 feet above sea level, that this imposing hotel was built as the new century dawned.

In the autumn of 1900 the *Buxton Advertiser and Herald* reported that "a new hotel is being built in the Park . . . which promises to be, like Barnum and Bailey's show, the most extensive on earth. The universe seems to be a large order, but the Empire is a building of magnificent proportions, standing in its own estate and gardens, and commanding views of panoramic proportions."

The hotel was built four-square and facing the south. It enjoyed views across the upper Wye Valley to the woods on Grin Low, topped by that limestone lookout called Solomon's Temple which acts as a distant gazebo in the park-line panorama from the terrace that ran the whole length of the hotel's front. The 'Empire' opened at the height of the era of Edwardian opulence, and it seems that the place attracted many wealthy guests, driven by horse and carriage under the large, wrought-iron gate arches and into the courtyard on the northern side, overshadowed by trees on one side and the massive bulk of the hotel on the other.

All the outer walls of the building were stuccoed and all rooms had relatively large windows. Some of the better bedrooms had a small balcony, too. The steeply-angled roof—of green tiles— was crowned by a veritable grove of tall and well-proportioned chimney-stacks. Viewed either from close to or from a distance the building was handsome. It seems that the architect was influenced by Dutch or Flemish designs, and the whole scale and proportion of the hotel reflectd good taste and a contrast with the fussy and often drab lines of Victorian hotel architecture.

At the beginning of World War I the Empire was commandeered for the housing of Canadian troops; though it was not known at that time, the hotel had housed its last paying guest, and the carriages plying to and fro between the courtyard and the railway station were never to come back.

In 1919 the army left, but the damage done by the troops was so colossal that no one would undertake the expensive task of renovation. One of the troubles was that, if anything, the hotel was too large. There were other smaller hotels in Buxton, and the restoration of the 'Empire' could never be an economic proposition.

The place lay empty, the lower windows shuttered and the garden gates locked. The weeds grew, and nesting birds blocked gutters and chimneys. The wonderful white plaster mouldings of oak leaves and acorns which had adorned the ceilings of the public rooms slowly disintegrated away as the interior became damp.

At the outbreak of war in 1939 the War Office took the place over for a second time. Concrete drives and a parade ground were built in the gardens in front of the imposing southern aspect; and long, red-brick buildings were erected among the trees under the eastern front. By the end of World War II the damage wrought inside had become so great that a very large fortune would have been necessary to re-equip it as a hotel on the grand scale. Even so, the place had yet another purpose to serve. Soon after the war ended it was unofficially 'taken over' by 'squatters'.

A number of homeless families established themselves in the monstrous ruin and made good use of floorboards, beams and even a staircase. All went up in smoke in various fireplaces throughout the building. More 'squatters' arrived and the colony grew, as did the accumulation of refuse, both inside and out. A plague of rats threatened the entire area surrounding the 'Empire', and the inhabitants of Buxton decried the whole business as a social scandal of the first order.

I well remember visiting the 'Empire' while the 'squatters' reigned there. Most of the communicating doors on the ground floor had been chopped up for firewood, the ceiling of the Grand Foyer bulged downwards threateningly, and huge piles of tins and kitchen refuse lay piled in one of the main public rooms.

From the top of the elegant sweep of the grandiose main staircase children's playful calls drifted down; while the white plaster acorns and oak leaves broke off occasionally from the ceiling as vibrations from the first floor increased in intensity!

After some years the new community was removed, and the place was never occupied again, except by the jackdaws and field mice. Children sometimes played in the overgrown grounds, and the braver ones explored the dark angles of the building. Not many years ago the rooms of the first floor on the south front somehow got on fire, and the local fire brigade spent some time in controlling the blaze. But the 'Empire' was well built, and subsequently the only outward evidence of the fire was blackened stone window frames and charred plaster.

The most recent and, as events have since proved, the last plan for putting the ruins in order and using it again came from the Derbyshire County Council. It was proposed to adapt the place for use as a College of Further Education—in theory an admirable idea, but the cost of renovation would have been fantastic. The great size of the place, the havoc wrought by troop occupation, 'squatters' and the long years of neglect made the plans impracticable.

The 'Empire' always had an air of apartness, stillness, of being a forgotten palace not far from the comings and goings of one of the Peak District's largest towns. Something of an enigma, something now a little unreal for the demolition contractor's hammer has sounded through the empty halls. They are no more and there is a great feature missing in that view of Buxton from Axe Edge Moor.

Far across Peakland to the east and actually outside the district in the strictest sense stand the remains of a mansion with a long and fascinating history. It lies in the parish of Sutton cum Duckmanton close under the magnesian limestone escarpment dominated by Bolsover Castle. The word Sutton is derived from the Old English terms 'suo'—'south'—and 'tun'—'farm'. Literally 'the south farm' in relation to the village of Staveley. The Earls of Scarsdale lived here in the seventeenth and eighteenth centuries, and their family name has been added to the original village name. At the Domesday Survey in 1086 the name was 'Sudtun' and by 1243 it was known as 'Sutton en le Dale,' the dale being the shallow valley over which the village looks towards the magnesian limestone escarpment crowned by Bolsover and its pale-yellow castle. Draining this valley is the tranquil River Doe Lea, flowing from the Great Pond and other nearby pools close beneath the finest Elizabethan house in England and the gaunt ruin across the drive—Hardwick Halls, new and old. The coming of the motorway along this valley is a tragedy as far as the peace and quiet of the prospect is concerned, though completely predictable in a way

The keep of Bolsover Castle from the south–west

The south front of the Empire Hotel, Buxton

The east front of Sutton Scarsdale Hall

in which the horrible opencast mining of the fifties was not. This rape of the slopes to the north and east of Sutton Scarsdale has now been healed, but the regular fencing which inevitably replaced the former hedgerows, trees and fences still looks rather incongruous.

Sutton Scarsdale Hall stands a tree-girt ruin. According to no less an authority than Sir Nicholas Pevsner it is "easily the grandest mansion of its date in the county" of Derbyshire. To appreciate properly the story of Sutton in the Dale and particularly of the remnants of the Hall it is necessary to look back distantly to the commencement of the eleventh century. In 1002 the will of Wulfoic gave the Manor of Sutton to the monks of Burton Abbey, and eighty-four years later, at the time of the Domesday Survey, it was given to Roger de Poicton. There were several changes in ownership subsequently, but the first great period of the history of the Manor began in 1415, when it passed by way of marriage to the ancient Leake family, descending from Leak in Nottinghamshire. At this time came William, younger son of Sir John Leake of Gotham. The family of Leak (or Leake) is the one most closely and longest associated with Sutton in the Dale, later to become Sutton Scarsdale. In 1643, for instance, one of the family would not bow to the Roundheads and so subsequently lost his estates by forfeit, regaining them by purchase for the sum of £18,000. J. Charles Cox refers to the notable tradition connected with the same family in the first volume of his monumental *Churches of Derbyshire* (published 1875). A Sir Nicholas Leake (there is no record of such a knight ever living at Sutton) left for the Holy Land as a Crusader and was taken prisoner by the Turks where he languished many long years. As time passed he became ill and prayed that he be given the chance to see once more "his fair domains at Sutton". Upon waking next morning he found himself in the porch of the parish church of St. Mary at Sutton. He was turned away from the doors of the hall for everyone believed him to be a worthless beggar on account of his wretched appearance. Remembering that he possessed half the gold ring broken and shared by his wife and himself before he left for the Near East long before, he sent his half via a servant and his wife immediately recognized it. He was happily re-united and lived as master at Sutton Hall for many years afterwards. After his death his will was found to contain instructions that eight bushels of wheat be baked into large loaves and distributed on St. Nicholas' day ever afterwards to the needy of Duckmanton, Sutton and Temple Normanton.

The Sir Francis Leake (Lord Deincourt) who upheld the King during the Civil War and so temporarily forfeited the estate at Sutton is recorded as becoming so "mortified after the horrid murder of his rightful sovereign" that he clothed himself in sack-cloth, had his grave dug and lay down in it every Friday right up to his death on 9th April 1655.

The Earls of Scarsdale followed as lords of the manor later in the same century, and early in the eighteenth century work began on completely rebuilding the old Hall. The original building was not demolished but subjected to metamorphosis by building around it. It was the work of Smith of Warwick, the building programme covering a period of four years between 1724 and 1728. Constructed of stone, its major architectural feature is the giant fluted pilasters on each front of the two-storeyed building. The north front, now largely shrouded by ivy, contained the principal entrance and the finest rooms, once renowned for their fabulous decorations. Some of these were removed to the Philadelphia Museum in the United States, where they are still to be seen, giving an impression of what the interior of this noble house must have been like within the memory of many older local inhabitants. A fantastic amount of money was spent on this modification, the plaster work being executed by the outstanding Italian experts of the period—Vosscie and Artan. As work on the house was completed the three lakes in the park to the north of the mansion were made and several of the estate farms were improved. Nicholas, Earl of Scarsdale, the instigator of all this noble improvement died eight years later owing so much money that the estate was sold to one Godfrey Bagnall Clarke of Somersall, an ancient Derbyshire family.

For ninety-five years (1824–1919) Sutton Scarsdale Hall was the home of the famous Arkwrights. Sir Richard Arkwright never lived at Sutton, but his descendant Robert was the first member of the family to make his home here. Nearby Arkwright Town of long, gaunt red-brick rows is named after this illustrious family, as is the adjacent Arkwright Colliery. After 1919 the property was owned by successive owners, whose only interest was to make capital out of the great house. It remained empty, the grounds invaded by willow-herb and nettle, the plaster and fireplaces torn out and sold and much fine stonework removed.

Some years ago the last owner decided to demolish the entire building, but fortuitously three days before work was to begin the late Sir Osbert Sitwell of Renishaw Hall came with friends to visit the ancient church and, meeting the sexton in the graveyard, learned of the forthcoming demolition. In the nick of time he bought the estate and so saved the Hall. And so this wonderful ruin stands inviolate above the shallow dale where the River Doe Lea drains, across the fields from the nobler ruin of Bolsover Castle. On a bright, warm summer evening my friend, Frank Needham of Wilday Green, brought me to the quiet countryside about Sutton in the Dale for the first time. Swallows were congregating upon the overhead wires, and the midges were biting as we explored the empty halls. Brambles and nettles made progress difficult and looking up to the dappled rolls of fine, white cloud in the azure where the roof once stood we were able to make out the positions of what must have been impressive bedroom fireplaces.

Many noteworthy mansions are complemented by the close proximity of the parish church, but there is no other in this country built so closely as that at Sutton in the Dale, Sutton Scarsdale to most people nowadays. A passage leads out of the Hall into the north aisle of the church and the north side of the church tower supports several outbuildings of the Hall. J. Charles Cox suggested, probably correctly, that a section of the graveyard was taken over at the time of rebuilding of the Hall because access to the church from both northern and eastern sides is impossible. The fact that a recent addition to the existing area of the graveyard is to be seen on the western side seems to substantiate this theory.

The church is the parish church of St. Mary and was completed in the first half of the fourteenth century. It has a fine Perpendicular tower and there are windows of the fourteenth century. This church has suffered severely of late at the hands of vandals and has had to be locked to prevent further damage to the interior. Anyone interested to go inside during reasonable daylight hours can contact Mr. Taylor, great friend of the church and Hall, who lives in the cottages by the main road almost oppositie the main gates leading to the Hall. He will be pleased to take anyone and show them the simple treasures of stone and glass and filtered light, and the recently exposed ancient wall paintings.

Two ruins indeed, one has come and gone in the relatively short space of time that the other has fallen into disrepair. Both had or have a special fascination; one is gone, the other remains to remind the visitor of gentler days before the coming of Arkwright Town and the motorway. It remains as a monument to the individualist lately deceased who saved it from final, ignominous destruction at the hands of the Philistines.

FOURTEEN

The Tors of Peakland

Second only to the fine hill shapes of the gritstone areas of Peakland, it is the tors which command the greatest interest and fascination. They are not quite unique, for similar tors may be seen upon the broad wastes of Dartmoor and close to the plateau-surfaces of the Cairngorms.

The hundreds of tors on the face of Kinder Scout are well known. Seen by far fewer who explore at the 2,000 feet contour are the great quantity of outcrops upon Bleaklow, the heights to the north of wide Longdendale and on the extensive tracts of moorland forming Howden, Upper Commons, Bradfield, Broomhead and Derwent Moors. Yet again there are many noteworthy outcrops of this coarse, carboniferous rock in the west, overlooking the Dale of Goyt and Wildboarclough and forming the mighty Roaches in north-eastern Staffordshire.

Mountains are formed from the deposits laid on ancient sea floors, they are made from the material of volcanic outpourings and yet others have been built of still older mountain masonry. More recent activity has led to the development of the details which are so much a part of our present mountain scene—arête, cliff and scree, cwm and hanging valley. The weathering caused by wind, rain, sun, snow and ice; heat and cold, downpouring and drought, has produced these features which might be designated subsidiary.

During the Pleistocene era ice sheets advanced from the north over much of the British Isles at least four times, covering some of the land surface to a considerable depth. Recent research, however, would suggest that the ice never built up to such a depth as previously thought. In fact, it is probable that many of our mountain tops never had an ice cover at all! They doubtless occupied the same position in the Pleistocene period as the nunataks of Greenland and other rock islands standing above present-day glaciers.

The following facts should help to prove the point.

It is generally accepted that the south-western peninsula of England never had an ice-cover. In this area we have a region of upland which is technically a mountain land. On the tops of the highest (e.g. Dartmoor) are the famous tors. Had the ice advanced over the area these tors would have been wiped away completely. Tors are formed by the rotting away of the rock along its lines of weakness (fault lines), the debris being slowly weathered away to reveal these features. In fact, many tors-in-the-making can be seen in quarries in south-western England. Here the gravel, dust and stones have been pulled away to reveal the granite blocks, formed by horizontal and vertical fault lines.

This tor formation was taking place before, during and after the Ice Age and it is still taking place. In Peakland these tors are outstanding in isolation upon the summits of the highest land. They are comparatively weak rock structures which much have stood higher than the highest advances of the ice sheets.

Professor David Linton has done much valuable research into the problems of tor formation and has exposed tors-in-the-making, new tors not far below the surface of the debris in several mountain regions. Though there is evidence of glacial work in the upland hollows of the region how did these frail piles of gritstone withstand the immense forces of the advancing ice? The logical answer is that the higher plateaux—where most of the great tors are found today—were never entirely covered by ice, but remained just above the ice, which clawed powerfully at the plateaux-sides and help to create the extensive gritstone 'edges' or short cliffs which protect extensive lengths about these tablelands. It is possible on these plateaux to dig deeply into the gritstone gravel which is the remains of tors long since vanished in the face of aeons of erosion. Upon the northern side of the Kinder Scout plateau and on the wild and distant wastes of Bleaklow it is easy to discover the tops of new tors lying on the same level as the peat deposits. With the passage of time the peat will be removed at a faster rate than the gritstone rocks, and, slowly over the centuries, new towers and turrets of coarse and blackened rock will rise above the general level of these heights.

Here and there are tors which toppled long ago, caught in mid-air and locked in precarious positions. As I have mentioned, a closely related feature of the tors are the [illegible] ces of millstone grit dropping from the plateau-top t[illegible] ep heather- or bracken-covered slope descending to a [illegible] greater dale. These rock edges reach heights approachin[illegible] hundred feet, and where it has been exploited by quarrymen [illegible] the past some very impressive faces have evolved: edges used in recent times for the extraction of millstones for corn grinding and, particularly, for the sharpening of steel cutlery, weapons and implements in Sheffield, which is never far distant over the moors to the east. Nowadays vertical and overhanging routes of great severity are done with the aid of artificial aids (pitons, etriers and double ropes) on many of these former quarry sites—notably at Dove Stones, high above Saddleworth near to the Lancashire-West Riding boundary, and at Millstone Edge above Hathersage in the Derwent Valley.

Upon the extensive broken faces of the natural edges the early climbers of the district practised their art. Men like J. W. Puttrell were wandering along Stanage Edge in 1890 in the search for suitable rock for climbing. At this time routes like Hollybush Gully and the Twin Chimneys were first ascended. Edges to become attractive to those pioneers were Laddow overlooking Crowden Great Brook in far north-eastern Cheshire and grimy Wharncliffe Crags overlooking the confines of the Don Valley between Oughtibridge and Stocksbridge. Stanage Edge came into its own after World War I, when Morley Wood and A. S. Pigott joined others—like the Kellys—who had found routes upon this long escarpment previously. It has been called the 'Golden Period' and the following extract from the historical notes prefacing the 1951 edition of *The Sheffield Area* gritstone climbing guide sums up efficiently that era upon the edges: "Easy access, friendly gamkeeepers and delightful days picnicking amongst the millstones at the foot of High Neb and wandering rubber-shod up new, unscratched routes on splendidly sound, steep rock."

Of all the characters of those far-off days the name of Rice Kemper Evans is perhaps best remembered. Of all things he was the American Vice-Consul in Sheffield at this time, and, though he never became a 'tiger' upon gritstone, he was a strong and well-loved climber. He is best remembered for his modest statement—"I guess I thought I'd write my name on Stanage, but it just didn't turn out that way."

After World War II these same edges were the nursery of such notable men of the mountains as Joe Brown and Don Whillans, who raised the standards attainable upon these steep, coarse, rounded-hold cliffs to an undreamed-of degree. Two of the most interesting gritstone outcrops are in rather unlikely places. One is Wharncliffe Crags, virtually the birthplace of outcrop climbing and undoubtedly the dirtiest climbing rock in the world, a distinction for which the steelworks of Stocksbridge must accept responsibility. Fire-breathing monsters inhabit the wooded steeps below the crags and cross the open hilltop leading to Wharncliffe Chase at dead of night, but few climbers have met the Dragon of Wantley. Soon after 1880 J. W. Puttrell came here regularly with friends to explore and practise their climbing craft. The most notable feature of the crag is the detached buttress known as the Bass Rock. It is really a tor. For more than three decades attempts were made to scale it by the steep front, but it was not until 1931 that Harry Scarlett climbed the centre crack and produced a first-class 35-foot-high route of 'very severe' standard. The other outcrop is called Rivelin Edge, more than 6 miles to the south-west and overlooking the Rivelin Valley beneath Lodge Moor. Here stands a most impressive tor, called the Rivelin Needle. Though Puttrell attempted to reach the top of this tall tor, even resorting to lassoing it from the summit of the adjoining edge before the turn of the century. Time passed and the Needle stood virgin, defying the several attempts of strong parties. During the early thirties it was first vanquished by a party using combined tactics and a top rope. In 1934 another party top-roped to the summit and found evidence of the first party's visit; the following year saw it climbed by Eric Byne and Clifford Moyer at the south-western corner, but two pitons aided them. It was not until March 1950—over half a century after Puttrell's first explorations here—that the Rivelin Needle was climbed without any artificial aid, by a route known as the Spiral Route and 75 feet in length.

Perhaps the finest tors of all stand upon the lonely crest of Derwent Edge and on the plateaux of Kinder Scout and Bleaklow. Derwent Edge overlooks the line of reservoirs in Derwent Dale, attaining 1,765 feet at Back Tor. To the south of this are the several scattered tors seen so well from the road by the side of those reservoirs; the rounded, dumpy trio called the Cakes of Bread, the shattered face of Dovestone Tor (a name derived from the Old English 'dufe', 'stan' and 'torr'—literally 'the crag of the dove's stone') and the unusual Salt Cellar. This last rock is 20 feet in height, and the central part has been weathered to form a narrow stalk supporting the more resistant upper mushroom. Many have been the scramblers marooned upon the top of the Salt Cellar after climbing onto the top, unable then to make the more difficult descent.

Ringing Roger from Grindsbrook Clough near Edale

Half a mile to the south of the Salt Cellar is one of the most interesting of all tors, called the Wheel Stones. A local name for this group of high rocks is the Coach and Horses. Looking from the western slopes of Derwent Dale near Ladybower Reservoir one sees a profile of a stage-coach drawn by galloping horses a mile away and 900 feet above the surface of the water. Even upon closer inspection, from east or west, the group resembles a coach and horses in certain lighting conditions when details on the face of the rock are not clearly discernible.

Upon the smooth and peaty ridge of Bleaklow are numerous tors, the Barrow Stones, Grinah Stones, Bleaklow Stones and others. Among the scattered Bleaklow Stones is the Anvil, a small tor similar to the Salt Cellar but so sharply etched out by the elements that it could well have been designed for use by Vulcan.

Right around the perimeter of the plateau of Kinder Scout, at the 2,000 feet level, are well-developed tor formations. Along the northern edge are the various tors making up Seal Edge, rounded rocks which indeed resemble sea lions. Beyond Fairbrook Naze are the Boxing Glove Stones, upstanding rocks which resemble a pair of boxing gloves to a remarkable degree, made famous in photographs by W. A. Poucher. On the other side of the plateau there are the weird Madwoman's Stones, the castle-like turrets of Upper Tor above Grindsbrook, the Mushroom Stone and the most fantastic group of all—Whipsnade or The Mushroom Garden. On a high, level shoulder between Edale Head and Crowden Tower (both tors) the exposed gritstone has been eroded into hundreds of small rock groups so as to resemble nothing less than animals in various attitudes. Come here in misty weather and it is quite easy to identify many of the beasts—the Dog, the Camel, the Hippos in their pool (a peaty pool surrounding the rock group), Sea Lion and so on. Wandering among this moor-top maze gives a most peculaiar feeling of other worldliness.

High on the edge of Gibbet Moor and overlooking Chatsworth Park is the well known Cannon Rock, a huge rectangular block which points out high above the road and is a landmark for motorists. A couple of miles to the north, above Baslow Edge, the Eagle Stone stands 25 feet in isolation above the heather and is scored by countless scratches, many made by the young men of Baslow village long ago when it was customary to climb the Eagle Stone to prove one's manhood.

On the 1,200-foot top of Hathersage Moor stands a particularly impressive sight, the great bulk of the tor known as the Mother Cap. It is particularly attractive because of its general tilt to the west, a leaning which does not suggest imminent collapse but grace and a quality which comes close to dynamic aestheticism. Not far away, overhanging the main road to Sheffield, is that best known of all Peakland tors, a large, flat gritstone block complete with 'eyes' and 'mouth' which has been the Toad's Mouth for longer than anyone can remember. But tors of the district with historical associations are few; one is Robin Hood's Stride, near Birchover, where two gaunt towers—the Weasel and Inaccessible—stand above encircling trees of great antiquity. Between the two turrets the indomitable Robin is said to have strode, a feat which it is difficult to believe as the distance is so great. The name of this tor is mentioned in an Enclosure Act of 1819, and there is another old name which seems more appropriate, one which befits the place to perfection; it is Mock Beggar's Hall. A poor man's palace rising gaunt above the sweet chestnuts, a draughty hall of hard rock where the winter wind whistles and shared with magpie and carrion crow and tawny owl beneath the frost-laden sky.

Of all the tors of Peakland none are better placed in relation to their surroundings than the little group atop Howden Moor called the Rocking Stones. They comprise several conspicuous towers of roughly equal size rising from the crest of the steep plunge towards Derwent Dale a third of a mile below (and to the west of) Outer Edge. From that edge they present a fascinating profile against the hazy horizons of Bleaklow which float away to the west. On an August afternoon we watched from Outer Edge as a small shooting party circled with their dogs about those tors; it was a day of warm sunlight when the needle of Holme Moss television transmission mast stood clear in the sky 7 miles away. All was still as the last of the marksmen and his black Labrador disappeared beyond the bilberry brow from which the upper confines of Derwent Dale are visible below. When we reached the Rocking Stones no one was to be seen, we might have been the only inhabitants on earth.

On an autumn afternoon I raced with E. Hector Kyme from the King's Tree at Ronksley, through the coniferous forest and over the re-erected packhorse bridge at Slippery Stones. It was a race against the setting sun, and we had little hope of gaining the Rocking Stones ere the light had gone. Yet by pushing forward up past the ruins of the Bull Stones shooting cabins and onto the crest by the Crow Stones we reached our goal in time to see a most spectacular sundown. The sky over Bleaklow was decked in fragmented cloud—strato-cumulus and fracto-cumulus crossed paths in a pattern of unique geometrical pattern while an island of lower, darker cumulus lay strategically above the southern fringe of that great plateau. While I explored the familiar turrets and enjoyed the sunset tapestry Hector was hard at work with his camera, producing more of those works of art for which he is justly famed. Then as quickly as the brilliance had come it faded, a perceptible fading to pale blue and mauve and valleys filling with indigo.

FIFTEEN

Shooting Cabins in Decline

The monastic foundations of the Middle Ages were the first to use the high, brown plateaux of the Peak District to any great extent. They established outlying farming settlements, or granges, in the valleys under the tops in order to use the moorland for the grazing of sheep. They were the first important sheep farmers in England, and extensive flock management became the prerogative of the Augustinian, Cistercian and other orders. The high ground surrounding upper Derwent Dale was the property of the Canons of Welbeck in Nottinghamshire.

Large, private landowners followed the monasteries as the users of these heights of Peakland, and with the growth of field sports it became increasingly fashionable to turn the wilderness into areas where game was introduced, maintained and encouraged to breed. On the plateaux of the Saddleworth Moors, Black Hill, Bleaklow and Kinder Scout and upon the grit-stone edges to the east of the Derwent Valley the red grouse *(Lagopus scoticus)* and the Scottish or Mountain Hare *(Lepus timidus scoticus)* were the favoured animals. They were well suited to the heather and bilberry and the severe winter conditions.

Wanderers were not only frowned upon, they were actively discouraged from setting foot upon these delectable heights for fear of disturbing the birds and the hares, and for fear of any physical damage that might be caused to the moors by burning and to boundaries and to buildings erected at that time for the convenience of sportsmen and their employees. In 1886 the Duke of Norfolk became the owner of much of that vast and fascinating moorland to the east and north of the upper Derwent Valley, which rises to the watershed extending from Derwent Edge, by Margery Hill to Howden Edge and Swains Head. The Big House of the estate was the now-vanished Derwent Hall.

The considerable distances up the valleys and narrow cloughs were covered by the sportsmen in due season using ponies or on foot. Likewise the dedicated countrymen employed as keepers, labourers and beaters reached the plateaux on foot throughout the year—whenever there was a job to do upon the moor. For the convenience of employers and employed, shelters were erected from an early date in convenient places on the heights. These came to be known as shooting cabins.

The pioneer ramblers enjoyed two things which today linger as little more than memories. The first was the thrill of avoiding the hawk-like eyes of vigilant keepers, for access to all the best parts of the gritstone plateaux was strictly forbidden, and any keen walker venturing there without permission did so at the risk of a chase over the heather. The keepers of the moors in the first third of this century were men dedicated to the task of preserving the plant and animal life in their charge. For that quality they deserve our highest regard, such dedication to an employer is rare indeed now.

As I have stated no trespass was tolerated upon the plateaux far into this century. Only a very few non-sportsmen were favoured with official permission to ramble upon the sacred ground. My father was one such favoured rambler.

Kinder Scout was the most popular high ground of the Peak District, as it remains to this day; it has a popularity resulting from the fact that it is the very highest ground by a narrow margin in the whole of England south of the central Pennines. Also its gritstone rock scenery is nowhere bettered, and at its southern foot runs the main Manchester to Sheffield railway route, so that when most ramblers relied upon public transport Edale was the obvious mecca. Now Kinder Scout was shared by three landowners, and any serious rambler wishing to traverse the plateau without fear of prosecution had to gain the permission of at least two of these landowners.

The western flanks of Kinder Scout, including Kinder Low (2,077 feet) and the Downfall area, were the property of a Manchester wholesale warehouse proprietor called James Watts. His keepers kept a vigilant eye upon this western ground and were quick to take action against the trespasser. It must be recalled that it was relatively easy for an owner of these grouse moors to bring an action successfully for trespass, because disturbance of the birds could be said to legitimately constitute damage to the landowner or his sporting tenant. So it was when my father and a friend were seen close by the Downfall on an October day in 1922. Of course, it was the wrong time of year to be caught for the shooting season was at its height. Names and addresses were taken and a few days later James Watts's solicitors sent the following letter:

17th October, 1922.

Sir,

We are instructed by Mr. J. Watts of Hayfield to communicate with you as to a trespass committed by you on the Downfall at Kinder on Friday last, October 13th, and unless we receive an apology, and an undertaking not to repeat the offence, together with 6/8d. our charges, by Friday next, the 20th, we are to take proceedings against you without further notice.

Wisely the apology was made and the charges paid. In time my father was in a position, by judicious courtesy in the right quarters, to get written permission to explore the plateau from time to time. In answer to a request for permission to cross the western part of Kinder Scout in the autumn of 1925 my father received a printed notice from James Watts:

Manchester

It has been my practice of late to allow members of the public, who asked for such permission, to walk over my portion of Kinder Scout, when I could do so without detriment to the value of the ground as a grouse moor.

Were I, however, to accede habitually to the ever-increasing number of such applications, the moor would soon lose its entire sporting value. The continual crossing of the ground is quite enough to make the grouse—a most shy bird—depart.

I trust, therefore, that those who apply will not think me unreasonable if on account of the breeding and shooting season, or for other reasons connected with the proper management of the ground, I am from time to time compelled to refuse the desired permission.

James Watts.

On the reverse side of the notice was written the following message:

3rd November, 1925

Permit Mr. A. L. Redfern and party to visit the Downfall on Sunday, November 15th, 1925.

James Watts.

J. T. Marriott.
R. Barnes. Keepers.
S. E. Barnes.
W. Wall.

With compliments.

The Dukes of Devonshire were for a long period the owners of the northern and eastern sides of Kinder Scout, and most of the plateau-top. With the sudden death of the tenth duke after World War II this extensive area was given to the Government in lieu of death duties and it was handed over to the National Trust for safe keeping. The third owner of Kinder Scout was the family of Champion, who had long been associated with Edale. The big house of Edale village is Grindslow House, close beside what is now the southern end of the Pennine Way. The eldest son died early so never inherited the Grindslow Estate; his brother William came into the property but lived and farmed at Thetford, Norfolk. There were four sisters. One of these girls married the engineer who came to the valley to survey the route of the Midland Railway's new line between Manchester and Sheffield, which was opened in 1894. The eldest sister was Anne, who lived at Grindslow House with her maiden sisters, Pattie and Alice. The Misses Champion were friends of my father's mother so that permission was always forthcoming to enter the sacred ground by way of Grindsbrook Clough: "Edale, 12th November 1926. Certainly come up this way if you get permission to go to the Downfall. You are most welcome. . . ."

The Champions let their portion of the plateau-top (which extended from the head of Grindsbrook Clough and Grindslow Knoll to Crowden Head), to Samuel Skinner of Throapham Manor, Rotherham. He was the owner of the Waleswood Colliery between Swallownest and Killamarsh and had the shooting rights from the Champions. So in order to cross from Edale to the Downfall area in November 1926 my father had to obtain the permission of three parties. The Champions, of course, were always co-operative. Samuel Skinner was also obliging:

Throapham Manor,
Rotherham.

Dear Sir, 11th November, 1926

I have no objection to your visiting Grindsbrook on November 28th if you can obtain the leave of Miss Champion, but Mr. Watts objects to people going over his ground.

I am,
Faithfully yours,
S. C. Skinner.

My father had already written to James Watts and, by chance, the latter replied on the same day as Samuel Skinner. He was a severe man to deal with, though his memory of the 1922 incident did not seem to interfere with later requests for permission to cross his ground. He refrained from allowing permission on that occasion, stating that as he paid rates and taxes on sporting values the passage of even a few visitors could ruin any sport for which he claimed he was paying dearly. He concluded his note by stating that he would be "grateful if you would forego a visit during the next season".

How strange it was that in the future, when Kinder Scout's northern side came into the hands of the National Trust, my father should have been mistaken for a gamekeeper looking for trespassers. It was at the time when this part of the plateau had only recently left the hands of the Dukes of Devonshire and we were descending high above Fairbrook Naze in wet and windy conditions. Two ramblers were going down in front of us at some distance. They stopped and we approached them; seeing my father's trilby hat and plus-fours they passed a few hurried words to each other, turned quickly down the path and were soon far away near the Ashop River. We thought it a good joke!

The second feature of high Peakland enjoyed by the early ramblers were the shooting-cabins placed strategically by those landowners for the convenience of sporting parties. Many of these cabins or shelters fell into disrepair at an early date, but it is only in the last ten years that most of those remaining have been ruined at the hands of an increasing number of vandals who, for some unknown reason, come to the wild places and destroy wherever possible. One thing is certain, this element does not come from a love of mountains or wild-life; their very actions upon the hills prove that.

E. Hector Kyme near Edale Cross, looking towards Crowden

Grindslow Knoll from the head of Grinds Brook Clough in winter

As an example of the disappearance of these shooting cabins we may look at the southern flanks of Kinder Scout, where Mr. Fred Heardman, B.E.M. of Edale remembers that there were once at least eight such buildings. Most of these fell into ruin before the coming of the masses, and very few ramblers will recall them all. The first one was near the Swine's Back, close to the 2,077-foot top of Kinder Low to the north of Edale Cross. Fred Heardman remembers it as intact about 1912, but after the Great War it had become ruined. The next was beneath Edale Head, high above The Cloughs, where there is one of the finest springs in the entire Peak District. On a dark night long ago Fred Heardman and a friend arrived here intending to sleep within. The door was locked! Such a thing was unusual, but the visitors knew that access was possible through a trap-door in the wooden floor. Through this trap-door the keeper let down a stone jar of ale into the stream which flowed right under the cabin from its nearby source. During the night it rained hard and by next morning the stream was almost lapping the trap-door. How would they escape? Pushing their rucksacks ahead of them they headed through the flood beneath the cabin's floor and bobbed out into the open in a decidedly bedraggled condition.

Peat Moor Cabin was the next shelter coming eastwards. It stood at about 1,600 feet upon the eastern slope of Grindslow Knoll and most of the stones of its foundations are now incorporated into a nearby wall. Half a mile away and in sight steeply below Peat Moor Cabin once stood a most elaborate cabin. It was more like a bungalow and in it people lived for some years. An old photograph in Fred Heardman's possession shows an open-fronted marquee standing beside the bungalow, as it often did on shooting days in late summer and autumn when the weather permitted. Here the guns were stacked and the dead birds hung to be counted. It actually stood beside the Mill River, above its confluence with Grinds Brook and was demolished by the Champions between the wars in order not to attract the attention of vandals. Its site can still be made out beside a sheltering group of silver birches. Five hundred feet higher, close beneath Nether Tor and beside the upper reaches of the same stream, stood the Mill River Cabin. It was built of stone, and its foundations can still be made out above the true right bank of the steep stream from which it gets its name. If Fred Heardman had spent the night secretly at the lower, elaborate cabin, he always came up to this one to cook breakfast. From this 1,650 feet vantage point one would be in a better position to see the approach of a keeper and to make good one's escape.

One of the most romantically situated cabins stood upon the very top of the plateau near the 2,000 feet contour. It was close beside the infant Grinds Brook, where it meanders in a gritty bed between the frowning crests of complex peat grough scenery. The original cabin was built here by a man called Mike Tym, a notable Methodist who lived in the Vale of Edale but who, now and then, had regrettable lapses into drunkenness. He was a stone-mason and builder by trade and was set on to repair the cabin. While there he delivered a lecture to his men on the horrors of alcoholism and the old cabin came to be known thereafter as 'Mike's Church'. The new cabin replacing the original was constructed in two halves—one side for the shooters and the other for the beaters.This is a common theme throughout the Pennines, though most examples consist of two separate cabins. This new building came to be known as 'Four Jacks Cabin', as the Edale men who built it were called Jack Belfitt, Jack Tym, Jack Rowbotham and Jack Burdekin—the latter a member of a family who have lived in the district since the Domesday Survey.

High above Nether Booth and not far beneath the rocks of Ollerbrook Tor a seventh cabin is recorded, though nothing but its flattened site remains. Less than a mile to the east, overlooking Lady Booth Clough, another cabin existed long before Fred Heardman came to live at Edale over forty years ago.

Round on the northern flanks of Kinder Scout stand the remains of several other cabins in lovely positions, most with extensive views towards the wide desert country of Bleaklow. Wood Moor Cabin stands at 1,350 feet, high above the River Ashop and directly beneath the frowning gritstone profile of Seal Edge. A steep pony track leads up from the valley, and when one is ascending it there is a strong resemblance to mule tracks winding up the stony steeps about Saas-Fee in the Valaisian Alps. Turning a corner the brook comes into view as it tumbles beneath one's left hand and perched surprisingly nearby is the cabin. Little more than a decade ago this cabin was in remarkably good repair. It was constructed with timber and had an inner lining of timber. From the windows there were fine views down to the toy cars upon the

The ruined shooting cabin on Black Ashop Moor

Snake Road and along to the west, towards the bold headland of Fairbrook Naze. Quite suddenly, about 1960, it suffered at the hands of vandals; the furniture was smashed, the lining ripped out for firewood and the windows broken. The weather got in and accelerated the process of destruction, so that today the place is little more than a rotting pile of timbers.

About $2\frac{1}{2}$ miles away to the westward from Wood Moor Cabin, upon Black Ashop Moor at 1,800 feet, lie the ruins of Black Ashop Cabin. It was a substantial gritstone building with a good spring close by but has not been fit for use since the twenties. Fred Heardman once told me how a friend of his who should have known much better was responsible for stone-rolling from the top of The Edge almost 250 feet above the cabin. He was not content until he had scored a direct hit with one of his boulders, which crashed through the roof of the cabin.

Continuing but half a mile northwards—and 500 feet lower down the slope—stands the ruined cabin in Ashop Clough, a little way below the old footpath connecting the Snake Inn with Hayfield via Ashop Head. Being so close to a well-used footpath this cabin was damaged from an early date and the former keeper at Snake Cottage, Joe Townsend, once told me how he caught two men in the act of chopping up the cabin door for firewood! Both vandals appeared at the magistrates' court and were fined heavily.

Such short-sighted actions are hard to understand but continue apace. A wide, stone shelf of stones which had been plastered over was built into this cabin to serve as a permanent table but a party was found hacking at this quite recently, effectively loosening the stones of the back wall. The ruins of this cabin are squalid and now possess little romance.

A pleasantly sited cabin stood well up the clough branching off the head of Lady Clough and known as Upper North Grain. A substantial pile of gritstone blocks mark the site of the building where Fred Heardman sheltered in 1922 when completing the first ever 'Three Inns Walk' (now the 'Four Inns Walk'). Lack of maintenance and general weathering led to the early demise of Upper North Grain Cabin, assisted at a later date by the ravages of motorists who had wandered up this little clough from the Snake Road.

Shooting cabins upon Bleaklow are few, though many were built in and above Derwent Dale. A pair were erected on the Duke of Norfolk's estate near the head of Abbey Brook, at the heart of the Howden Moors. The old one stood a few yards to the north-east of the larger, more recent building. It was a wooden hut and fell into a ruinous state in the twenties, though its foundation is still visible by the mound which helped to shelter it from the nor'-easters which rage off Middle Moss and Broomhead Moor. To the other cabin we often came and ate our sandwiches, and the first sign here of vandalism was the appearance of communist slogans written on the inside walls. During the last ten years decay and destruction have been so great that by 1968 the front of this wooden building had been pulled out, and in July 1968 the cabin finally collapsed. Fred Heardman has amongst his collection of historic Peakland photographs a picture of this fallen cabin, the corrugated iron roof toppled to the ground and the whole thing looking tragically forlorn.

It must be remembered that all these cabins were of use, not only to their owners and their employees, but to any ramblers who cared to make use of the shelter they offered in the years since much of the high plateaux became 'open country'. As an instance of this I recall the case of two girls who were crossing these very Howden Moors some years ago. They became separated from the rest of their school party and wandered until, in failing light, they came upon the remaining Abbey Brook

Cabin purely by chance. They took shelter here and passed a dark night of high winds and rain in comparative comfort—it is quite likely that the cabin saved their lives. No longer can the lost and exhausted make for the head of this deep-sided clough with any hope of a sheltering roof for the night.

A mile and a half to the north-west there is marked on the one-inch Ordnance Survey map a pair of shooting cabins at Penistone Stile, at 1,350 feet and due east of the head of Howden Reservoir. There haven't been cabins here for at least forty years, and no sign remains of their exact whereabouts. Such features marked upon a map can be inconvenient and positively dangerous to the walker who hopes to find shelter in bad conditions and spends energy fruitlessly in an attempt to reach cabins which no longer exist. Proceeding northwards from Penistone Stile the two hollows of Cranberry Clough and Bull Clough are crossed with the expenditure of much perspiration before the upper part of Broadhead Clough intervenes, with the narrowing steeps of Derwent Dale down on our left side. Here, close to the top of the long slope above the River Derwent stood the two buildings known as the Bull Stones Cabins.

Beaters used the old, stone cabin at a slightly lower level while the shooters' cabin was a well-built timber construction something like a miniature climbing hut in the Alps. This timber cabin was in excellent order until the early sixties. In fact, Mr. R. L. Ollerenshaw of Derwent repaired it during that period, fitting three new window frames. Within two weeks of these repairs having been completed Fred Heardman recalls that all fifty-two window panes had been smashed. Being sited on a conspicuous shelf which can be seen from near the re-erected packhorse bridge over the Derwent at Slippery Stones it was inevitable that these cabins would fall victim to the increasing numbers of vandals who plague the fringes of the high ground. Mr. Ollerenshaw finally resorted to burning the pathetic ruins so that irresponsible elements would not be attracted up here. Nothing but the foundations remain today.

Where the Land-Rover track terminates in the upper reaches of Derwent Dale, upstream from the Deer Holes, one can look down to a marshy patch close beside the river. It is the site of the former Upper Derwent Cabin where Fred Heardman and his friends often slept the night before a long day on the incomparable horizon-country that is Bleaklow. It was here that Tom Vernon, that fine keeper of the Derwent Estate for half a century, caught them in the cabin after an early morning 8-mile walk up the dale from Derwent village where he lived, a village which now rests below the waters of Ladybower Reservoir.

Coal for the cabin fire was kept in a hollow nearby and a few years ago on Bleaklow, Fred Heardman met a rambler friend who said that he had never realized that there was actually coal in the rock strata of Derwent Dale. He explained where he had seen lumps of coal beside the path that day, and on their return that evening Fred Heardman saw it for himself—lumps of coal which he had hidden there for future use in the Upper Derwent Cabin over forty years ago and which had only recently been uncovered by erosion.

The coming of the Land-Rover has meant that shooting parties and keepers no longer need the protection of cabins so much, but for serious walkers they can still be of considerable interest and service. It is the irresponsible vandal and hooligan who has done far more than ever wind and weather could have done in the time to reduce most of these buildings to either useless ruins or nostalgic memories. There are, however, two or three rarely visited and little-known cabins which remain in good repair. I have no intention of divulging their whereabouts. If any reader does come across one of them I trust his good sense and judgement will guide him to treat them as if they were his own property. In such a way the handful of remote structures will continue for a long time yet as useful shelters for the true hillman and as monuments to an age not long since passed when the Peakland bog-trotter was a pioneer who ventured into the plateau-land knowing that he would see fellow spirits; though the hawk eye of the keeper may not be far away in the next peat grough or spying on his progress from a distant tor silhouetted grotesquely upon the level skyline.

SIXTEEN

A Combination in the Country

Had William Cobbett been born a century and a half later, I am sure he would have used a motorcycle of some sort for his notable rides. Apart from anything else, such a means of transport offers a more elevated and clearer view over roadside boundaries to the fields, the woods and the far country beyond. How restricting and unimaginative are all but a few older models of motor-car, with their low-slung seating, darkening roof and all-enveloping windows. A lot has been said and written about the 'convenience' of the motor-car, particularly from the viewpoint of bad weather protection. I have found this ill-conceived contraption—one of the most inefficient ever devised by man—very much an inconvenience; as for excitement, of course, it is virtually designed to stifle the meaning of the word. The makers of today's finest motorcycle state quite correctly that the motorcyclist is "one of the last adventurers of our time. . . . When others are leisurely travelling in comfortable cars, he braces himself against the wind with tingling senses and experiences the soaring feeling of speed and perfect control over his machine while seeing all the beauty of nature".

It is that ability to see and feel at one with the world about one that sets the motorcycle apart from most motorized forms of transport. Along the leafy, summer lanes between my home and the Barlow Valley I used to meet my first motorcyclist friend. He could be heard far away upon that memorable 500T Norton long before he appeared around some sharp curve of the way, the evening sunlight glinting on that small, alloy, petrol tank of fine, purposeful shape and the polished 'Roadholder' forks. It was those early pillion rides sweeping up to Hill Top from Lee Bridge that set me on the road which is shared with none save fellow motorcyclists.

My first motive power consisted of a 49 c.c. two-stroke engine attached to my bicycle. It took me up and down the escarpment country about home, to work and back again. The power produced was severely limited, particularly so as it drove the rear wheel by friction upon the tyre. Having such power assistance prompted great feats of endurance, for to be seen pushing such a machine up even a really steep hill would have been ignominous in the extreme. Consequently it was a lung-burster and caused me the expenditure of vast amounts of energy I could rarely afford on early morning journeys to the farm or when returning in the dark after a long day's threshing or manure spreading. It was on such an evening of winter darkness that I ran over a large beam or sleeper—it was invisible in the inky blackness of Stubley Lane—and completed my journey on a pair of rectangular wheels.

Not long afterwards I became the proud owner of a new 197 c.c. James Captain, its brilliant maroon enamel-work and chromium-plated wheels inspiring me to keep it, as far as possible, in show-room condition. How I enjoyed that first motorcycle, riding it through deep woods and across open hillsides; out of Peakland westwards and across the Cheshire Plain into the heart of the Welsh mountains in driving rain, winter snowstorm and warming sunlight. For taking friends to the mountains I had to find transport with greater carrying capacity, and there was no question of purchasing a van or car—there was no interest in that direction. The answer was a combination. Herein lay the solution to the problem for there is no better way of getting three or more people about in exhilerating manner.

An advertisement announced the sale of a very sporting side-car outfit, and within a few days I was the proud owner of what proved over the years to be a most economical and exciting means of transport. The motorcycle was a 1952 R.67 600 c.c. B.M.W. and the side-car a slightly more recent Swallow Jet 80 single-seater. From the first it proved a powerful outfit and with a low centre of gravity was great fun to handle at high speed. Soon after getting it I set off westwards on a winter day to climb in Snowdonia. On the outskirts of Congleton the engine began to develop terribly expensive-sounding noises. I became worried as the noises increased and finally stopped and discovered the engine and my legs drenched in hot engine oil. A brief search of what was then an unfamiliar power unit didn't reveal any obvious cause of the trouble so I concluded that both big-end bearings had gone and that I was well and truly marooned.

The cold wind blew out of the north so lunch was taken in cramped but sheltered circumstances inside the limited space of the side-car. A critical eye cast over the oil-drenched engine casing to the right revealed what appeared to be a most peculiar alignment of the near-side cylinder *vis-à-vis* the engine. I leapt from the confines of the side-car with a mouth full of sandwich and in a matter of seconds had diagnosed the cause of the breakdown—both horizontally-opposed cylinders had worked loose on their cylinder base bolts because non-locking washers had been used. I had soon tightened the eight bolts and tried the engine. It ran once again quietly and smoothly; but now there was a car racing from the east to relieve my apparent plight, complete with tow-rope and spare number plate, for I had summoned aid when first the machine had broken down. There was only one thing to do and that was to turn round and shorten the journey of the relief vehicle as much as possible. The Sapphire 234 breasted the climb out of Wildboarclough at high speed, the explanation was given and both vehicles turned round and went their separate ways.

Apart from high-speed journeys and soaring climbs about the lanes of Peakland, the combination served the useful function of beast of burden. When we had a quantity of cart harness to bring from the farm some miles distant, where it had been bought, the side-car was laden with leather bridles, reins, a collar and chain saddle. When we had several hundredweights of basic slag to carry up the fields from the farm buildings at Horsleygate the side-car was again well laden. Then there were the several rolls of wire netting and stakes which we transported across the ridges to Birley; a small bookcase and the large quantity of *The Countryman* bought at a country house sale on a hot August day years ago. A dozen point-of-lay pullets rode quite comfortably in the side-car one day, as did a shepherd friend and his ample sheepdog, Trib.

One day I got a message from a little girl that a Mrs. Hoyle would like me to have a stuffed barn owl if I cared to fetch it. This lady was moving from her Moorhall cottage into a bungalow in the valley, and on an October evening brilliant with stars and sharp with early frost we rode up the old ridge road to the hilltop hamlet. It was warm and bright at the fireside and the barn owl looked unblinking from behind his dust-proof glassy dome as we talked of all the years Mrs. Holye had lived in the storm-blasted cottage close by the hilltop road. Then we were off into the twinkling night, my friend balancing the owl on his knees in the plunging and weaving side-car close by my side.

Another autumn evening stands out in memory for its terrible and intermittent fog. On a motorcycle one is far, far better off in misty weather than when driving a car, for there is nothing to interfere with vision. Even so on this occasion I completely lost my whereabouts on a well-known lane, the verge being completely invisible. Eventually I found that the combination was standing on the off-side and right upon the path of any vehicle which might have come towards me. Turning around it was possible to climb to higher ground and, quite suddenly, my head was out of the fog in bright moonlight! The tops of the hedgerows and nearby trees were likewise standing clear of the vapour but had I been sitting within a car visibility would still have been very poor indeed.

In all but the worst of snowy weather a combination can proceed where few cars can go. There is no finer motorcycle fun than riding a side-car outfit in bright weather after a good snowfall. Controlled sliding and spinning is quite safe with a low-slung machine, as my B.M.W.-Jet 80 outfit certainly was. Once, I remember, we nearly came to grief when I swung off the road to park on what appeared to be deep road-side snow. The front wheel dropped into a drainage ditch running parallel to the road and I was almost catapulted over the handlebars. Only once did the combination meet its match—in the form of drifts of frozen snow several feet deep at the top of a familiar lane on a February day in 1963. We stuck well and truly in the snow that day, and only after considerable struggling did we manage to turn around and return valley-wards relunctantly. Even so the outfit proved its worth a few days later when we carried my large Swedish sledge upon the side-car's crash bar to sledging slopes some miles distant.

The time came to sell the remarkable and reliable combination, but to replace it I had a newer R.69 600 c.c. B.M.W. solo machine in almost new condition. It was eight years old yet had only been used for pleasure by the first owner so consequently had covered only 13,000 miles. The combination, I heard later, stood in rusting decay in a muddy backyard, and a year after selling it could have been bought for ten pounds. I would dearly have loved to get it back but had neither space to put it nor the heart to restore it back to its former condition of shining black enemal and chrome; it would have taken too long. So now the R.69 carried me high above the hedgerows and clearly through the fog. I harbour a secret plan to attach a Steib single-seater to it so that once again the great pleasures may be had of owning a combination in the country.

SEVENTEEN

The Vale of Amber

As I lay and dreamed upon that sunny, summer's bank above the valley of infinite promise, as I saw and felt the cloud-wash sliding on a liquid sky, another vision was revealed. It was a wide and winding valley-trench and embracing the small waters of an upland stream. Where the vale wound down beyond me and my belvedere on high it was lost to sight as it entered a lower, wider stage in its seaward journey. The vague lighting crystallized, the vapours passed to reveal a clear downward view of a valley of familiar detail.

My first encounters with the Vale of Amber in the long ago leave few happy memories. It seemed a miserable sort of place, with Victorian houses of dull and massive gritstone and the sun never shone. But independent explorations at a later period showed the valley to be one full of promise. The hollow, or trench, has been carved out over thousands of years by the waters forming the clean little River Amber. The name of this watercourse is wrapped around with mystery. According to the Egerton Charters in the British Museum the river was the 'Ambre' in the late twelfth century, and in the Cartulary of Darley Abbey about 1269 it had become 'Omber'. It has been suggested that the word has come from old terms for water, though it cannot be traced in the Celtic language. The River Amber rises close by Roach Farm at 1,000 feet above sea level close by the long, straight lane leading from Chesterfield to Two Dales in the Derwent Valley. There are in this area many scattered and interesting farms, all with alluring names. Roach House (or Farm), for instance, was 'Paystonhirst Roche' in 1448—'the rock at Peasonhurst'. All about are stone quarries; it is an area long exploited for its good-quality gritstone.

Downstream as far as the hamlet of Kelstedge is the upper basin of the Amber. Below Kelstedge is the middle basin, downstream by Ashover and Milltown as far as Ogston. Below Ogston the River Amber enters its lower basin and turns directly southwards close to South Wingfield and Pentrich. The waters join the Derwent at Ambergate, approximately 15 miles below Roach House and 775 feet lower in altitude.

The river starts life as the Hodgelane Brook, after Hodge Lane which dips into the valley here and which was so called before 1724. Its major tributary is the Smalley Brook, draining from the northern slopes of this upper basin and running into it in the shadow of Eddlestow Wood, not far upstream from Amber House. The major settlement of the upper basin stands fair and square at its centre, on sloping ground at 900 feet. It is Uppertown, a not-unique name in this part of the country. How old the designation is cannot be discovered with accuracy but it is called 'Over-town' in the Wolley Charters of 1724 in the British Museum. Uppertown or Overtown, the name is fairly clearly one given to a hamlet standing on elevated ground above others within a limited geographical region—in this case within the bounds of the Amber's drainage system. It is Upper to Kelstedge and Ashover. I like the place for its quiet aspect at the meeting of three lanes, where stands an old chapel where we once had a happy encounter with a talkative farm cat. Now the chapel has been sold and no longer serves the purpose for which it was built. Likewise the little school up the hill beyond the tree-shaded farms. Here is the start of straight Cullumbell Lane, along which stands the tall and tiny, amusing Cullumbell House. In 1409 there was a John Columbell living locally and it is a well-known family name over the hill in and about Darley Dale to the west.

All about this upper basin are scattered holdings and isolated cottages, which are relics of an ancient settlement pattern. Many of them are far from any public road and retain the atmosphere of former insulation beneath a wide, upland sky. Their names tell a vivid story of worlds now so readily overlooked, swept aside as of little consequence, when in actuality these are the things of permanence—roots in native soil which possess a dynamic energy, self-renewing and an anchor for the spirit of those discerning the treasure of simplicity and the unique beauty wrought when man works with Nature, as in the long ago. Tree-girt and sad upon the open hill stands lone Buntingfield, off Cullumbell

Lane. The farm is named after the medieval family of Bunting. In local Court Rolls for 1392 there was a William Buntyng. However, it has been suggested by Dr. Kenneth Cameron that this elevated holding was probably called 'Dyneleswude' at an earlier date, a name derived from the Old English terms 'dëofol' and 'wudu', 'Devil's wood'. There are the remains of a hilltop wood to the south, and a narrow valley-wood not far away to the west. Maybe this wood was much larger and darker than it is today, a sinister vault where evil was worked beneath the howling moorland clouds a little distance away towards the western horizon. Half a mile to the south-west of Uppertown, at about the same elevation across the upper basin, stands Shooterslea Farm. In 1328 it was 'Shetley', and it is most likely that the name originated from the Old English 'scitere' and 'leah'. This is literally 'sewer' and, 'woodland clearing' so that this was a 'well-manured clearing' or 'a clearing with a sewer or ditch'. It has been suggested that the little brook which rises here and drains northwards to the Hodgelane Brook was called 'scitere', an 'open sewer'. A name which occurs at least three times within a small area of this upper basin of the Amber is charming Robridding—there is Robridding, Robridding Farm and Robridding Lane which winds steeply down the northern slope to the brook. According to the Court of Requests of 1543 the place was 'Obrydynes'—actually Robert's 'rydding' or 'clearing', an area of land cleared by a long forgotten Robert for agricultural purposes.

But, for me, the most attractive single place within the upper basin is that called Brockhurst not far from the valley-bottom, where stands an old, disused corn mill on the tributary Smalley Brook. My first close acquaintance with this sheltered backwater amongst scattered trees was on a bright autumn day. The delightful thatched cottage set the seal on the basin, for all its decay and workaday appearance. The little garden was bright with dahlias, those finest of all late-year cottage garden plants. The giant blooms and the thatch and the ancient face peering ominously from a tiny window were straight out of a Victorian seed merchant's calendar. Brockhurst stood in its fading autumn, and that face still stared from behind the cobwebs and the torn lace. According to the Calendar of Patent Rolls for 1316 the place was 'Brokhurst' and it can be assumed that the name was a derivation of the Old English 'brocc' and 'hyrst', 'a badger copse'—and it doesn't require great imaginative powers to believe that hereabouts were extensive badger setts in scattered woodland in medieval and earlier times. Brockhurst—Brock's Country—has altered remarkably little in the past century and is luckily well off any main road. The proper way to see Brockhurst is on foot or by bicycle.

The most noteworthy house of the upper basin is Eddlestow, really Eddlestow Hall Farm, which looks out from 860 feet above sea level along and down the side of the Amber Valley near the crest of Slack Hill. It is the home of the Hole family and their well-known Amber Herd of Dairy Shorthorn cattle, successful in the show rings of this part of England. The house is a dream of Elizabethan architecture, something of a jumble of styles but all the more attractive for that. Behind the house stands a building of probably greater antiquity with two fireplaces. It is quite possible that with increased wealth the Elizabethan yeoman farmers moved out of this ancient homestead to a new and larger dwelling and relegated the former to service as a cowshed or barn, which is what it has remained. Now there were four manors in the Ashover district from the thirteenth century, and Eddlestow Hall was always thought of as the hall of one of these, the Musters' manor. It is known that Roger de Hynfield was living here in 1737, when he purchased the lordship of Musters' manor. Following this several families lived at Eddlestow before the Gladwins arrived later in the same century. Now this family had lived within the parish for a very long time—there was William Gladwin in the Parish Register of 1656—and the boundary of the Musters' manor formed a 'corner' at the high, level ground over 1,070 feet above sea level 3 miles to the north-west of Eddlestow. This area of wind-swept hill country came to be known as Gladwin's Mark, derived from the Old English term for a boundary, 'mearc'. So this ground was the boundary of Gladwin's land or territory or manor. A large farm developed here, close to the highest ground, and it has ever afterwards been known as Gladwin's Mark Farm. At the beginning of World War II this upland holding was in a poor state and unproductive. It was taken over by the War Agricultural Committee and the husbandry improved by that pioneer agriculturalist James R. Bond, O.B.E., M.Sc., N.D.A. (Hons.), alongside other large farms up and down the county. He demonstrated that with the application of scientific methods and sound common sense productivity of all upland farms could be greatly increased. Gladwin's Mark became a household name in Derbyshire farming circles during and after the war.

A long and almost straight lane follows the western watershed of the Amber's upper basin from near Gladwin's Mark, by Revell's Hole, the coniferous plantations upon Upper Moor, Middle Moor and Bottom Moor (names given to relatively small divisions of Matlock Moor surrounding neighbouring Cuckoostone Dale) and so over Amber Hill and southwards above Holloway to the hill-end at Crich. It is the route of a very old ridge-way or packhorse track which kept to the open country and so avoided the dense scrub and woodlands in the surrounding valleys in the Middle Ages and at an earlier date. The demand for good stone led to the development of small quarries along the ridge and this ridge-way remained in use, to be improved with limestone chippings and, latterly, tarmac. Anyway, this long, straight way takes one by the shortest route back from Gladwin's Mark to the slopes just above Eddlestow. About 1250 this place was known as 'Ethelstowe' and down the centuries it was altered slowly to 'Edenstow' and 'Edellstall'. It may be derived from the Old English personal noun 'Ædel' and the Old English 'stow', that is, 'Ædel's place' or 'the habitation of Ædel'. Alternatively, and just as likely, it could have originated from the Old English terms 'ædele' and 'stow', literally 'noble place' or 'splendid place'. This could have referred to the building, but it could equally well describe accurately the elevated yet sheltered place with its commanding view over half the Vale of Amber.

Across the fields from Eddlestow the road between Chesterfield and Matlock climbs to the summit of Amber Hill by way of shadowed Slack. It is generally called Slack Hill, of notorious inclination and bends, the nightmare of carter, coach-driver and threshing contractor. At the top of the first, straight upthrust of the hill-slope, called Amber Lane, there stood until recently a public house—the Lord Nelson Inn—which suffered damage mightily from runaway vehicles over the passage of the years. Often have we paused here when crossing the road on our valley explorations and seen hard-laboured wagons and lorries come almost to a halt, or lady drivers in ancient motor-cars who missed their gear and avoided a fearsome run-back at the bend by the

Lord Nelson only by a last minute use of brakes or a quickly applied stone beneath the rear wheels by an athletic passenger. There is an escape road for any vehicle which runs away on the higher part of Slack Hill. Just below the bends, at the side of the site of the old 'Lord Nelson', a lane runs around the slope to the south-east. A little way along this old route there stands, high above the open valley and just below lane-level, the fine old Goss Hall of Tudor gables adorned with summit balls of local gritstone. The name is an adulteration of the seventeenth-century 'Gorse-hall', a name obviously given on account of the rough, steep and shaded bank on this southern side of the valley, a veritable thicket of gorse in former times.

The old lane swings on and down at an angle into the valley of the Amber to come to Overton Hall a mile from Slack Hill. Overton—or 'uferra' and 'tun', the Old English terms for 'upper farm'—was really an outlying hamlet of farms and hovels in the possession of the Le Hunt family. In 1556 Thomas Hunt sold Overton to a Richard Hodgkinson of Northedge Hall, another ancient property near the north-eastern edge of Ashover parish, about 2 miles distant from Overton. A descendant of the Hodgkinsons married into the family of Banks of Revesby Abbey in Lincolnshire. In due course the property devolved to the Right Honourable Sir Joseph Banks. He inherited Overton Hall in 1792 and spent some time here every autumn in the quiet of a typical Derbyshire valley. Banks was one of the greatest botanists of Georgian times and had been elected a Fellow of the Royal Society at the age of 23 in 1766. In the same year he had begun a botanical survey of Newfoundland. Two years later he went with Captain Cook around the world and became the first botanical director of Kew Gardens. From 1778 until his death in 1820 Banks held the responsible position of President of the Royal Society. In 1829 Overton Hall—much altered over the years from its original ancient structure—was purchased by Dr. John Bright and has had a very chequered history since that time. Latterly it was owned by the Clay Cross Coal and Iron Company, then occupied as a retreat for old people. On a damp and foggy autumn day we came again to Overton, a day when the leaves from the tall sycamores and beeches surrounding the place were falling wet and soggy along the lane. The contents of the hall were being auctioned and through scores of rooms we wandered, dark, forlorn rooms of cobwebs and broken plaster; dank, stone-flagged passages and back kitchens; shabby bedrooms piled with old bedclothes smelling strongly of bed-pans; a great, cold room with a moulded plaster ceiling which was piled high with discarded toys. In a soily corner of the garden we found heaps of toys and signs of recent play. Where they had come from or why they were there we never discovered, Overton the sad became even sadder after that damp autumn day for me.

Swinging right round above Goss Hall and Overton Hall, really forming a western rampart or wall or impasse for the middle basin of the Amber, is a fine, though broken, scarp of exposed gritstone. Along its bold, east-facing profile, are several notable 'heads' or noses of higher rock. From the north, above Goss Hall, they are Bradley Tor, Cocking Tor and Ravensnest Tor. Here and there this scarp slope has been excavated for building stone. The boldest brow is above Overton Hall and is known locally as Gladstone's Nose for from certain situations the rock profile bears a resemblance to an aquiline masculine profile. Nearby is the site of the ancient Turning Stone and from this scarp-top viewpoint one looks out in clear weather northwards over the width of the valley to Ashover itself.

This is, of course, the real place of the whole valley, the township of a large and scattered parish. Indeed this is one of the largest parishes in England, an extensive parish and township which formerly included Lea, Holloway and Dethick over the watershed of Eastmoor and on the slopes towards the River Derwent. In 1846 this combined parish had "11,290 acres of land and 3,482 inhabitants, of whom 46 were persons in tents".

The settlement was called Essovr at the Domesday Survey in 1086, a name derived from Old English words meaning 'Ash tree slope'. With the passage of time it became Esshorr (1278), Asschour (1330) and Ayscheover (1519). Even by 1086 there was a church and priest here, and at this time it came into the possession of the De Ferrars, one of the oldest family names deriving from this period when the Normans came. Ashover was split into four manors, the church being part of the manor of Newhall (called at a later period Eastwood Hall and referred to in Chapter 12). The oldest part of the church of All Saints dates from about 1270 and consists of the south doorway, inside the porch. That it is one of the loveliest churches of Peakland is an undisputed fact, and its crowning glory is the tower and spire, traditionally attributed to the notable Babbington family from little Dethick over the watershed to the south-west and erected in 1419. In his monumental work on the churches of Derbyshire, J. Charles Cox states that it is remarkable that the tower "has no west window of any dimensions, as though it had not been intended to be opened out into the church. . . . The spire is of very elegant design, and is ornamented with eight crocketed windows. Seven yards of this spire were blown down and rebuilt in 1715." During mid-Victorian times the topmost part of this eighteenth-century rebuilding had to be restored. The top of the weather-vane is 128 feet above ground level, 4 feet lower than the steeple-top at Dronfield —a much more powerful spire, more masculine and proud.

Of the features of Ashover church's interior there is room here to mention but two, both unique and well worth close examination. The first is the old lead font upon a more recent base. The font measures 25 inches in width and is one foot high. Upon the outside are twenty upright figures holding a book in their left hands. J. Charles Cox has pointed out that "the age of this font has been much over-rated by Lysons and Glover, who attribute it to the Saxon period". As far as was known by Cox, twenty other lead fonts were extant in England in Victorian times, and none farther north than the example at Ashover. In 1953 Pevsner stated that there were in all approximately thirty such lead fonts. Had it not been for the Reverend Immanuel Bourne, rector of Ashover at the time of the Civil War, the font may well have been defaced or, at worst, taken away and melted down by the Roundhead troops who destroyed Eastwood Hall, Bourne's residence, in 1646. They came to the church to hear a sermon on the evils of the throne and popery delivered by their leader, a Muster Master Smedley. However, the quick action of the vicar resulted in the font being removed from the church and buried in the graveyard temporarily.

The other feature is one of the five bells hanging in the tower. It is believed to be unique for no other English church bell possesses an inscription including the name Bonaparte. The full inscription states: "The old bell rung the downfall of Bonaparte, and broke April 1814. J. and E. Smith, Founders, Chesterfield. George Eaton, and S. Banford, Churchwardens."

Perhaps the most notable person to live in the district was

Leonard Wheatcroft. Besides versatility in labour—he was tailor, parish clerk, village schoolmaster and poet—he recorded for posterity the everyday life of the district, and much of it still exists. His most accurate and detailed descriptions date from about 1722. Describing the boys' school Wheatcroft states that "at every corner of the garden is a birch tree, that the master may not want for the more moderate correction of his unruly scholars, and between every birch tree there is placed a handsome sycamore for them to sit and shade themselves from the violent heat of the sun". Correction and kindness go hand in hand.

But it is Wheatcroft's reference to "excellent water" and 'eighty springs' that brings to light the fact that this valley has long been renowned for its mineral waters. Few of those "eighty springs" of crystal water are marked upon the $2\frac{1}{2}$-inch Ordnance Survey map (Sheet SK 36), but one which is stands out for special mention. Close by the winding valley-road between Kelstedge and Ashover is a Chalybeate Well draining into the Marsh Brook. Chalybeate waters get their name from the Greek word 'chalyps' —literally meaning 'steel'. Such water contains iron salts, chiefly as a carbonate or sulphate and occasionally as a chloride. A worn, paved path leads to a substantial slab foot-bridge by the well, pointing to the fact that this was an important place formerly—for general utilitarian use in addition to 'the curing of several distempers'.

In his autobiography of 1682 Leonard Wheatcroft gives many glimpses of life in and about the Amber Valley of three centuries ago. For instance, he records planting 'about 200 trees' in 1681 and 1682 "about a new hall, which was new built, called Clattercotes". That would have been in the now-named Clattercotes Wood, by Clattercotes Farm due south of Ashover Hay. The named Clattercotes is derived, incidentally, from two Old English words—'clater' and 'cot'—meaning "hovels near a heap of stones". Wheatcroft's sense of beauty was well developed, as evidenced in his descriptions of landscape and in his simple coverage of facts and figures, as here in a further description of the parish: "Four spacious commons, well furnished with all sorts of Moor game, besides foxes, hares and the like, and ten fair woods".

In 1691 Wheatcroft records that he built "ye fabrick upon the top of Ashover Hill". The gritstone outcrop at Farhill, to the north-west of the village and at 982 feet above sea level, has long been known as the Fabrick, probably referring to the tradition that stone used in repairs to the fabric of the parish church were taken from small quarries hereabouts. The Fabrick Road descends northwards from this ridge-top to the hamlet of Alton, the 'old farm'. This is a truly remarkable viewpoint because in even average climatic conditions one is able to look steeply down into the intimacy of the Amber Valley in one direction and out over the slope-away to the far and wide-flung coal measure lands the other way; Wingerworth, Clay Cross, Glapwell and, farther, to Hardwick and the promise of level arable country over that distant height. Looking back to the confines of this enclosed Amber country several notable houses are revealed not far below us. There is Marsh Green standing off the beaten track quite close to Kelstedge, the home of Miss Jemima Nodder in the middle of the last century. Then, much closer beneath us, are the turrets and chimney-stacks of imposing Eastwood Grange. This was a former home of the late Sir George Kenning, founder of Europe's largest motoring organization, who started in business at nearby Clay Cross. This large house is today a Youth Conference Centre. Next along the valley-side stands the ruin of Eastwood Old Hall, referred to earlier and in Chapter 12. From here the ivy-clad remnants look romantic in the extreme, a tower of dark stone rising from the sloping fields and backed by the wider country of this middle basin.

All along this southward-pointing, tapering ridge millstone grit outcrops in a front of fine tors, though now largely hidden by the wind-bent trees of East Wood itself. Though I know this escarpment well, a warm June afternoon stands out in memory: when we clambered here upon the rocks and found several interesting climbing routes of steep inclination and uniqueness. Later we sped across the valley and had tea beneath the opposite crags, at Cocking Tor. The sunset tore at our wind-driven hair as we explored this last face of the day and as the last light bled from the vale.

From the Fabrick this southward view down the narrowing ridge only gives a hint of the position of Stubben Edge Hall, one mile distant. This ancient place was much altered in 1821 but long before that it was the home of the well-known family of Crich. In Elizabethan times William Crich's widow married a member of the Daykeyne family. Later this Daykeyne married the favourite maid of honour to Mary Queen of Scots. It is recorded that this woman, later the mistress of Stubben Edge Hall, faithfully attended Mary to the scaffold at Fotheringhay in 1587. The Hall passed to the now extinct family of Hopkinson of Bonsall in 1720. Today it is the home of one of the late Sir George Kenning's sons, a very proper and fitting association of local industry and genius with one of the valley's finest houses. In 1319 it was known as 'Stubbyng' and by 1588 had become 'Stubbinedge'. Actually the name is derived from the Old English terms for an edge or ridge which has been cleared (or stubbed) of trees—'the place where trees have been stubbed'.

Just below this hall the River Amber cuts through a neck or narrowing of the vale. Rising up on the far side is a most picturesque ridge of land, steep and well patterned by the field boundaries which fall away on both sides. It is Ashover Hay, named in the register of Felley Priory (about 1500) as "la Haya". A 'haeg' was, in Old English, 'an enclosure', so this steep ridge was land enclosed for the inhabitants of Ashover.

A last look out from the Fabrick reveals the contrast of steep, gritstone slopes overlooking the valley on east and west with the flattish fields around the village, bounded by whitish walls of limestone. The middle basin of the Amber Valley is, in fact, a geological curiosity. It represents a break in the surface uniformity of the rocks of Peakland. The overlying gritstone has been cut through by erosion to reveal the underlying, and older, limestone. This has been exploited here and there for both the pure limestone and for the associated fluorspar. There are still fluorspar mines being worked here. The Clay Cross Coal and Iron Company built the Ashover Light Railway for the purpose of carrying this quarried limestone from their own workings near Fallgate and Hate Wood, Ashover, to the blast furnaces at Clay Cross. Between the wars the little railway also carried passengers; on a summer afternoon visitors would take the little train up the valley, through the trees, by the river and close to the grazing cows. At the terminus near Hate Wood was the Rainbow Café, a finely proportioned wooden building well remembered by hundreds of regular travellers on that little line. After World War II the quarries proved uneconomic and the passenger traffic fell off with the spread of the motor-car and motorcycle. Today the Ashover

Light Railway is no more, and the Rainbow Café stands in less beautiful surroundings, serving as a social club at Clay Cross.

There was some volcanic activity here, in association with the weakened limestone surface. Evidence of this volcanic out-pouring can be had in old quarry workings in the vicinity of Hockley (close to Ashover itself), where the dark, knobbled toadstone is exposed here and there in the shadow of the tall trees above the valley road.

A last look out from the Fabrick in good weather will not be soon forgotten for:

Gritstone hangs on either side
The vale of Amber deep.
Far below the limestone fields
Crowd in where cattle sleep.

Tall trees rise from those green fields
To shelter well the spire
And hide the browns of slated nave,
Suggested by the sexton's fire
Of fallen leave and curling blue.

The old halls ring the vale about,
Dotted here and there.
They recall the long ago
For those who really care
To remember trees to climb
And horsemen's calls across the steep.

Memories of corn stooked fields
And humming threshing drum.
A memory of smoking kilns
To where the rail had come
And brought its puffing narrow gauge
To carry off the rock.

The views from gritty outer rim remain,
The cattle still lie sleeping
Where limestone fields crowd green.
The blue-towered sky is weeping,
The wind still blows the same.

Where the river breaks through from the middle basin to flow due southwards, where it is joined by the north-south Press Brook (called the Smithy Brook in its lower course alongside the main line railway south of Clay Cross Tunnel), stands impressive Ogston Hall in the adjoining parish of Brackenfield. Though greatly modified inside and out, this old home of the Turbutts stands a mile to the north-east of Brackenfield's spired church of the Holy Trinity. The hall is bowered around with well-matured trees, but its position is clearly seen from trains on the main railway route between Derby and Chesterfield as they pass through the valley, hidden intermittently by cuttings on the true left bank of the river. Now in the thirteenth century the Manor of Ogston—then known as 'Oggedestun' or 'Oggod's farm' (the personal noun is probably of Germanic origin, as suggested by Cameron)—was held by the Heriz family. About 1369 it came into the possession of the Revel family, and after 1706 it came by marriage to the Turbutts of Doncaster. Until recent years the late Colonel Turbutt lived here, and the family still retain part of the house, the rest forming a Church Conference Centre.

Just below Ogston Hall the impounding wall of the new Ogston Reservoir was constructed so that now one of the features of the Amber Valley, where it turns southwards out of its middle basin, is a great level of water where sails dip before every passing wind. Most of the water is used for cooling purposes at the Coal Carbonization Plant 5 miles distant near Wingerworth, and I believe that this part of the basin, below Woolley and Fletcherhill and South Hill, is today more interesting than before. Water fowl have come here and may be best observed close to the banks, and particularly amongst the reedy waters of the inlet under Woolley Moor. From the hill slopes about Ogston the smooth journeyings of the wind-driven vessels below are a thing of infinite variety and considerable interest. Lying upon the waving sward on South Hill of a June evening to watch the passing to and fro' of the sailing boats below is a pleasure not at once associated with Peakland, and all the more memorable for that.

Away, behind Ogston to the south, lie Brackenfield and Wessington; villages of unusual Derbyshire greens, extensive and well suited for grazing donkeys and sheep. They are not cluttered about with houses but lie open to the sky as do few greens in this part of the country. It is known that there was a green in existence at Wessington prior to 1254, when it was referred to as "Wystanton Grene". Rising up towards the

850 feet high ridge which looks down upon the wider, greater valley of the Derwent is steepening farmland dotted with trees and scattered farms. Up there lies the angled hamlet of Wheatcroft, crouching from the west wind on this eastward-facing slope. Up there on the ridge the treasures of the Amber Vale are hidden, but the lovely hollow containing them is in full view, often below a ravishing sky.

EIGHTEEN

Robin Hood in Peakland

Fable or fact? Yeoman of the Greenwood or last of the Saxons? There certainly was a character roaming the north Midland country who made a tremendous impact upon the life and law of his and subsequent times. Probably he was the last of the Saxons, holding out against the Norman invaders as late as the twelfth century. What literary justification have we to support the legend? The oldest existing record of him is in the second edition of Langland's *Piers Plowman*, dating from 1377, where Sloth coupled him with Randle, Earl of Chester. Whoever this Robin was he would seem to have been contemporary with the Earl who "flourished in the reigns of Richard I, John and Henry III", and his tradition was fully-grown by the first half of the fourteenth century. The doings of the gallant greenwood band are localized between Doncaster and Nottingham, especially in Barnsdale and Sherwood, but it is pretty certain that Robin and his followers spread further afield from time to time. Take the Peak District for instance, a wild and sparsely peopled region in the Middle Ages. Consider the number of places which are married to the myth, in name and by tradition.

Under the gritstone shadows of Gibbet Moor is the hamlet of Robin Hood, on the road from Chesterfield to Baslow, and taking its name from the gaudy hero on the signpost of the rebuilt inn only a couple of miles from Chatsworth. Then, of course, there is Robin Hood's Stride on Harthill Moor, near Birchover, already referred to in Chapter 14. As you approach this tumbled gritstone tor from the east it is easy to see why it was called Mock Beggar's Hall long ago. Surrounded by aged oaks and framed by a nearer sweet chestnut stand it resembles nothing less than a great mansion. The two tallest pillars are called Inaccessible and Weasel, standing all of 50 feet apart. Despite this gap tradition states that

Robin made a single stride from one to the other. A feat which would have given even Little John considerable difficulty to accomplish.

Twenty-two miles to the north-west, 2 miles south-west of Glossop, are Robin Hood's Picking Rods. There upon the rough grazings of Ludworth Intakes stand two upright gritstone pillars set in stone sockets and not far from the Monk's Road. Conjecture has been the historians' tool here too, though a current theory would seem to provide the true answer to the origin of the Picking Rods; that they are, in fact, a pair of stones erected by medieval archers for the purpose of leverage, so that the bow could be bent in order to fasten the bowstring; like the Bowstones on a similar hilltop to the south, high above Lyme Park and the Goyt Valley. Whatever their origin and purpose, the Picking Rods are now officially linked with Robin Hood, as evidenced by the Ordnance Survey Tourist Map of the Peak District. If the village simply takes its name from an inn sign, if the stride story is pure fantasy and the Picking Rods coincidental with the legend, the environs of Hathersage, in the Derwent Valley, bear evidence more weighty, evidence believed as authentic by great historians and local inhabitants alike.

Stand by the 4-foot-tall stone pillar on Offerton Moor called Robin Hood's Stoop and look a mile and a quarter to the north-east, to Hathersage Church. Robin is said to have shot an arrow

Robin Hood's Stoop on Offerton Moor, looking to Bamford Edge

from this spot into the churchyard. And down there in the graveyard is a similar stone pillar; does this mark the spot where the arrow landed?

A few yards away beneath two yews is the grave of none other than Little John. In 1776 a Walter Stanhope of Cannon Hall, near Barnsley, made thorough investigations of the site, and this Stanhope's cousin, one Captain Shuttleworth, opened the 10-foot-long grave under the yews, and 6 feet down a thigh bone thirty inches long was found and taken away to Cannon Hall. Obviously this was the grave of some giant of a man! The great seventeenth-century Oxford historian Ashmole records having seen John's longbow hanging inside the church in 1625. About 6 feet long it was fashioned from spliced yew, tipped with horn and needed an effort of 160 pounds to draw it.

A. M. W. Stirling, writing of Stanhope's inquiries, state that

> this famous companion of Robin Hood, who had been a native of Hathersage, was brought up in the local industry of nail making, till his wonderful strength and prowess made him try his fortunes elsewhere. Little is known of his career, however, till the Battle of Evesham in 1265, when he fought with the rebels under Simon de Montford, who was defeated. Little John with Robin Hood and many of the Earl's followers were outlawed. They forthwith retired to the woods and, escaping the arm of justice, lived a jolly, free life till old age overtook them. Robin Hood died at the age of fourscore and was buried by Little John in Kirklees Park, after which Little John sought out his native village, where he wished to lay his own bones. As he approached the Vale of Hathersage, it is said he remarked that his career would soon be ended, and shortly after he breathed his last. From that time his great bow with some arrows and some chain mail were hanging in Hathersage church, together, it is said, with a green cap suspended by a chain; but when William Spenser became possessed of Hathersage he caused the bow and armour to be removed to Cannon Hall for safe keeping.

This bow can still be seen at Cannon Hall. And as far as the grave is concerned, the old rhyme is still sometimes heard in wooded corners of the village:

> His bow was in the chancel hung,
> His last good bolt they drave
> Down to the notch, its measured length
> Westward from the grave.

And root and bud this shaft put forth,
When Spring returned anon,
It grew a tree and threw a shade
Where slept staunch Little John.

J. Charles Cox investigated the Little John tale too, and reported in his *Churches of Derbyshire* (published in 1876) that:

> On the whole the evidence warrants us in assuming that a portion of the weapons and accoutrements peculiar to a forester were hung up in the church, that the said forester (both from the bow and the grave) was of exceptional stature, that both weapons and grave were popularly assigned to Little John more than two hundred years ago, and that the said weapons must have belonged to a man of extraordinary fame, or they would not have found such a resting place.

What of watering places? Well, there are wells of course. Three miles eastwards from Hathersage church, up on the moors of the Longshaw Estate, is Robin Hood's Well. A dripping spring in the heart of a dark greenwood 1,100 feet above sea level, while half a mile to the south is Little John's Well, out on the open moor, complete with a metal cup on a chain attached to the rock. Then, finally, 4 miles to the north the high gritstone ramparts of Stanage Edge stand out sternly above the dale, haunt of climber, walker and grouse. Near the Black Hawk end of this edge is the dark recess of Robin Hood's Cave. It is high up on the cliff face and difficult of access. Lots of climbing routes pass this way —Robin Hood's Chockstone Chimney, Robin Hood's Crack, Robin Hood's Cave Gully, Robin Hood's Balcony Cave Direct —yes, balcony is a fitting word, for behind a balcony of rock the recess opens into a natural hiding place; one could lie here undetected for long enough, especially before the Edge resounded to the calls of climbers. An obviously inconspicuous place for an outlaw to retreat—whether Robin came this way or not.

Arthur's equivalent in the yeoman world certainly left his mark in Peakland. It would be hard to explain away all the place names and other associations as fable, but let Dr. Charles Cox have the last word for he accurately summed up the subject by stating that "the opponents of the accuracy of the tradition seem to us to have far more difficulties with which to contend than those who accept it".

NINETEEN

The Quiet Hills

Silence is a rare thing, the true silence of nature. Standing on a frosty winter's day above the gleaming hollow of a Peakland valley may seem silent, but in actuality such utter lack of sound is an unlikely phenomena. The crackle of ice breaking from a nearby bough, a rook's distant calling, the sough of the cold breeze off the snow-deep moors, one or other or all may break in. Often such occasional natural sounds go unregistered by the mind, but they nevertheless destroy the silence.

One of the greatest qualities of hill country is the quietness there—soft calls and varied sounds, at once interesting and restful. Real silence, even in the hills, is so unusual that once experienced it will remain clear in the mind as an almost living thing, a dynamic tension poised threateningly. High mountains are rarely silent, for there is the incessant whisper of distant falling water, heaving ice or the sighing of the wind across some far ridge on the stillest of days. In the depths of the forest birds rarely go for long without some voice. It is only in the great deserts of the earth that long silences can be experienced, as among the deep red sandridges stretching to a serrated skyline of the fearful Simpson Desert at Australia's heart. Even here, where no birds dare stray, the occasional yapping and howls of dingoes sound through the living silence beneath a frosted night sky of many stars.

For a few minutes at a time it is possible, even in highest Peakland, to experience what one believes to be utter silence. Its transient quality gives to it a well-loved magic. I have been upon the top of Kinder Scout early on a winter's morning and watched the dawning sky in many shades of grey and deeper mauve move up over the white-crested horizon, where drifts were piled one upon another to block out farther views. There was silence for a time, as far as I could judge, on that winter morning though quite soon a cold wind sprang out of the north-west and whined over the plateau surface for the rest of the day. In the secret, peaty hollow of Swains Greave where the River Derwent gathers itself close beneath its source on Bleaklow the sun can build up heat excessively in certain summer conditions. On one occasion I remember there was great silence for some time as we rested near the slow wanderings of the stream, below steep banks of chocolate peat where the ancient timbers of silver birch have been exposed by the cutting power of the water. But that particular silence was short-lived too, destroyed by the sudden and explosive rocketing of a family of red grouse from the heather slope not far from where we lay. The far rumble of an approaching thunderstorm kept silence at bay thereafter as we quickly crossed the top of Bleaklow into the Westend Valley as lightning flickered over south-east Lancashire.

In all my wanderings in the wild I suppose that some of the most satisfying days, at least in retrospect, have been those involving intimate encounters with animals. Animals, especially, which I have been able to help in some way—animals in danger, in illness and animals injured.

Many years ago, on a cold January morning, a friend and I were ascending the steepening heather slopes below a rocky outcrop in order to climb directly by one of the many rock routes there. As luck would have it we kept on below the outcrop for some way, then, just as we began to turn up steeply over great boulders amongst the heather, we heard a metallic ring over to our left and were just in time to see a fox disappear amongst the boulders, dragging a gin-trap on one hind leg. We soon came upon the poor creature, a fine dog fox, cowering and snarling in a crack. Blood was still pouring from the wound made by the cruel gin-trap's jaws, which had all but severed the leg to which it was fastened. To attempt to get hold of the fox bare-handed was to invite a bad bite so I borrowed a pair of gloves and got the animal behind the neck. He struggled and would have bitten me but he was weak and there was barely any flesh on his bones. The animal must have been trapped for some time, probably on lower ground at the foot of the moor where there are two farms. He had managed to drag himself up here, searching instinctively for the security of solitude.

My friend released the jaws of the trap and the bone lay fully exposed. What could we do? It was decided that all we could do, apart from destroying him, was to let him go and hope that he would recover. The last we saw of him was a russet streak hopping along below us, finally disappearing into the boulders.

Naturally enough encounters with sheep have been many. There was a sheep we came across standing in a frozen pond on Ramsley Moor. She had evidently wandered over the ice, gone through and, unable to get out, was waiting in the freezing water waiting for the end, or the ice to melt. I walked carefully out to the edge of the ice and bent down to get hold of the sheep's fleece. As I hauled her out of the water the extra weight broke the ice beneath me and we both crashed into the water. Now, however, I was able to lift her onto the ice and push her to the bank, then clamber out myself. Heavily encrusted in ice we went our separate ways little the worse for wear.

Not far to the south of Ramsley Moor, on the long levels of Beeley Moor, I came upon a large ram not so very long ago. There were a few inches of snow covering the heather and the wind was cold. I was following a high gritstone wall which divides a coniferous plantation from the open moor. There, in front of me, lay the ram, on his back with his four legs sticking in the air. He appeared to be dead, but suddenly a leg moved so I rolled him over on to his right side. He must have been there in the bitter cold for some time for he was very stiff and one eye was damaged, either by frost or crows.Propping him up with some stones I ran off down through the trees to Park Farm, a mile away above Chatsworth House, to raise the alarm. The farmer knew the shepherd of the moor and promised to tell him. When I walked back the way I had come later in the day I found the tracks of a Land-Rover leading over the moor to the spot where the ram had been. About a week later I heard from a neighbouring shepherd that the ram had eventually died.

One of the less obvious dangers for mountain sheep in winter is that of becoming entangled in the runners sent out by blackberry bushes. On a fine and frosty afternoon a year or two ago a friend and I went down into sunlit woods. The dead bracken shone russet and added a little warmth to the pale, wintry sky. A number of sheep were foraging among the oak trees. We soon came across a ewe which struggled to flee from us but seemed unable to do so—closer examination showed that it was held firmly by a

Sunset from the Rocking Stones, Howden Moors

Looking down the Amber Valley from the Fabric

strong bramble runner, the spines caught by the animal's long wool. After a struggle of several minutes we managed to liberate the ewe. It was obvious that she had been caught for several days as the ground within her reach had been stripped completely bare and torn up by her efforts to get free. Soon we came across another victim of the briars and by the end of the afternoon had set free half a dozen sheep. The importance of regular cutting-back of brambles during the summer cannot be over-emphasized to avoid such dangers to sheep in the winter when they come down from the high sheep walks with their long coats.

In more distant country I have had several encounters with wild goats. One was an adult nanny which had strayed onto a narrow ledge upon a steep face of rock. For days she had been trapped on her ledge and the heart-rending bleating echoed down to the bottom of the valley. We planned to get to the prisoner by roping down to the ledge from the top of the cliff, then, if possible, we would lower her down to the bottom of the crag. On a sunny evening we planned the rescue and had everything ready for the next morning. However, when we reached the cliff next day the goat had gone and though we searched the top, sides and bottom of the crag we never found a trace of the animal. Had someone rescued it during the night? Or had desperation driven it to undertake a difficult traverse and so led it to safe ground? We shall never know.

A much younger goat was the subject of another encounter a year before the cliff-locked nanny. I was with a young friend—it was his first visit to the mountains—in an ash wood which grows at the foot of a tall cliff in a remote valley. It was a cold, bleak February day. Suddenly a young goat kid appeared between the trees a few yards away and stood bleating at us. It must have been only a few weeks old, its soft coat pale grey. There is a herd of goats in this area, and often when one has completed a route up on the cliff one faces a dozen bearded faces on the grassy level which forms its top. However, on this particular day there were no other goats about, and though we searched high and low we never solved the mystery of the lone kid.

In gentler country more recently the same friend, now grown up, and I came across a Friesian bullock lying on its back on a steep slope of frozen grass above Ogston Reservoir in mid-Derbyshire. It appeared to be dead with its legs pointing skywards, around it half a dozen other young cattle were congregated, inquisitive as always. The inverted bullock blinked an eye —obviously still alive! So we pulled lustily at its legs and got it over on its side, from which position it stumbled to its feet, looked unsteadily round and galloped off down the slope with its tail erect. It is, I have found, a peculiarity with cattle and sheep that if they get into an unnatural position, one from which they cannot easily recover, they give up the struggle quickly and lie waiting—for what? Often, of course, this procedure saves valuable energy but it can, too, mean that they die needlessly when the expenditure of a little more effort would have freed them.

A happier encounter came one winter's day on the southern flanks of Kinder Scout. It was a day of low cloud, and the 2,000-foot-high plateau had a covering of several inches of new snow. Descending from the rim of the plateau into the deep trough of Crowden Clough I came out of the cloud and made for a coniferous plantation at the lower end of the Clough. Around the edge of the plantation of spruce and Scots pine was a 5-foot-high stone wall. I looked over it into the silent trees. Their trunks rose straight up to the snow-laden foliage of needles and beneath them the forest-floor lay white and unbroken. Everything was still, and just as I was thinking that here was a scene straight from a Breughel canvas I saw, quite close beneath the nearest trees, a mountain hare squatting with ears pressed flat along its back. The picture was complete.

These mountain hares were introduced into the Peak District from Scotland at the turn of the century and have adapted themselves well on the high plateaux. In winter they turn white like the ptarmigan, which renders them difficult to see against their world of snow and ice. However, this particular hare had not changed for some reason and we eyed each other under the still trees for some minutes. Had I had a cine camera with me it would have been a wonderful chance to procure some really close shots of this elusive and fleet-footed rodent. At last it turned and raced off to safer ground at the far end of the plantation.

Of all my close encounters with birds in the mountains my most vivid memory is of puffins upon St. Kilda. For that reason I will mention the experience here. We were exploring Hirta, the main island of the archipelago 100 miles west of Scotland's western coast and 50 miles westwards from the Outer Isles. Until 1930 there was a human population on Hirta, but in that year these rugged islanders were evacuated to the mainland.

St. Kilda is the breeding ground of the world's largest gannet colony and of one of the world's largest fulmar colonies. It is estimated that a million puffins breed here each year, too. The eggs, flesh and feathers provided the St. Kildans with much of their meagre wealth. It was August and the time when young puffins were leaving their burrows in the hills and making for the open sea. Parent puffins forsake their young, but hunger eventually drives them into the open and instinct dictates that they fly out over the sea, where they stay for anything up to three years before returning to their island base to breed. Many of the young puffins fall prey to gulls before they leave St. Kilda. Another hazard now is oil. The generating house at the army camp has lights burning all night and the innocent puffins are attracted by them as they fly out from their hillside burrows to the sea. Many land and waddle in among the generators to become hopelessly covered in diesel oil. On most mornings of our stay we took a large cardboard box down to the army camp and rescued upwards of thirty poor young birds completely covered in the thick, black oil. They looked pathetic and left as they were must surely have died. We took them up to the old Factor's House, where we were staying, and washed them in warm water and detergent. They lathered up well and despite angry pecks and violent struggling we got most of the treacle-like oil out of their plumage. To have set them free immediately would have been useless, for the detergent had washed out all the natural oil from their skin and feathers and without that they would soon have become waterlogged at sea.

After drying them they were placed in a box in the warm attic of the Factor's House and after thiry-six hours or so they had become the fluffy balls of 'sea parrot' that nature had intended. Of all the puffin patients we cared for the most memorable was Peter. He was a cheeky, inquisitive bird and scampered around the attic, his feet slapping the floorboards much as a large penguin's would. When the time came to liberate the puffins after the natural oil had returned to their plumage we took them down to the little jetty overlooking Village Bay and carefully threw them into the air seawards. Most of them flew off with strong wing-beats and soon were lost to view. Peter, however, flew off then dipped towards the choppy water and finally splashed headlong into it! Instinctively he turned about and swam straight back towards us and landed on the shore by the jetty and looked at us as if to say, "You know jolly well that I wasn't ready for that yet!" We took him back to the attic for another twenty-four hours then tried again. The water was calm and this time he flew off, sank towards the sea, gathered himself and rose again. Soon he was out of sight and making for the wide seas beyond the Dun. I often wonder if he ever came back to St. Kilda to breed.

The countryside of fifty years ago was generally quieter than it is now for the internal combustion engine had only slightly impressed itself upon the land. The calls of the horseman to his team did not carry over the same distances as does the roar of a diesel tractor; the passage of a car along the lane was a welcome diversion, in complete contrast to the incessant clamour and the fumes produced by the nose-to-tail thunder of week-end motorists 'enjoying' the rural scene. Something of that far-away quiet was experienced in the valley hollows of Peakland in the terrible autumn of 1967, when an ogre was abroad, ravaging the farms suddenly here and there. That fearsome shadow was the scourge of Foot and Mouth Disease. It is really a highly infectious condition which derives its name from the blisters which form upon the body of sheep, cattle and pigs—particularly on the feet and within the mouth. A virus causes the disease and this virus is present in the blood, milk and urine of infected animals. Though the disease rarely causes death in adult animals it results in a declined milk production and loss of condition in fattening animals. For this reason, linked to the fact that the disease has the ability to spread very rapidly, all outbreaks must be instantly reported to Local Authorities and all animals on an infected holding are slaughtered.

The first outbreak of that particular and notable plague occurred on a pig farm at Oswestry, upon the Welsh border. The disease spread throughout Salop and Cheshire; dairy herds were slaughtered wholesale, the funeral pyres leapt across the grassy plain towards the brown heights of western Peakland. Then, quite suddenly, an outbreak was confirmed at Ollerbrook Farm, Edale. If the disease spread to the sheep on the open sheepwalk of Kinder Scout it could rage unchecked northwards through the flocks of hill sheep which inhabit this great watershed of the Pennines right up to the Scottish border. All visitors were turned away from the autumn moors, the birds and sheep enjoyed a seclusion reminiscent of pre-war years. An outbreak then was confirmed among cattle at Foolow and at Stoney Middleton in the White Peak. It was now hoped that no further outbreaks would occur in the Vale of Edale and each passing day would mean increased safety for the hill flocks. But by midnight on 17th November 1967 the animals at Grindslow House, Edale had been pronounced infected, and 600 sheep and cattle were subsequently slaughtered. These animals had been infected by a new and more virulent strain of the virus; it was a black week-end for the Peak District and adjacent areas.

Some time later an outbreak was confirmed at Bowling Green Farm, adjoining Haddon Hall above the lower Wye Valley. All animals were slaughtered on neighbouring farms upon the ridge. And a week later there were two outbreaks at nearby Rowsley; a Friesian herd at Hall Farm and ninety-two Guernseys at Bridge House Farm. The very next day, 7th December, two more farms were infected—Pike Hall, Winster and at Ashbourne. On 8th December there were outbreaks at Marston Montgomery, in south-western Derbyshire, and at Coombes Farm, Bakewell. On 13th December ancient Mouldridge Grange, near Elton, was infected. And so it went on, and into the next year. A friend of mine farming at Foston in south Derbyshire remained on his holding for weeks, and there was no physical contact between his stock and that of his neighbour. Nevertheless, when the neighbour's cattle suddenly contracted the disease my friend lost all his animals, too, as it was the policy of the Ministry veterinary officers to slaughter all animals on closely adjoining holdings in an attempt to halt the black advance of the plague. My friend never re-stocked his farm at Foston and later moved to a holding overlooking the Cornish coast.

With the advance of spring 1968 the disease lost momentum and slowly died. The land of Peakland stood quiet and serene, scoured by the winds which had earlier spread the virus in a haphazard and unpredictable manner.

The hills themselves, and all of nature, stand quietly—not silent—and regenerate in due season the life which causes constant wonder and delight.

TWENTY

I Know a Valley

And so as I lay upon that high vantage point where my eyes had closed at the beginning of the travels through this book the sun came from behind a small and passing cloud. The intensifying light caused me to rouse and to come back to the present. The cavalcade of other years which has gone into the previous chapters slid vaguely out of sight, down a long, green avenue of trees which melted into a distant wisp of cloud vapour, burnished by the summer sun.

The valley which opened at my feet, which stretched away from the slope below me, was revealed once more in all its astonishing loveliness. A. E. Housman's Salopian vistas were similar for they, too, contained these "blowing realms of woodland" and the "cloud-led shadows" which, as I gazed, were "sailing about the windy weald" which caressed the steep fields and woods on either side and clasped at its heart the jewel of still waters.

My viewpoint was near the ancient bridleway which curls between Grange Hill and Wigley; my valley far below, wherein dwelt those curving woods and silent, summery waters, was Linacre. I had first heard of this hollow in the hills when my friend Billy Pickering had visited it while camping with the Scouts. It had thereafter been an imagined valley with water conserved in reservoirs for nearby Chesterfield. I never knew, or bothered to find out, its exact location. Then one day in early April 1960 I walked with friends the footpath way from Dronfield, by way of Cowley and Moorhall and Barlow Grange, to come down that ancient bridleway which winds across the head of the Vale of Linacre. Children were gathering the wild daffodils in Nutterall Wood, through which the Birley Brook tumbles valley-wards. The memorable features of that day were the loose, brown rocks which rear above the headwaters of the brook and are surrounded by thickets of almost impregnable gorse; also memorable were the glimpses of water as we traversed down into the valley, glimpses through the slim and graceful sycamore trunks of Birley Wood to the surface of the upper reservoir. The floor of the wood, I recall, was bright green with sprouting bluebells and all around us in the sky were towering peaks of cumulus clouds, white in the full sunlight and blue-grey where they fell into shadow. We crossed the fields and passed through the fresh-budding larches of Kitchenflat Wood on our way northwards towards home.

Since that time the Vale of Linacre has become a place well known to me, a valley of quiet woods and winter gales and spectacular atmospheric clarity on midsummer evenings, when the whole eastern world has been revealed in great detail by the westerly sun. I am lucky to know many of the secrets of this valley of few men.

The complete length of the valley is four miles, running approximately from west to east. The stream draining it rises as Birley Brook at 850 feet beneath the smooth, southern side of Grange Hill and in less than 2 miles becomes the Linacre Brook. The name Birley which is found about the head of the valley can be traced as far as 1154, when it was referred to as "Birleiam" in the Calendar of Charter Rolls. By 1273 (or thereabouts) the name had become "Byrley" in the Registrum Antiquissimum of the Cathedral Church in Lincoln. It is a name which can clearly be traced to the Old English terms 'byre' and 'leah'—'byre or cow-shed in a clearing'. The other important name of the place is Linacre and this is likewise derived from two Old English terms. In 1189 the central valley area was called 'Lynacra', literally 'lin' and 'aecer'—'flax land', an area of cultivated land where flax grew, a not-unlikely crop in the moist soils of the valley-bottom.

Birley Grange is the most important place in the upper-vale. It is a long, ivy-clad farm-house and substantial buildings forming a sheltered quadrangle on a level terrace of land at 850 feet above sea level on the northern slope of the valley. The Grange belonged originally to the monastery of Louth and was an outlying farm with space for the storage of grain as at other granges belonging to monastic foundations—Barlow, Harewood and the like. The abbot and convent of Rufford in Nottinghamshire had lands hereabouts in Brampton parish, granted by Henry VIII to the Earl of Shrewsbury and Birley Grange had passed with the manor. A short distance up the slope from the Grange is Bluster Castle, a farm in a blustering position which catches all the winds that blow. It was so called on the original one-inch Ordnance Survey maps of 1840 and probably got its designation by way of ironic humour, several examples of which remain in this part of Peakland.

Close in front of Birley Grange stands a cottage where a labourer and his family lived when the farm employed more men. Today it stands empty; empty, that is, of human inhabitants. It is filled with families of rabbits which are fed daily by one of the old bachelor brothers who farm the Grange. The first time I went around the cottage was at dusk, when we went from room to room in the failing light, careful to close each door behind us so that the families did not become mixed and so upset the breeding plan. White rabbits bobbed in the shadows and darker animals melted imperceptibly behind the scant furniture still in place in several rooms.

Just across the valley of the Birley Brook, across the steep angles of Nutterall Wood, stands little Birley Farm. It has always seemed to me that this is the original 'crooked house' of the nursery rhyme, for not only was it narrow when viewed from front or back but it seems perched, ready to topple, at the edge of a steep pasture field which drops through a row of lime trees to the brook below. In the field before the little farm is a deep well which is kiln-shaped, opening out below ground to twice the diameter at ground level. In the scattered trees above the farm are the ruins of an older farm and another well. Mr. Ernest Hasman was born at Hare Edge Farm in December 1884, and he recalls the last occupants of the ruined farm at Birley. They were called Wragg and he remembers having a meal beneath the low-raftered ceiling about 1904. The house needed a considerable amount of structural repair by this period and the family moved across the valley to Wigley about 1909. Since that time the farm has slowly fallen into a ruinous state, though part has been repaired and used as out-buildings for the newer Birley Farm across the bridle road. This newer place is remarkable for so small a holding in that the south front of the house is faced with excellent dressed stone and there is a considerable weather stone above the front door. For very many years up to the thirties it was the home of the Misses Botham, countrywomen of the old school who lived almost entirely from what they produced. They took butter and eggs down the length of the valley to sell them in Chesterfield and returned with their baskets laden with those provisions which they could not produce at home—tea, salt, sugar and flour. A longer walk took them across country the 6 hilly miles to Dronfield station, where they caught a train to Sheffield to sell butter and eggs. In later life and especially in winter their laden return by way of Dronfield Hill-top, Barlow Commonside and Grange Hill must have been hard work. Despite their simple, rugged life they both lived to a good age.

Mr. Hasman remembers that they had comparatively little money. One summer the sisters asked him to mow their hay and lead it to the stack when they had made it. He agreed and cut the mow meadows on several fine evenings after doing his own work at Hare Edge. For a few days following the sisters turned the swaths with hay forks and raked the 'made' hay into heaps. Two or three labourers helped Mr. Hasman thereafter to lead the hay with horses and cart and make the stack. When all was finished he told the old ladies that 30s. would cover the cost, being rather sorry for them.

"That is a lot of money for such a small task", one of the sisters snapped. It was not that they were really without money but that they did not realize the value of time and labour in their lives, which were governed more by the season and the position of the sun in the sky than by the clock.

From the environs of Birley Farm there is an unusually unspoilt view down the valley towards Chesterfield; unspoilt, that is, except for the newly-come red-brick expanse of recent developments on that town's western perimeter. On very clear days, notably after rain, one can easily tell the time by looking down the valley with binoculars to see the clock on Chesterfield's parish church, topped by its famous crooked spire. From the lane above Birley Grange it is possible to see Lincoln Cathedral in similar conditions, all of 42 miles to the east.

The steep fields below the farm are habitats for a wide range of spring and early summer flora, especially lady's smock in the damp out-flows of field drains and cowslips in drier sites. Beyond, the gables of the very old and very well-preserved Birley Barn belonging to Birley Grange stand out of the trees, groves of deciduous giants ranging up the valley-sides into Birley Wood and Copy Wood. Cradled by the steeps of distant Linacre and Priestfield Woods the waters of the Linacre reservoirs are a surprise to the stranger and lead the eye on eastwards, beyond the town-top to the magnesian limestone escarpment at Bolsover and Palterton. Over to the south-east Old Brampton church spire pokes above the tree-tops, blunt and wide, and a corner of Hardwick Wood near Wingerworth crowns a conspicuous hillock to the south.

When cuckoos call from Copy Wood
And bluebell haze fills Birley-side,
When larks rise over Linacre
And cloud-isles cross a deep, blue sea
Towards the eastern world so flat and wide. . . .

On a sunny summer day this is the atmosphere of the place and even in winter there is tranquility. The bridle road that passes Birley Grange and Birley Farm descends to the main tributary of the Birley Brook below Freebirch Quarry and so up the far hill-side as High Lane to Wigley. This lane is the remnant of a very ancient, probably Saxon, route leading southwards out of the Barlow Vale towards mid-Derbyshire. High Lane leads up to Wigley, the original home of the family of Wigley. The Hall Farm looks out southwards with a face unusual in this district; a tall graceful front and windows on three storeys.

In the year 1254 this hamlet was called 'Wyggeley' and could have been derived from the Old English words 'Wiga' and 'leah' —literally 'Wiga's clearing'—or it may have originated as 'wigga' and 'leah'—meaning 'the clearing where beetles were abundant', 'wigga' still being used in this context to refer to the family of orthopterous insects we call earwigs, literally ear-runners. Beyond Wigley and the cross-roads at Wigley Green where stands the primary school (to which Mr. Hasman remembers carting stone during its construction) is the hamlet of Wadshelf. It is known locally as Watchell, claimed by some to be derived from Watch Hill; a vantage point from which the advancing Scots could be seen. However, a more reasonable origin will be seen if we consider the Old English words from which it must derive. At the Domesday Survey the hamlet was called 'Wadescel'. The man Wade is known to have held lands here and at Brampton according to the "tempore Regis Eadwardi", of the Domesday Book, and the Old English term 'scelf' describes 'a shelf of sloping land'. So this was 'Wada's sloping land' at 900 feet above sea level and facing the east.

From Wigley one could have looked out upon a scene of great industry fifty years ago, out to the north-west over Freebirch Quarry, when steam-cranes, horses and carts and many men toiled in the extraction of the useful Coal Measure sandstone. The Margerison brothers of Ingmanthorpe were the last to work the quarry, and Mr. Hasman recalls that one brother was the quarry foreman while the other one travelled about the countryside to get orders for this useful building stone. There were two traction engines working in the quarry and Mr. Conrad (Bill) Turner has recounted to me how his life-long love of steam-engines and railways stemmed from his very early days in this district, when the traction engines and steam-crane worked loud and long to win the stone. Kerb stones in particular were made from Freebirch stone, though farms, cottages and buildings over a large area are constructed from this material. Its only weakness is that some strata are liable to 'corrode' or erode quickly in the elements, leading to a broken face of stone in old buildings. Such 'corrosion' can be seen in many places within several miles of Freebirch. Trade fell off with the increasing use of bricks so that by the beginning of World War I work in the quarry had virtually ceased. A large block of stone stands beneath a sycamore tree at the north-western corner of the quarry. I had often wondered why it stood there, and quite recently Mr. Hasman gave me the reason. About 1916 he and a quarryman were taking the block—it weighs 30 hundredweight—in a cart to the stone-saw in the hut now ruined not far from the sycamore tree. The cart became bogged down in the soft ground and no amount of effort on the part of the horse and the men could move it. "Blow it", said the quarryman, "we'll never move her, let's tip it up and forget it!" And that is what they did. As soon as the stone had slid out of the cart the horse was able to proceed back to the quarry for a smaller stone.

A traction engine carrying stone from Freebirch Quarry towards Chesterfield once breasted the top of Puddingpie Hill above Wigley Green, the driver attempted to change gear while still moving, as was his habit, but the engine gained momentum on the long, straight descent past the school. He was unable to engage gear and his mate jumped for his life as the engine and load gathered speed. The driver attempted to slow the runaway by steering into the verge but a deep drainage ditch running at right-angles to the road locked the wheels on that side and the engine turned over, killing the driver. Mr. Conrad Turner has in his possession a photograph of the overturned engine on Puddingpie Hill. It is still remembered and talked about by older inhabitants of the district.

Today the quarries are covered by quaking grass and tawny owls and hares live with foxes among the tumbled stones.

At the edge of the quarries, by the road from Grange Hill to Baslow, is Freebirch Farm—the name for all this level district is Freebirch. It is a comparatively new name, being a corruption of the original name. The Old English names 'preo' (meaning 'three') and 'birce' (meaning 'birch tree') had become "Threbirches" in the Calendar of Charter Rolls of 1271. Even as recently as 1857 F. White referred in his *Directory of Derbyshire* to "Three Birch".

Lying comfortably in the trees between Wigley and Freebirch is Moorhay Farm. In a terrier (a book or roll in which the lands of private persons are described in detail) dated 1698 the place has its modern name but by 1712 it had been corrupted in the local dialect to 'Morrey' and to this day it is so pronounced by the majority of local inhabitants. The name was actually derived from two Old English words—'mor' or 'barren waste land', and 'haeg' or 'fenced enclosure'—so refers to 'enclosed waste land', the area now cultivated but in 1694 referred to as Wigley Moor. Moorhay Farm belonged to the Sitwell Estate and during the second half of the last century was farmed by a John Furniss. He was something of a romantic and social reformer, regularly standing in the Market Place at Chesterfield to address the crowds on the evils of class and creed. About his land he piled heaps of large stones roughly hewn from Freebirch Quarry, to give focal points of interest to the scene. When his wife died in childbirth in 1888 he made known his intention to bury her in a corner of one of his fields. The vicar of Old Brampton pleaded with Furniss to have her buried in consecrated ground within the bounds of the churchyard and even offered to pay for a church funeral but the widower would have none of it and buried his wife at the edge of his field, where stands a group of deciduous trees and from whence there is a fine view across to Birley and down the Linacre Valley. The stone slab marking the grave is carved with a heart and upon this is cut the memorial to the young wife. Subsequently John Furniss had a large block of Freebirch stone moved to the very top of Puddingpie Hill, just beside the road, for it came out of the ground just as it stands today—in the form of a useful chair where countless labourers, ramblers and cyclists have rested over the years. This man Furniss was something of an inventor, and about this period he put forward the idea of an aircraft but, Mr. E. Hasman recalls, few people took him seriously and his aircraft scheme never came to fruition. He had a twenty-one-year lease of Moorhay Farm, and when this expired he moved away. Today one of the Briddon family farms at Moorhay and keeps a Jersey herd.

Half a mile away to the north-west stands the little farm at Hare Edge where Mr. Hasman was born. He is one of that breed of hardy countrymen who seem to go on forever without the slightest change. He is notable throughout this district for the amount of hard work he has done throughout a long, healthy life. Longevity often runs in families and the Hasman family is no exception for Ernest Hasman has a sister who is well into her nineties at the time of writing. He has never been ill in the normal sense of the word, with the exception of a poisoning about twenty years ago. In his youth he was made to work long and hard and the following is just one example of this. It was a regular thing in the first years of the century for haymaking to continue until eleven o'clock at night in order to make the best of the fine weather. One night, after haymaking on a neighbouring farm with the team of horses, he stayed for supper and arrived home at midnight. He had been up since before five o'clock that morning. His father asked why he was so late coming home then added, "Don't go to bed, lad, I want you out with the mowing machine in a couple of hours." So young Ernest simply watered and fed the horses and lay down on the kitchen sofa until two o'clock. He went out to the horses—he hadn't bothered removing their collars—and fastened them to the mowing machine; soon he was off in the cold darkness to start cutting the next field of hay. This occurred day in and day out while the fine weather lasted. The haymaking season ended with everyone very tired and an odd day's rain was praised by many an exhausted farm-boy and labourer for the comparative break in the back-breaking hard work which it offered.

When his father died Mr. Hasman was still young and he continued to farm for his mother, but when the Duke of Rutland decided to sell the farm in 1920 (at Bakewell in a big sale of much of his property in this area and in Barlow Vale) he would not buy it. It was offered then for £800, but there seemed no future at Hare Edge so in 1922 he moved to Church Farm, Old Brampton as a tenant of the Sitwell Estate. In 1959 he retired and moved to a smallholding at Sutton Scarsdale, where he still does a good day's work at the age of 86 (at the time of writing) looking after his beef cattle, pigs and poultry together with his orchard and garden. If you see a wiry figure fencing, hedging or scything thistles in the open fields between Freebirch Quarry and little Birley Farm it will be Mr. Hasman at work in these outlying fields which he still owns. He normally sees to his livestock, catches two buses and then walks down the bridle road from Grange Hill before such work begins. At the end of his labours he climbs again up to Grange Hill to return to Sutton Scarsdale. He is a remarkable man with a mind as agile as is his body.

A mile and a half down the smooth-topped ridge eastwards brings us to Old Brampton, "Brantune" at the time of the Domesday Survey, the most notable building being the blunt-spired parish church. In 1846 it was aptly described as being "an ancient embattled structure on a bold elevation on the north side of the village; it has nave, chancel, side aisles, lower tower, from which rises a short contracted spire".

There were originally three manors here, two of which were joined soon after the Domesday Survey and given by Henry II to Peter de Brampton, supposedly a son of Matilda de Caus, a woman named in the Forest Book as owning a fee to Henry III for possession of the forests of Derby and Nottingham. She died in 1224 and her effigy is on the west wall inside the church, having been discovered under turf in the churchyard in 1739. Though the de Caus family became extinct in the male line about 1460 Caushouse Farm still remains, near the Chesterfield to Old Brampton road at Ashgate, built on the foundations of medieval Caus Hall.

About the year 1100 the Dean of Lincoln received the parish of Chesterfield, including the two dependent chapelries of Brampton and Wingworth, from William II. After rebuilding was completed early in the thirteenth century Brampton Chapel was consecrated by Bishop Brendan in the summer of 1253. Eleven years later a Chantry with 35 acres was founded and "given to God and the Chapel of the Apostles Peter and Paul, Brampton". There are early carvings of both apostles high upon the outside of the south wall, together with numerous others, one of which is the curious face with a man in its mouth. Relics of late Norman work include part of the outside wall of the south doorway, and upon the west wall of the porch is an enigmatic lion carved in the carboniferous stone with which the church is constructed.

The spire, battlements and the porch were added in the middle of the fourteenth century, probably at the time of Thomas Ball, a priest remembered by an alabaster slab which has been much mutilated and now stands at the foot of the west wall of the north aisle, utilized in the eighteenth century as a memorial to another family. Near this, leaning on the west wall of the nave was the effigy of one Hiskanda, Domina de Brampton. The effigy has gone but it has been suggested that the carved head at the spring of the arch at the west end of the nave may be part of it. Next to the arch is a large wooden cross made from the timber of Ypres Cathedral and brought from the grave of Major Lord Gorrell of Flanders, a member of a local family.

The church and its environs are mellowed with great age upon the rounded ridge-top and from the fields which fall northwards towards the Linacre Valley one can look back upon the quiet settlement and recall the busier days of previous centuries. In winter weather and particularly after snowfall the village takes on an air of former times, the peace increases and the silhouette of church and ridge-top cottages stand framed by old and naked trees. At that time comes to mind the medieval custom that the people of Brampton were bound to take the corpse of the first person who died in Brampton, Loades, Pocknedge, Wadshelf or Wigley after New Year's Day to be buried in Chesterfield, at the parish church of St. Mary and All Saints. The vicar of Chesterfield received all the fees and mortuary offerings that would normally have been paid if the body had been buried at Brampton. One of the notable Mower family of Barlow who resided at Barlow Woodseats Hall had in his possession an ancient book in which was recorded the quick burial of Godfrey Foljambe of Moorhall. This latter family originated at this hilltop hamlet of Moorhall and made their name in the Chesterfield district over a long period. A road is named after them. This Godfrey was the son of Sir Godfrey Foljambe. He died "on Monday at morn, about first cock-crowing" 15th November 1591 and was buried with all speed under the high altar at Brampton church. His body had this hasty burial "in the chancel under the high altar, where it stood the same day towards night, for it could not be kept". No tablet or memorial exists to record this burial or to mark the exact spot.

To the west of the graveyard stands the school, erected in 1830 together with the original master's residence, close by the thatched lych-gate into the graveyard. It is recorded that the National School Society gave £100 towards the endowment of this little school. There had been a school here for a remarkably long period, at least from the latter quarter of the seventeenth century—when Peter Calton left 10s. per year, along with six other benefactors who left sums ranging up to £2 per year and the interest on £40. In 1846 it was recorded that "in consideration of these sums the master instructs sixteen children free". The school no longer provides free education, the nearest primary school being at Wigley Green.

Across the road stands ancient Brampton Hall, embowered upon this side by old trees. It has been much altered on the eastern and southern fronts. Until recently it was the home of the Peak Pack of Bloodhounds, one of only three in this country. Now it has been disbanded and no longer does the romantic baying echo across fields and woods, no longer do the brown coats flash with erected tails from hedge to hedge.

A short distance west of the church and old school stands the cottage row where was Old Brampton's Post Office. Here lived Mr. Jack Collis, who was a collier at Grassmoor Colliery and it was he who dug a well 63 feet deep at Hare Edge for Mr. Ernest Hasman's father when work in the pit was scarce. Old Jack Collis had extended his cottage premises at the very end of the last century to make his place much longer to the west. The post office was retained in the old part of his cottage, where a deep well still stands in the front garden close beside a most unusual bird-bath. It is a small gritstone bath supported upon an elaborately carved stone pedestal which was the original top of Old Brampton church steeple, erected over 600 years ago. It was torn down by a great thunderstorm in the summer of 1911 and a new spire-top was incorporated in the reconstruction. Mr. Collis died at the end of World War II in his mid-nineties.

From the village two footpaths lead down northwards into Linacre Vale and the bewooded reservoirs there. Linacre Vale slopes up due westwards from Chesterfield and when fifty-eight

Sunset over the Emperor Lake, Chatsworth Park

The Lower Linacre Reservoir after drought, October 1969

The original top of Old Brampton Church steeple, now part of a bird-bath in the village

citizens of that town successfully pressed for a proper town water supply in 1825 this valley was the obvious choice for its collection and storage. In those early days of civic utilities a masonry weir was erected across the stream not far from Holme Hall and 51,000 gallons daily were taken into a pipe and fell by gravity to a reservoir in West Street. Pipes from this tank fed street taps.

The lowest reservoir was built after an Act of 1855, two-thirds of a mile above the original 1825 weir, and has a surface area of 8½ acres. Strangely enough, and for reasons best known to the Chesterfield Waterworks and Gas Light Company, the next reservoir to be constructed was the uppermost—Linacre Upper—in 1863. Its construction resulted in a boom for the Gate Inn at Pratthall for the navvies went there to drink. This probably accounts for the inn's rebuilding in an ugly Victorian style. This is the largest dam, having a top water area of 18 acres and reaching a depth of 61 feet.

Finally, in 1904, the middle reservoir was built, filling the valley-floor between the Upper and Lower dams, where previously had been rough woodland and grass; by 1909 the water undertaking was completed, with filter beds standing on the northern slope below the conifers of Kitchenflat Wood. For the first eighty years of its existence (until 1905), the Linacre undertaking supplied

Chesterfield with all its water needs and altogether there have been six different companies or boards responsible for this. In October 1963 a seventh took control, the newly-formed North Derbyshire Water Board.

It is a happy thought that no old house, farm or cottage was flooded when the reservoirs were made. However, in 1938 ancient Linacre House—which stood on the northern slope and almost in line with the Middle reservoir's impounding wall—was vacated by the Riggott family, who had farmed there for several generations. It was believed that drainage from the farm was polluting the waters of the Lower reservoir. The Riggotts moved to Over Newbold Farm beyond Cutthorpe village, and their old home fell into decay. That house was a rather ugly one with three storeys but stood upon the site of medieval Linacre Hall, the ancestral home of Doctor Thomas Linacre, who was born here in 1460 and subsequently became the first president of the Royal College of Physicians. He rose to favour with royalty, becoming a tutor to Prince Arthur and Princess Mary (brother and sister of Henry VIII). He also taught Sir Thomas More and Erasmus and died in 1524 at the age of 64. In 1938 new choir stalls in Old Brampton church were dedicated to the memory of Doctor Thomas Linacre and a bronze tablet is set in the north wall of the chancel behind them. The ruins of Linacre House (called "Lynacure Hall" in 1519) have finally all but disappeared, and with them the ancient mason's marks in the vaulted cellars which indicated that this was a place connected with a monastic foundation. The monks passed this way *en route* between Beauchief Abbey and the daughter penitentiary at Harewood Grange.

Half a mile away, towards the north-east, stands the straggling village of Cutthorpe at almost 600 feet above sea level upon a broad and open ridge rising in the west to almost 1,000 feet at Grange Hill. The Cutt family were resident hereabouts from the fourteenth century—there is a Roger Cutte mentioned in the Hardwick Charters of 1361 now at Chatsworth House. Literally, then, this was "Cutt's outlying farm". As early as 1417 the settlement was known by the name Cutthorpe.

Today it is in the parish of Brampton but has some claim to independence as an historic settlement in its own right for it contains several notable farms and private residences. Probably the most notable is the Old Hall or Manor. It is a very fine Elizabethan

Cutthorpe Old Hall from the northern edge of Kitchenflat Wood

yeoman farmer's house, remarkable in this area for the fact that the eastern portion consists of three main storeys, with the stairway in an attached wing. Viewed across the fields from the south it looks most impressive, giving the impression of a tower or turret—just a suggestion of fortification. To my mind it represents the height of an architectural style which has never been bettered in the three centuries or more since it was contrived and executed. At that time Cutthorpe Old Hall was owned by the notable Clarke family of Chesterfield. For a long period it has been the property of the well-known Botham family. To Mr. S. Botham and his family go congratulations for the sympathetic and tasteful renovation of their old home over many years. The place could not be in better hands for Mr. Botham is a most enthusiastic and knowledgeable lover of his native countryside and its people.

Almost opposite Cutthorpe Old Hall a lane leads directly down beneath an avenue of trees to the wooded slopes about Cutthorpe New Hall. This is a lovely old place, too, but is the result of several additions during the seventeenth and eighteenth centuries. On a warm, summer evening it is pleasant to explore the field paths in this part of the Vale of Linacre. Daffodils bloom in a copse close by the New Hall in spring, and it was from this colony that a local man called Heathcote prepared a concoction to cure "the distempers" of Queen Anne when she visited the district in the early years of the eighteenth century.

Quite close to the site of Linacre House there is an uphill path, through the fields by Linacre Wood-top to the hamlet of Pratthall. On this high ridge the trees below hide the faces of the man-made lakes but the views on every hand from close beside the ancient Hall Farm are extensive and, in clear conditions, remarkable. The name 'pratt' is derived from an Old English one meaning 'trick' and this, in turn, became the name of a local family—perhaps a name earned through sly dealings or by way of a joke—so this was 'the hall of a man called Pratt', though there is no trace now of a local family of this name. Here at sky-facing Pratthall is a small Methodist Chapel, identical with one at Hollins, one mile west of Old Brampton. At Hollins—the Old English for 'hollies' on account of the abundance of holly trees in the district—lived until recent years the Drabble family, well known throughout the district as good farmers who had the little chapel built close to their large holding. Today it is an outhouse.

From Pratthall paths lead down into the Vale of Linacre and one slants from Cowclose Farm across the level fields by Birley Grange to the very head of the valley. Where the old bridle road turns sharply to the south and crosses the head-waters of the Birley Brook there is a glimpse between the towering gorse bushes towards the lower reaches of the vale; to the woods and field slopes which have their successful culmination in the blunt, far-off spire of Old Brampton church. A further walk of some hundreds of yards brings one out, quite suddenly, onto the flat sward at the crest where the Vale of Linacre breaks away towards the east.

In any season, at any time of day or night, this is a fine belvedere. In the heart of winter one is inclined to wonder:

Did Breughel walk this way
After sudden winter snow?
The footsteps down through naked trees
Suggest he did, and so
I like to think he painted
From this wide viewpoint.

The white world opens out
Into the lovely vale.
The brittle drifts suggest great strength
Of an unexpected gale
That brought great flurries
From the north-east side.

With the advancing year the mood of the prospect changes. The daffodils bloom in secret Nutterall Wood—these are true wild bulbs but the quantity of flowers has decreased of recent years, due, it is thought, to the heavy demands made by pickers who came here each Easter on an annual expedition from Pratthall Methodist Chapel. Later the cowslips and bluebells come into flower and brighten the view once more:

This is, I always like to think,
A part of John Clare-land,
Where dainty maid trips with a stool
To milk the cows by hand.
Where aproned dame makes milk pail splash
By the open kitchen door.

After sundown the distance of the valley is reduced, it seems, by the coming of darkness. I have seen wonderful sights in the shades of autumn nights and at the depths of winter evenings:

Silver is the shade of the Birley moon,
Silver the light that is cast
Across the sloping fields and wood.
A silver skin floats o'er the lakes
To contrast the thick, black trees.

Only the line of distant lights
At the bottom of the vale,
Reduce the distance that in daylight
Separates the town from this far slope.

My particular guide, whoever he may have been I do not know, brought me to this grassy crest and I began an exploration of this and every countryside which will never be completed:

I walked this valley long ago
On a lovely, lonely summer's day.
This was a peaceful, unknown land;
If anywhere this was where God showed his hand.

For lovely, lonely summer days,
For widest eastward views above our fields
To distant ridges under clearing skies,
To watch the farthest smoke-screen rise.

It came to pass that as I lay upon the high vantage point where, in a semi-dream, all that has gone before was clearly seen between the very edges of the clouds the last vision occurred. There is an overflowing feeling of sadness or pleasure—perhaps a combination of both—in a landscape. That feeling must ever remain within the individual, within the bounds of the flesh wherein it was created, for no other living creature can ever enter into and experience exactly the same interplay of the senses and related associations. Dvorak's A major String Sextet conveys better than any words the magic and living reality which is the Vale of Linacre and the hanging woods of secret memory and long history.

And as I lay I saw that far, green hilltop which in actuality is hidden behind the Pratthall ridge from this place. It was that green hilltop of early memory and I could see Highgate Lane stretching close to the fields where larks were singing overhead. The soft, brown dust was blowing along the lane, driven by a breeze that has blown intermittently through all those intervening years. That, at least, has not changed.

INDEX